REVIEWS OF *THE ROB*

First, I think the content is very appropriate nowadays and the addressed topics embrace important and timely issue of the applications of this new technology. I liked the variety of social themes (like cellphones, bullying, education in general) merged with more technical topics. So the goal of explaining and discussing not only the technical achievements of artificial intelligence and robotics, but also their social impact seems to be fully achieved.

Technical issues are properly presented with precise terminology although being still appropriate for non-expert readers. Chapters are of a good size: not too short, not too long. All of them clearly explain the relation between technology and its societal impact. All the material is very well referenced, inviting the reader to go more in details and understand better the ideas developed in the book.

Overall, I think that this book would be particularly valuable for teachers and students (at different degrees). In fact, it rises many interesting discussion points to be developed in class. While teachers will probably enjoy reading the book with the current organization, for students, and more in general young readers, it may be useful a guide indicating chapters that may be more suitable for them in a first reading of the book, possibly also depending on age, interests, etc.

Congratulations for this big effort!

Luca Iocchi
DIAG, Sapienza University of Rome, Italy

"The Robots are already with us and we have to learn to live with them. The main issue is that the robots, combined with artificial intelligence, digital technologies and telecommunications were previously confined to help humans in the structured environment of the factory or in the clerical work of the office. Conversely, they are now entering our homes, leisure time and everyday lives. They are changing our habits and routines, so influencing our social behaviour. Thus, they are impacting on us humans in an unprecedented manner.

The enormous potential of the robotic revolution, with the urgent need to train the teachers of today and tomorrow to cope with it, has motivated the Practitioner Doctoral programme participants that have written the present book. The result is a very rich and accurate description of the technology, its impacts and potentials.

Far from being catastrophic, the book shows a strong awareness of the relevance of robots for our jobs, economy and social life, together with the importance of the ethical and legal implications involved. In addition, the book demonstrates awareness that the young generations are the most receptive to the present, pervasive technological revolution, so their education requires particular attention and care.

An intriguing book, easy to read and at the same time deep and technically rigorous. It is a must for educators and for everybody that wants to stay up to date, be prepared and able to assist others to cope with the fast evolutions of the present times."

Luigia Carlucci Aiello
Emeritus Professor of Artificial Intelligence
Sapienza, University of Rome

"*The Robots are Here* is one of the most interesting and entertaining books to appear on the difficult yet crucial issue of Artificial Intelligence, often known as AI. As the book's insightful authors point out, AI will have a profound impact on all aspects of human society in the years to come, much like other disruptive technologies did in previous industrial revolutions. AI's most important impact may well strike in the areas of economics and commerce, which could be transformed utterly. While AI will undoubtedly lead to a sometimes painful restructuring of current economic structures, it could also produce vast increases in productivity and living standards, if its introduction is managed well. The creative young minds that produced this important book have performed a significant service and made a major contribution to the public debate on artificial intelligence."

USA Ambassador Michael Gfoeller (R)
Washington

The University of Buckingham Press

THE
ROBOTS
ARE HERE

LEARNING TO LIVE WITH THEM

Edited by Rosemary Sage
and
Riccarda Matteucci

The University of Buckingham Press,
Yeomanry House, Hunter Street, Buckingham, MK18 1EG
info@legend-paperbooks.co.uk | www.ubpl.buckingham.ac.uk

Print ISBN 97817895501917
Ebook ISBN 9781789550924
Set in Times.
Cover design by Simon Levy | www.simonlevyassociates.co.uk

Publishers Note
Every possible effort has been made to ensure that the information contained in this
book is accurate at the time of going to press, and the publisher and author cannot accept
responsibility for any errors or omissions, however caused. No responsibility for loss
or damage occasioned to any person acting, or refraining from action, as a result of
the material in this publication can be accepted by the editor, the publisher or any of
the authors.

Charts and tables from other authored texts have been requested for use and referenced
accordingly.

This book is dedicated to children who are the future and will have to navigate the pleasure and pain, good and evil aspects of robots now they are here! Riccarda would like to dedicate this work to her delightful new grandson, Leonardo, born in 2018 and ready to run the race of enlightened progress. Rosemary is dedicating the text to her lively grandchildren, Arlo, Frankie, Stanley, Sonny and Esme, whose love of technical devices knows no bounds!

THE FOREWORD

SIR ANTHONY SELDON
VICE CHANCELLOR, UNIVERSITY OF BUCKINGHAM

I am delighted to write the introduction to this book, which compliments the one I wrote last year * *The Fourth Education Revolution*, with examples of how Education for Robotics is being thought about and implemented in schools across the United Kingdom as well as Europe. It is the output of the first **Practitioner Doctorate in Education** in Britain, which we are proud to have implemented at the University of Buckingham. This development followed a European Commission research project which initiated this qualification in order to further enhance the professional practice of educators, whether in schools, colleges, universities or workplaces. The aim of this programme is to produce leaders of the future, who have an understanding of global politics, economics and social issues that influence education. This background prepares participants, in a broader way than a PhD, to plan and implement policy and practice in their institutions and therefore make a direct impact for those they work with and for across the world. This professional record forms the evidence for portfolios in a live document to revise and review throughout a career.

The first part of the text introduces work in Italy, where they have had a curriculum for robotics over the past decade, which has been monitored by university research hubs across Europe. **Professor Federico Faggin**, who is listed in the ten top geniuses of the world for his invention of the micro-chip and touch screen, is connected to the *Italian Education for Robotics Research Hubs* and has written a chapter on *consciousness* for this text. The visiting *International Professor* to the *Practitioner Doctorate*, **Dottaire Riccarda Matteucci,** has coordinated the Italian contribution and the picture illustrations of the work produced by children are inspiring. This demonstrates how engineers are now working in schools to facilitate the creative and imaginative abilities of learners to solve ongoing complex world problems using intelligent machine technology.

The book provides a background to this topic area, which must be a priority now in educational policy and practice. A wide variety of view is established among the authors, who come from schools, colleges, universities and training departments in commerce and industry across the world. It will be a valuable resource for students at any level as well as for readers interested in promoting this area of practice.

Seldon, A. & Abidoye, O. (2018) *The Fourth Education Revolution*. Buckingham: The University of Buckingham Press. ISBN 978-1-9086-8495

THE EDITORS

ROSEMARY SAGE AND RICCARDA MATTEUCCI

The editors are both professors on the first **Practitioner Doctorate in Education** of this type in the United Kingdom (UK). It was originally piloted in a European Commission project * (*Policy for Educator Evidence in Portfolios (PEEP) 2011-16*), which produced a strategy for the continuing educational development of professionals in teaching, training, policy or practice development. The aim is to develop a practitioner qualification to international Level 8 criteria for prospective, professional leaders. The programme aims to equip participants with the political, economic, social and cultural context of today's education. It focuses on topics that are important to particular workplaces, such as well-being, change management, communication, the hidden curriculum, special needs and the parent-school interface, as examples. Those undergoing doctoral level study are developing initiatives to solve the problems presented.

The chapters are written by the first cohort to examine the issues of *Education for Robotics*, which is now becoming a hot topic amongst experts, as future employees will need a broader range of personal competencies for the higher-level jobs to come on stream now that routine tasks are being carried out by intelligent machines (robots). The doctoral participants are looking at how to implement more relevant ideas in study programmes for their learners and the chapters present their ideas and reflections.

As Professor Matteucci, a visiting professor from Rome, is involved with the programme, she has been able to introduce us to the work being carried out in schools and universities in Italy. This country has been implementing an *Education for Robotics* programme for 10 years, with careful monitoring by the universities on progress. Therefore, the first part of the book is dedicated to this background with illustrations of some of the projects that are presently undertaken in schools.

The second part of the book presents the ideas and views of the practitioner doctorate group in order to open up discussion on this important debate and develop a forum for exchange of ideas on how to assist students for their future employment possibilities.

We hope you will enjoy the content and that it will inspire you to take up the challenge of preparing learners for a brave, new world. Buckingham University is well-suited for this type of programme development, with innovative work carried out by the *Centre for Enterprise and Entrepreneurship*, headed by the Professor of Professional Practice, Nigel Adams.

*Project Title: Policy for Educator Evidence in Portfolios:
Project Number: 521454-LLP-1-2011-1-UK-KA1-KA1ECETB
Grant Agreement: 2011 – 4133 / 008 – 001: Sub-programme or KA: Key
Activity One: Policy Co-operation and Innovation

Audience:
The book is suitable for anyone interested in how education can be developed to meet the needs of the robotic age, but different chapters may appeal to varying audiences.

The Preface, prologue, chapters 1, 2, 3, 11, 14, 15, 16, 17 and 18 provide information for a general audience interested in technology development and social issues. Chapters 4-10, 12 and 13 are relevant and important for education stakeholders, including teachers in training, students, education staff, support services and parents.

CONTENTS

PREFACE

THRIVING IN THE AGE OF ARTIFICIAL INTELLIGENCE

ROSEMARY SAGE AND RICCARDA MATTEUCCI

The mystery of human existence lies not in just staying alive, but in finding something to live for.

Fyodor Dostoyevsky: The Brothers Karamazov

A WORLD OF POSSIBILITIES

With smartphones in our pockets, the world is literally at our fingertips. An artist, Charlotte Prodger, has just won the 2018 Turner Art Prize with a film recording a video-diary of her life on her iPhone. Judges praised the lived experience as mediated through technology. The Internet of Things (IoT) means we are more connected than at any other time in history, but remotely rather than face-to-face. Now with Artificial Intelligence (AI) all of us are having to face a future of living with robots, which are machines now in human-type forms. This is a brave new world and takes some getting used to! Chatting to a 'chat bot' (*robot machine*) about a tax form seems weird and was not a useful experience as it could not answer specific queries! There was no flexibility demonstrated!

Such a machine movement has been dubbed the *'Fourth Industrial Revolution'* and like previous ones has ignited fears over job security. The McKinsey Global Institute Report (2017) *Applying Artificial Intelligence for Social Good,* predicted that robots would eliminate around 30% of the global workforce by 2030, which is only a decade away! This equates to a possible loss of 800 million jobs world-wide, which frightens everyone! The report acknowledges that AI is not a silver bullet, but could help tackle some of the world's most challenging social problems. Does this possible job scenario, however, present us with the full picture? Are we being bombarded with too much doom and gloom about the demise of many work roles, which might change in nature rather than disappear?

Over the last century machines have increasingly taken over routine jobs, such as product assembly, but luckily the workforce has survived, as new roles have been created. The changes, however, have had social consequences. Textile workers in the 1800s burnt down factories because of the introduction of mechanised looms. This innovation made the workforce helpless, hopeless and raised their hackles! New looms allowed the textile industry to expand, however, creating the need for more workers in new roles, like sales and marketing. In the 21st century, the service industry has now overtaken the industrial one and led to a huge increase in employment possibilities. Nevertheless, this has meant that people have had to develop new knowledge, attitudes and skills, which has been demanding and challenging, because more personal abilities are required that have not been taught in education programmes.

While we cannot know for certain how AI will impact on jobs, recent views are that it will boost sufficient growth to create as many roles as it replaces, suggesting a more promising future for everyone. New, creative, innovative thinking will drive technology for the better. This is being encouraged and promoted with examples like the Telegraph STEM (*Science, Technology, Engineering & Maths*) Awards 2019, which facilitate undergraduate students to find novel solutions to UK real social issues. Just think what doctors will be able to do with intelligent machines speeding up diagnosis rates. Also, the Army will benefit from smart bots analysing the battlefield to make winning more certain. The Telegraph STEM Awards offer higher education students the chance to prove their talent to some of the biggest names in industry. Now in its sixth year, the scheme requires students to tackle problems from the personal to the global. Take a look at the challenges below from industry sponsors. The aim of the participants is to solve one of them. If the idea is chosen as the winner, it could mean a career-defining work-experience programme and £25,000 for the lucky person.

These STEM Awards encourage us to be creative with 5 major issues facing society today:

1. **The Innovation Challenge.** How can robotics be used to make industrial processes more efficient? The UK has 72 industrial robots per 10,000 workers, meaning we lag behind China, Germany and Japan. Increasing industrial robot use is a key driver for increased productivity and necessary if British industry is to be competitive in a post-Brexit world. This challenge encourages participants to demonstrate how robotics can make an industrial process more efficient. It considers wider productivity gains from the innovation and the broader application.

2. **The Electrical Challenge.** How can we improve the efficiency of electric machines? Electrification shapes how we live, study and work, demonstrated by the many electrically-powered appliances, like kettles, that we use in life. No electric machine is completely efficient and manifested in the heat given out while in use. Heat management is a key challenge. This award section encourages the use of ideas to reduce waste heat and enhance performance.

3. **The Automotive Technology Challenge.** What new products or processes could be used to achieve weight benefits for high-performance sports cars? Using lightweight materials like carbon fibre brings efficiency benefits to all vehicles – not just sports and supercars. The UK McLaren Technology Centre is at the forefront of developing the new, future carbon-fibre technologies, to achieve higher performance levels and efficiency. This challenge encourages participants to achieve weight benefits that have the potential for wider uses in society.

4. **The Healthcare Challenge.** How can engineering, science and technology tackle the epidemics of tuberculosis (TB), malaria and neglected tropical diseases (NTDs)? The United Nations has outlined 17 sustainable goals (SDGs) to improve global well-being. A key aspect is ending TB, Malaria and NTD epidemics by 2030. Vaccines are being developed and medicines for prevention and treatment. Where will the emphasis be – prevention, diagnosis, cure, health-system strengthening or bioinformatics? The challenge is to develop solutions that tie into existing strategies and help people to feel better and live a quality life.

5. **The Defence Technology Challenge.** How will future armed forces stay connected in operations? What equipment might they need? The Army, Air force and Navy are increasingly inter-connected today. Technology knows their status continually and communicates with people and assets in operational fields. This must be maintained, sustained and developed, with equipment suitable for hostile battles, enabling armed forces to interact over time and space. How do we develop new personnel roles in this connected world? The challenge is to design battlespaces, explaining important features to be considered and how the vision can be realised.

These challenges will be faced by students in schools, colleges, universities and workplaces. They demand team cooperation, collaboration and engagement, requiring effective communication to share and develop ideas together, with competencies in production, presentation, performance, argument and negotiation. Presently, there is little emphasis on these abilities, needing expert instruction for success from teachers who understand such processes and provide development opportunities.

We have examples from Italy, with a tradition for developing knowledge and its implementation in educational opportunities. They have taught a robotics education for 10 years, monitored by university researchers. Italy leads the way, with STEM subjects encouraged in schools and engineers assisting children to invent and create robots to solve real-life problems. They then present achievements in spoken presentations locally and nationally in similar award challenges described above. This requires students to be in control of learning, encouraging motivation and self-discipline, through cooperation and collaboration with others. Initiatives are happening earlier in education than in the UK. Pulling together and pooling knowledge and skills is vital to save the planet. The United Nations Report (2018) showed climate change impact with stark conclusions and 12 years to save the planet and human beings.

Scientists agree on the major problem facing us. The rate at which humans produce CO_2 is heating the atmosphere and changing climate patterns. Ice caps are melting and raising sea levels. What is the solution? Partly, this depends on engineering technology, but the challenge is finding lasting solutions, as opposed to quick fixes, along with motivating people to collaborate to solve complex, multi-faceted problems. Education is vital in making us aware of present dangers and wasteful life-styles, while helping to develop competencies to find answers to troubles. Upgrading our energy systems is vital for clean, affordable, secure supplies in the long-term to meet targets for reducing carbon emissions.

AI provides the next leap for controlling local and national energy consumption. It interprets live data at a speed beyond any human to help power grids and individual persons to optimise energy use and consumption. This is taking place with the Google-owned British AI business, *DeepMind*, working with the National Grid to assess demand from data sets. Included are detailed localised weather forecasts and online searches, hoping to reduce fossil fuel use in the grid. Another factor is local energy storage, so the Government has invested in the landmark '*Faraday Challenge*', aiming to bring business and academia together for new thinking on micro-energy storage. This will propel the next electric cars as well as solar storage and other forms of sustainable energy, which our machine world must have ready.

A connected net-work of millions of smart batteries could provide clean energy for transport needs and give some back to the grids when needed. Moixa, a British Tech Company, offers battery systems to make better use of solar energy. Using AI, the company brings together large numbers of home batteries and connected devices to deliver service to the gird. Benefits are increased solar yields and storage to manage the gird infrastructure. It will only be possible if we achieve teams to share and develop ideas.

HELPING POOR COMMUNITIES

Small-scale storage solutions offer a brighter future for energy to poor communities, where renewable sources are available but storage problematic. Robotics are used to help optimise energy sources so that engineers, environmental and other experts can work together in a nuanced way to meet demands. Robots are accurate, precise, strong and reliable and are employed to meet many needs. Multi-discipline teams, with engineers, environmental, cultural and people experts, work with academics, to adapt robots for niche purposes. Saving the planet is urgent, but producing people to do so is vital to prevent global catastrophe. Partnering with robots and educating people to work with them is the world's future.

Cyber-utopianism promises magic outcomes for poverty, but old methods work in classrooms: well-qualified, knowledgeable, skilled teachers, fresh air and exercise with exploration of the real world. This is also what '*digital natives*' want. A study of e-learning showed that students preferred ordinary, real-life lessons with a smart person at the front of the class to facilitate activity. (Warschauer, 2004)

Children are on the conveyor belt of an '*information economy*' in present schools. We do not want them to be robotic competitors in future jobs. Students can opt out of Religious Education, but where technology is concerned, they are bound by blind determinism. Surely we should choose the direction technology is taking with education an example? Children turn up in schools with undeveloped brains and must learn to design a future in collaboration with others. It is time for schools to think again about the system, which originated to teach *compliancy* for factory and office jobs but must focus now on *creativity* for new world solutions.

WHAT EXPERTS SAY

Technology for children is questioned, as innovations have ups and downs. The Children's Commissioner for England warns that youngsters are facing a social media '*cliff edge*' as they encounter online cyber-bullying and pornography. According to Public Health England, extended screen use correlates with emotional distress, anxiety, depression and disruptive behaviour. The American College of Paediatricians links it to sleep problems, obesity, increased aggression and low self-esteem.

Other reasons suggest screen technology is harmful to children with little evidence it helps either personal or academic learning. The Organisation for Economic Cooperation and Development (OECD, 2015) found computer impact on pupil performance was mixed and in most cases was '*hurting learning*'. Kucirkova (2014) in *Frontiers in Psychology* said there is '*an absence of research supporting the enthusiastic claims that iPads will revolutionise education*' (p.3). Durham University found '*technology-based interventions tend to produce just slightly lower levels of improvement*' compared with other approaches (Higgins, 2012). The Head of the e-Learning Foundation says finding if technology improves results remains the '*holy grail*'. Education technology is justified on grounds that it boosts disadvantaged children, yet Warschauer (2004) says it widens not bridges socioeconomic divides. The *One Laptop per Child* programme, distributing 25 million low-cost computers, with learning software, to children in the developing world, failed to improve language or maths results.

Such evidence does not dent the faith of technology proselytisers who say children must be prepared for the future. Companies do not want children who learnt PowerPoint in primary schools, but employees who can think and express thoughts in speech and writing from first principles. Software programmes rapidly become obsolete. Coding classes only teach children to assemble pre-made building blocks. Silicon Valley executives restrict social media use. The Waldorf School of the Peninsula bans technology in classrooms, where Google, Apple and Yahoo staff send their offspring with not an iPad, smartphone or screen in sight.

Instead, teachers prefer experiential learning that contrasts sharply with the rush to fill classrooms with the latest electronic devices. Pedagogy targets communication and imagination in learning, taking a holistic approach to integrate pupil intellectual, practical and creative development. The fact that pioneering technology company employees query computer value in education begs the question – are high-tech classrooms in the best interests of the next generation? Beverly Amico, leader of outreach and development at the Association of North American Waldorf Schools, says their approach uses time-tested ideas on how children learn best. Teachers encourage students to learn curriculum subjects, by giving opportunities for them to express themselves through talk and activities like painting, drawing and performing, rather than consuming information from a tablet.

For example, a typical 4th grade lesson might include learning about Norse mythology, by making story pictures. Pupils acquire problem-solving mathematic skills through knitting or speaking a modern language and even playing a game of catch. They then share ideas with each other in spoken presentations. Amico says this creative learning approach brings lessons to life and is more effective than showing a series of images on a screen or hearing a teacher monologue about a subject.

> '*Lessons are delivered by a human being that not only cares about the child's education, but also about them as individuals,*' she says. '*What do you remember as a child in the classroom? It is usually field trips, getting your hands dirty in a lab or a beautiful story. Those are the things that stay with you 50 years later.*' (Guardian Press Interview, 2017)

Waldorf classrooms are designed to make pupils feel relaxed and comfortable, with natural wooden desks and plants. Removing the distraction of electronic media encourages stronger, interactive, spoken engagement between teacher and pupil. A reason parents in the digital industry choose a low-tech, no-tech education is that it teaches innovative thinking and language expressive skills that employers desire. Students weaned on technology often lack ability to think outside the box, problem solve and articulate this knowledge clearly and concisely to others.

The London Acorn School questions the assumption that limiting or removing technology use in class has a negative impact on student future employability. Children, under 12, are banned from using smartphones, computers and watching TV of films at all times, including holidays. The ethos is a gradual integration of electronic devices throughout child development. Students can watch television when 12 years old, but only documentaries vetted by parents. They cannot watch films until age 14; the Internet is banned for under 16s, at home and school, with computers only used for over-14s.

A considered approach to class technology use allows teachers to help students develop core skills like communication, executive decision making, creativity and concentration – which are more important than ability to swipe an iPad or fill an Excel spreadsheet. Technology, considered cutting edge today, will appear primitive tomorrow. The problem with instant information is that the ease you get from A to B for answers does not reflect life, so making children think that everything is readily obtainable.

Restricting technology use is a challenge for today's teachers, used to accessible resources and information from interactive whiteboards and computers. Educators suggest that digital devices inhibit imaginative thinking, movement, interaction and attention spans, with no place in teaching youngsters. You must be more creative in *how* lessons are delivered and work with your voice *(loud/quiet)* to engage and give incentives. Pupils must be interested in what comes next. Teaching is about human contact and interaction. Children are disadvantaged by being taught by machines at a young age.

The neuroscientist, Catharine Young (2015), encourages teachers to '*appeal to all senses*' and employ repetition to help pupils remember information. Technology can be useful, especially for learning-based games, where students engage with familiar and new content interactively. Ideas that technology is one-way traffic and not interactive is untrue. Another neuroscientist, Judy Willis (2015) focuses on *balance*. She suggests that computer-assisted learning cannot replace good teaching but does not overlook its advantages. Online games help students to build skills to an automatic level at an appropriate pace for them. If we spent more time discussing an appropriate balance then perhaps more people would realise how technology can boost cognitive and creative development.

Educational Technology is predicted to be worth £129 billion by 2010. The world's largest Ed Tech convention (BETT) is about creating a better future by transforming education with the latest gadgets. Google, Microsoft and

Facebook sell expensive kit to cash-strapped schools, promoting *engagement* and *interactivity*. The traditional teacher-pupil hierarchy must be '*flipped*' to *empower* pupils to control and direct learning. In reality, children tap away on tablets, whose workings are as mysterious to them as outer space. They are often required to stare (*in dark classrooms*) at a giant, interactive whiteboard. Although temporarily attracted, attention spans eventually shrink if they do not have opportunities to interact and share ideas with others to produce new thoughts in novel ways.

The University of Buckingham, School of Education's new **Centre for Educational Practice**, has participants on the **Practitioner Education Doctoral Programme** piloting initiatives to be proactive for future, holistic, creative learning. Links nationally and internationally share knowledge and increase awareness of the need for radical, education changes. Assessing the political, economic and social factors that influence policy and practice, as well as student issues preventing learning, help in making decisions that could contribute to improved personal and academic abilities that life today demands. This book presents some ideas so we hope you enjoy reading it and reflecting on some interesting experiences happening in schools.

REFERENCES

Flynn, J. (2013) *Intelligence & Human Progress: The Story of what was Hidden in our Genes*. Els. Inc.

Higgins, S., Xiao, Z. & Katsipataki, M. (2012) *The Impact of Digital Technology on Learning*. University of Durham Report. Education Endowment Foundation

Kucirkova, N. (2014) *I pads in Early Education: Separating Assumptions & Evidence*. July. Frontiers in Psychology

The Mckinsey Global Institute Report (2017) *Applying Artificial Intelligence for Social Good*, 2018 https://www.mckinsey.com/mgi/overview. Accessed 27 Nov. 2018

Organisation for Economic Cooperation and Development (OECD, 2015) Report into Students, Computers & Learning. OECD Publication.

Public Health England (2013) Report: *Sedentary Lifestyles and Too Much Screen Time Affects Children's Well-being*. Published by Gov.UK

The Telegraph Stem Awards 2019. Tgr.ph/stem. Accessed 27 Nov. 2018

Warschauer, M., Knobel, M. & Stone, L. (2004) *Technology and Equity in Schooling – Deconstructing the Digital Divide*. Educational Policy. September 2004. Sage Publishing

Wills, J. (2015) *The Science of Homework*. Teacher Network

Young, C. (2015) *Don't Forget the Science of Memory*. Teacher Network

PROLOGUE

THE ROBOTS ARE HERE: HOW TO SURVIVE THEM

Technology is giving life the potential to flourish like never before or to self-destruct (Future of Life Institute)

ROSEMARY SAGE

AN INTRODUCTION

SUMMARY

Our world awaits transformation by intelligent machines (artificial intelligence/robots), which break down human tasks and are programmed to carry these out more effectively than us. We now have machines with capacity to pick those shy, red strawberries hiding lush beauty behind copious, green leaves! Whether robots relieve workers of dangerous, tedious tasks, enable medics to diagnose illnesses and prescribe more accurately, help carers lift and carry patients, or through adaptive learning allow students to be educated in line with personal needs, they have potential to make life easier for everyone. The UK is only average in world rankings for robot use and bottom of advanced nations. This contributes to low outputs and wages with Germans producing 35% and Americans 30% more than us. The need to produce goods and services more quickly, efficiently and in greater quantities is vital to sustain huge human population growth worldwide. The Czech Academy of Sciences is paving the way by writing data 1000 times faster, on copper manganese arsenide crystals (antiferro magnets). This will lead to supercharged computers, so speeding up processes, solving more problems and extending activities. Policy makers, employers and educators must quickly grasp present opportunities to expand, enhance and educate lives in new ways. It is vital to adapt to a changing political, economic and social backdrop as, more than ever, innovation is key to stand out in a competitive landscape. We must work with change and not against it to survive. Robots are here to augment what humans do and we need to be comfortable about this new presence in our lives and use intelligent machines judiciously.

INTRODUCTION

THE HISTORY OF ROBOTS & ROBOT LEARNING (R-LEARNING)

Humans have long imagined machines that can perform their tasks – depicted in drawings, books, plays and science fiction. The word '*robot*' comes from the Czech word, '*robota,*' meaning '*forced labour*' with initially evil connotations. A robot was first used in a 1920 play – *RUR-Rossum's Universal Robots-* by the Czech writer, Karel Copek. The plot was – *man makes robot and then robot kills man*. In 1977, the Star Wars movie represented robots as *human helpers*, made to look like people and called *androids or humanoids*. Recently, there has been an explosion of industrial robots to assist workers, with China (*a major developer*) building 52% more for world-wide distribution, in the first 6 months of 2017, than in the corresponding period of the previous year. In Japan, 5,000 construction sites are manned by robots doing all tasks, with just a highly qualified human engineer coordinating actions from a comfortable office. No longer do workers have to endure the dirt and danger of a building site!

The first industrial robots were employed in 1961 by General Motors, New Jersey, to assemble cars. With sophisticated voice and image-recognition, language translation and automated game-playing technologies now in operation, the *International Federation of Robotics* forecasts an enormous boom in sales worldwide. An example is Amazon's Alexa voice recognition, employed by the BBC for interactive audio adventures. In *Inspection Chamber,* a science fiction story, users were able to control the direction of the narrative, allowing them to experience interacting with the drama characters. *Alexa* is now a common acquisition, enabling people to interact with the machine to play the music they want or find out specific information like weather forecasts for the next football match! You just ask the small black box and a female voice obliges. The '*Once in Royal*' carol was requested and Alexa immediately responded, saying that the descant was by Wilcox. How impressive! Alexa, an intelligent '*virtual assistant*', whose functions include answering questions and playing music, is a surprisingly useful, smart investment. Recently, reports suggest that Alexa does not cope with strong dialectal English. In the UK, we have moved away from encouraging Standard English (SE) as elitist, with increasing problems in understanding each other's communication. Perhaps Alexa will play a role in facilitating a move back to teaching SE for public use, as is normal in other languages.

Below is a picture of *Professor Dottaire Riccarda Matteucci* teaching Practitioner Education Doctoral students at the University of Buckingham, UK (*November 2017 study school*) on robot learning across the World. Dubai has appointed a *Minister of Robotics* to support appropriate educational development that will prepare future employees for new jobs and different directions in present ones.

DEEP LEARNING

An approach called *deep learning* has transformed the field of AI, rebranding an earlier computer learning method, *artificial neural networks* (ANNs) in order to gain knowledge from data and make speedier classifications and predictions than is humanly possible. Deep learning has developed more efficient ways to train neural networks containing many more layers. Although a very simplified model of brain functions, it relies on unprecedented networks of thousands of millions of neurons, simulated in software, to enable them to adapt and learn in response to copious data.

Copyright picture of Sally Elvin, Marketing Manager in the School of Education with permission for use

The School of Medicine at Mount Sinai, New York, has used deep learning to analyse 75,000 patient records and 78 diseases, predicting severe diabetes, schizophrenia and many cancers with high accuracy. Google AI is now being trialled at London Moorfields Eye Hospital and is spotting disease better than doctors. This brings ethical concerns. How can a medical practitioner tell a patient they will develop a disease or must alter their lifestyle because a deep network says so? Can preventive treatment be started when no explanation is available? Researchers are working on this, suggesting that these are possible, using cognitive psychology methods to understand what the neural networks are responding to in making predictions. Other AI techniques, however, have explanations from formal mathematical underpinning, allowing us to judge our trust in such methods. AI is a plethora of different approaches applied for different needs and contexts. Deep learning impacts on life and work in ways that we are unaware of its use, such as monitoring shopping habits and web contacts. Whether we find this terrifying or not is important, because public sentiment drives education, investment and regulation, making outcomes self-fulfilling prophecies. New technologies disrupt and cause distress before producing benefits that change views. Concern is that if a proliferation of autonomous, intelligent machines hits lower-income people the hardest, to rid them of routine jobs, will inequality increase? Like all inventions, AI is capable of being used for good or evil and morality matters. Making better humans is more important than smarter machines. Today's solutions to technology problems (*like abusing personal data*), are vital for tomorrow's successes, with monitoring and regulation necessary for responsible robot use. DeepMind has set up a research unit focusing on ethical and social implications of AI and this is important now that systems are regularly hacked by cyber-terrorists.

Fullan & Langworthy (2016) collated international research exploring the curriculum needs for the future, which advocates learning '*in more challenging and engaging ways*', ensuring pupils gain '*real experience in creating and using new knowledge in the world beyond the classroom*' (p.22). This approach advocates digital mastery but anticipates future key learning competencies to comprise:

Communication, creativity & imagination, critical thinking & problem solving, collaboration, character education and citizenship. These reflect the European Commission competencies: *communication & cultural awareness, learning how to learn, mathematics, digital, scientific & technical abilities, social & civic engagement plus initiative & entrepreneurship.* The book, Paradoxes in Education (Sage et al., 2017), shows how these competencies are all underpinned by communication and this is explained with suggestions for mastery in different models for learning (p. 56).

ROBOT ROLES

Today, robots are changing the world as *computer-controlled performers*, doing all manner of tasks. Fascinating robot facts are in the media, such as a cornfield yielding 1000 loaves in 1968 would produce 33 billion in 2018 had agriculture improved at the same rate as computing power! Robomart is a driverless vehicle the size of a SUV and the first self-driving store. Customers order on smartphones and it rolls up to your door in less than an hour later. Pick the perfect produce and Robomart bills you for items taken. The CX-1 is a smart suitcase that follows you at speeds up to 7mph with a built-in 'eye' to map a face. A GPS tracker lets out a loud wail if you wander too far! Trevor Paglen, who produces surveillance *art,* is sending a sculpture into orbit and making images with AI to encourage people to look up into space and think about what is looking back at them!

In Japan there is a hotel chain run by robots which are also in use as surgery, nursing and therapy assistants in hospitals, as well as teaching aids at all educational levels. In the UK, Dr Penny Dodds has been leading research into the suitability of *'Paro',* a Japanese robotic seal responding to touch and speech for use on dementia wards to reduce stress and anxiety. Research shows that these robotic seals promote social interaction and improve mood and speech fluency. They have AI sensors that allow them to learn and respond by wriggling, turning to the patient, opening their eyes and squeaking! In today's world machines are not only assistants but main companions!

Lord Darzi's National Health Service (NHS report, 2018) calls for *'full automation'* suggesting swathes of work by health professionals can be done by intelligent machines to save £13 billion annually. The Royal College of Surgeons (2018) predicts that healthcare assistants, with robot help, will carry out key procedures in caesarean sections, now undergone by 1/4 mothers. Their *Future of Surgery Report* argues that big data advances will standardise ideal methods of performing surgery. This revolution will focus on the development of higher-level competencies to deliver rewarding parts of jobs like more contact with patients. Automation should also encourage demand. Radiology, analysing body and brain images for diagnosis, is expensive but machines can make this more efficient opening up new applications. Improved efficiency leads to higher production, lower prices and more demand for tasks that machines cannot perform. For example, *'expert systems'*, the AI technology of the 1970s & 1980s, has led to automated diagnostic aids allowing procedures to be undertaken that required a doctor. Dr Mahiben Maruthappu is the co-founder of the *NHS Innovation Accelerator*, tasked with introducing new ways to counter today's health challenges. The app, *HaMpton,* monitors pregnant women for hypertension; *WaitLess* enables patients to fast access urgent care for minor injuries; *Lantum* uses AI to match available clinicians with open shifts; *Respira Sense* allows medics to identify deteriorating patients and *Dip.io* is a smart phone urinalysis device for patients to test at home and share results with clinicians. These innovations enable the NHS to be sustainable with rapidly growing populations.

In a National Health Programme, residents have *health trackers* for GP monitoring without leaving home. Fingerprick tests for heart patients mean blood testing is regular with webcam links to medics providing advice and support. Reminders for flu jabs and infant checks, with apps tracking life styles, are operating. Fitbit-style bracelets monitor cancer patients and pink heart patches (*FreeStyle Libre*) monitor blood sugar levels for those with type 1 diabetes. Results are sent to surgeries and hospitals.

New-build homes will have movement sensors and other smart tech linked to a computer. The UK NHS has a project to design '*healthy homes*' – nagging families into better living habits and checking on the sick and elderly. There is a '*smart bandage*' to monitor the healing process. Dorset's virtual hospital Ward uses an electronic clinical system, *SystemOne*, for patient details to be available to all practitioners. This breaks down care '*silos*', allowing people to be managed at home rather than in hospital. *DoctorLink* and *Ask NHS* apps encourage patients to use a symptom checker telling them if they need a pharmacist, GP or to call 999. This saves valuable time. Exercise and other health tips can be flashed on screens if occupant activity levels fall. Alerts are sent if there are suspicious changes to routines such as failure to switch on a morning kettle. Many thought processes are being carried out by machines and some are anxious about his for human communication and intelligent behaviour.

Malaysia has service robots, in real-estate companies, welcoming prospective homebuyers and raving about house or flat features! The cute creation, *Mento*, performed on the catwalk in the 2017 London Fashion Show, attracting curiosity from city fashionistas. Robot fashion shows, in Nordstrom, demonstrate that the same robot dressed in different outfits – *bride, superhero, 'frilly girly'* etc. – elicited different reactions, with people more likely to ask about a robot's role than its hard or software. Robot priests have been customised to conduct Buddhist funerals (Nirvana) and dispense holy favours in 7 languages (Blessed-2).They have become popular now abuse allegations have diminished trust in human beings. Google has invented a baby-sitting robot, isolating sockets and activating digital door locks if an infant moves, sending texts or emails to parents.

Intelligent machines infiltrate all aspects of life! iPAL came to the UK in 2018. It can sing, dance, tell jokes, play games and chat about your favourite movie! The Haier smart mirror chooses clothes to wear if we are unable to decide and delivers work-out videos to keep us looking our best! Are the robots taking over? They are definitely here to stay but are we comfortable about this intrusion into our lives?'

iPAL

Photo from robotics competition, Italy February 2019

WILL ROBOTS REPLACE ALL HUMAN ACTIVITY?

Robots can be programmed to carry out routines faster and more accurately than us but do not yet have ability to respond flexibly to changes in all circumstances. Presently, they are unlikely to replace humans in higher-level jobs, because of *'Polanyi's Paradox'* – we know more than we can tell. Humans have a soul (*character*) and spirit (*energy*), as well as inherent, tacit knowledge (*intuition & consciousness*) to make judgments and act flexibly. These attributes are difficult to translate into programmed machines. Thus, instinct and reason (*gut feeling & inner voice*) counters the cultural belief that rationality prevails in decision-making. Using machines to gain knowledge and interpret data quicker and more accurately than experts creates new understanding for improved outcomes, so freeing humans for higher-level thinking, problem-solving and improved actions. An example is the BBC harnessing robots to direct and film comedy and discussion shows at the Edinburgh Festival. After analysing shows, the computer learnt to direct the formulaic genre of panel-type performances. This marks a shift in the way they intend to solve problems and serve audiences in a wider way. One potential use is to increase the range of live events the BBC covers, like music concerts, where cameras focus on limited points of action. This enables the director-producers to concentrate on more complex projects.

Google's DeepMind AI programme, *ALphaZero,* shows signs of human-like intuition and creativity, hailing an historical turning point. It has mastered chess from scratch in 4 hours and developed a unique playing style, improvising like a human being. Unlike *Stockfish,* the world's best chess machine, which calculates millions of possible outcomes while playing, *AlphaZero* learns from past successes and failures. Professor Silver, who leads DeepMind's *Reinforcement*

Learning Group, says it has a subtle, intuitive sense to balance out the different factors. This suggests that intuition and creativity, previously thought to be only human, are now accessible to machine intelligence. Researchers hope to use this system to solve world problems, like why proteins become misfolded in Parkinson's and Alzheimer's diseases. Results show that it may find things that humans would miss (Stajic, 2018).

ROBOTIC EDUCATION (R-LEARNING)

From first seeing bread pop up in a toaster and a kettle boil one has happily accepted and trusted machines to make life easier. In a world where cost, inconvenience and unreliability of travel increases, we will soon be likely to rent a robot to check on elderly relatives or help in disasters, say the experts! Technology has brought the world to us – *phone, radio, television & internet* – but now brings it to us immediately. You can sit in an arm-chair running the show or witness something as it happens anywhere. Examples are a *farmer* monitoring a milking robot, operating a computer from home, or a *teacher* using it to assist students remotely when unable to attend school because of ill health. Switch on a television and you observe events occurring in real time through many types of media machines.

Many worry about the loss of traditional jobs with robots taking over routines. However, new employment will emerge, such as trainers for robots, who demonstrate tasks to be done, providing feedback on performance rather than programming machines. This is happening at some airports, where robots assist passengers to gates and are trained to do so by human teachers! There will also be roles for designing, developing, making, maintaining, marketing and selling robots. These jobs require more interdisciplinary interaction than presently occurs with excellent communication, high-level thinking and empathetic understanding, which Flynn (2017) suggests are in decline.

For students, the impact will be when robots enter classrooms to assist learning. The test is whether we regard this as good or bad. In our model of quality that includes mechanical, electrical, information-processing, machine-intelligence, business and social influence, it is the latter that is difficult to assess. What we consider as '*good*' depends on attitudes and values. If robots free us to work **1** day for salaries instead of **5**, perhaps we will quickly learn to love them! A role for future education will be to engage people in interesting activities that are not job-related but benefit them and their communities.

Experts suggest that education must focus on improved inter & intra personal communication for problem-solving, interaction and behaviour now that robots take over routine roles. This will facilitate increased innovation and creativity, depending on group-sharing, discussing, reviewing and refining ideas, to fit students for more interactive, discursive, future roles. At present, communication is an under-developed competence, witnessed when people shout rather than conduct rational argument. Psycho-linguists are presently examining this discourse because political polarisation has increased antagonistic exchanges. Talking to *win* (*objectivist*) rather than talking to *learn* (*relativist*) means we are less inclined to legitimise ideas that are different from ours (Fisher et al, 2017). Future employment will rely on *interdisciplinary* communication and collaboration to jointly focus on solving present complex, political, economic and social issues, like people inequality. Team work is dream work but needs cross-cultural appreciation for effective results (Ilieva, 2010).

In education, robots fulfil learning targets more quickly, accurately and successfully, allowing teachers to concentrate on character and competence building for students. LEGO EV3 robots are invaluable for STEM teaching (*Science, Technology, Engineering & Mathematics*) and also Humanities, as in philosophy and poetry, allowing students to articulate through technology. Mindstorm robots focus on story-telling structure to encourage assembly of ideas, formal communication, cooperation and creativity. Students, in groups, are challenged to come up with solutions in fictional formats. Humanoid robots help improve oral languages and support those with special needs, using designed, programmed input by experts, like linguists, therapists and psychologists. This is more common in Eastern nations, as they view objects as *animate,* so feel comfortable with robots operating alongside them. In the West, we have a more sceptical attitude, derived from differentiating animate and inanimate things.

Teachers are naturally concerned about their traditional role but *Learning Management Systems* (LSM) and *Adaptive Learning* allow them to eliminate repetitive, lengthy tasks, like building and sequencing subject content or checking and analysing pupil progress. This makes educators available to talk and engage with students face-to-face, offering individualised coaching, alongside humanoid robots who can help them reinforce and support learning with a variety of relevant practice tasks.

A COMPARISON OF TRADITIONAL AND ADAPTIVE LEARNING

Traditional Learning Adaptive Learning

Teachers: seek, edit & organise lesson content; respond to students Decide what is taught; coach & manage

Adaptive Technology :
- finds& analyses best content;
- explains & links concepts;
- adjusts material to suit individual student needs

Students: receive same content, learn at same pace; many fail to cope Have personal learning plans;
* work at own pace;
* learn what is relevant for level of ability

CONCLUSION

In America, robotic teaching has developed *dream-team projects,* with student groups communicating and collaborating to solve problems, promoting interactive talking, thinking processes as well as technology competencies. This enables individuals to enter the workforce with vital communication, cognition levels, confidence and resilience to cope with rapid, world changes, where flexibility and adaptability are key to survival (Goodrich & Schultz, 2007). In Italy, universities, like Florence and Pisa, collate inter-discipline teams to assist schools with education that produces competencies for the future. Professor Faggin, in the top 10 geniuses of the world for his invention of the microchip and touchscreen, is a leading academic focusing on future needs of society and influential in looking at issues about *consciousness,* which is a hot debate in robotic development.

Predictions that many jobs will disappear is no surprise because we all engage with machines and have used them for chores increasingly over time, releasing us from tedious tasks. They now possess superior cognitive abilities (AI) to the human brain, designing and operating complex nano- and macro-technologies. These comprise anything systemised, with the objective of engineering labour out of manufacturing and other processes. In human services, like medicine, robotic assisted surgery and nursing are estimated to bring $60 billion dollars of annual benefits to the USA along with many others to do with administrative and organisation roles in clinics and hospitals. (Accenture, 2017). How long will it take until machines super-cede human general intelligence (AGI)?

Humans have moved from the stone-age to silicon-valley and from a simple life to one of huge complexity. Psychologists estimate we make at least 35,000 daily decisions, with choices exploding recently. In 1976, the average supermarket stocked 9,000 products which has ballooned to 40,000 today. Decision-making comes at a cost, as neuroscientists alert us to a loss of productivity, motivation and increase in stress. Facing many decisions creates neural fatigue, compounded by continual media exposure and information overload. More than a 1/3 of UK students receive medical support for anxiety, with a 42% increase in 2016. Student surveys reveal their inability to cope with life and depression about the future (Sage, 2017). Our traditional component approach to both managing ourselves and learning has prevented a holistic philosophy for personal as well as academic development. There is a mismatch between teaching-focus on academic goals and life-needs for better transferable competencies, like effective communication, which underpins all such abilities.

Today's world is mind-blowing. In September 2017, a robot, *YuMi* conducted a Tuscan orchestra, while Andrea Bocelli sang from Verdi's Rigoletto. Students invented a '*rowbot*' faster than the Cambridge and Oxford boat annual regatta crews, challenging rivals to compete in a *Rowbot Race*. Australians developed *Hadrian X,* laying 1000 bricks an hour, a task taking 2 humans 2 days. De Laval International cow-milking robot replaces humans! Tokyo has a robot '*Café Dawn'*, where people with disabilities can be paid to wait on tables via remote-controlled robots. This allows those with paralysis or conditions like motor neurone disease to control waiters over the web. Soon, all routines will be carried out by robots, worrying students, striving for jobs and overwhelmed by the enormity of life.

Zhuying Li & Floyd Mueller, at the Royal Melbourne Institute of Technology, invented an experience that we might find hard to stomach! They have made a sensor you can swallow to work alongside a smartphone called *The Guts Game*. The sensor measures body temperature changes and is swallowed to play the game. Over the next 24-36 hours players try to change their gut temperature to kill a virtual parasite on their smartphone. This is done by taking hot or cold drinks, eating spicy food or doing vigorous exercise, but temperature changes are small to eliminate risk. The winner is the one to hit the target temperature the most times before the sensor is eliminated in a bowel movement.

The tech world is full of surprises and the question is: *how will humans interact with these machines?* Humans are not like machines, lacking patience to follow complex instructions. They are unpredictable and not always logical in thoughts and actions, tending to muddle through life by responding intuitively to experiences. Today, people are required to work with programmed machines, subject to rigid, algorithmically driven work regimes like call centres manned by chatbots, or warehouses where movements are dictated by an electronic voice in the ear. We are forcing humans to act like robots and the difference between them must be recognised, as the debate is framed to imply computers can substitute for people. We need to build a world fit for humans not robots. The latter are unlikely to be comfortable navigating complex, unpredictable environments. Today, user experience (UX) is taken seriously, with anthropologists and psychologists employed by tech companies to understand the role that humans play in their systems. However, this is far from saying that corporations put people first. They require workers who are agile, flexible, adaptable and willing to embrace changes that AI and automations deliver, while creating an ethical framework to manage responsible implementation. Employers must ramp up worker abilities speedily and education has to change to meet this revolution.

Mass education promotes *compliant* not *creative* learners, with outdated teaching methods preparing them for largely routine work, now taken over by AI. Greater attention to learning needs and personal development is necessary for higher-level work, to be ahead of robot rivals! Students require excellent communication to collaborate, create and cope with a changing, challenging, complex world.

New job opportunities will occur but not at the rate fast enough to absorb large numbers of disposable employees, from both low-skilled and professional employment. This, in turn, will affect *consumption* key to a functioning, flourishing capitalist economy. If the unemployed are unable to consume – how will taxes be raised to finance social infrastructure, like education? This threat will only be solved by a society educated to communicate better and cope in innovative ways. Ability to share ideas - reviewing, reflecting and refining them for optimum outcomes is crucial as an entrepreneurial spirit is required when jobs disappear. The Wall Street Mart predicts that we will enter a new age of artisans, who were the elite of medieval times. We are a nation of small industries, with the human interface valued and these will increase. On-line marketing makes it easier to present goods and services to the world.

World pundits, however, note our diminished speaking ability now that technology is our preferred way to connect rather than talk (Sage, 2017). France banned mobiles in schools from 2018, because students do not play and talk together at break-times but fiddle on smart phones, with negative impact on interacting for learning. The BBC and Asda Supermarkets commissioned a poll of 724 6-12 year-olds and 986 parents to launch a *Power of Play* campaign, supporting physical activity and improved confidence, well-being and friendships. A favourite way to play is on a computer, tablet, games console or mobile phone. This screen-time was the first pick of 84% of children, confirming that interactive opportunities must be encouraged to gain abilities to cooperate with others successfully. With reviews saying children now spend 7+ daily hours on phones, this change in behaviour must be monitored.

The recent Leverhulme TABLET project (*Toddler Attentional Behaviour & Learning with Touchscreens,* Smith et al. 2018) reported that babies of 6 months are losing sleep because of using touchscreen tablets, raising fears that technology harms brain development. For each hour of using an iPad or similar device they lost about 17 minutes of sleep. The study of 715 families, by Birkbeck, University of London, found that 75% of 6-36 month babies used touchscreens daily for 20-40 minutes rising to 92% at 3 years with 2 hours of use. Although children showed better hand and finger dexterity there are concerns that sleep lack leads to food craves, obesity, loss of cognitive performance and a reduced immune system. Research by *Screen Education*, a US campaign group, found 20% of teenagers spent 2+ hours on phones in bed, with a further 22% 3+hours, when supposed to be resting! These are issues for public concern as mental and physical health are at stake here. Schools are warning parents that the online game, *Fortnite*, is making children aggressive and violent to fuel bullying. They are running daily sessions in Gloucestershire schools to warn against addiction risks. The game has 200 million players and because they can spend money for add-ons for their online characters, like weapons and costumes (*skins*), this is leading to rising cyber-bullying.

More interaction will help us think and reflect more deeply, as addictive technology is proving harmful, with children as young as 5 years old falling victim to online abuse (*Barnardo's report to the Parliamentary Science and Technology Committee, July 2018*). Illinois State University and Michigan Medical Schools report *'technoference'* in parent relationships with children, resulting in increased likelihood of behaviour problems and accidents. Manchester is the first UK authority to launch a public health campaign to tackle a breakdown in communication between parents and children, caused by smartphones and other digital technology. Speech and Language Therapists have strongly suggested that communicative and thinking developments are seriously under threat. Challenges are to increase awareness and alter present life-styles with nudge-style *'texts'* to parents, suggesting *how* and *when* they could talk to children, like meals or bath-times, with advice on when to put down phones. Health visitors are receiving training to provide family guidance.

Voice-activated machines are normal when you ring an organisation – a female robot's patient tone reveals she has been programmed to assume you are probably stupid. If visiting a restaurant in Poland Street, London, you will meet the robot waiter, *'Yo'*. When customers block his route, Yo says: *'Please move out of the way'*. After the 9pm watershed, the message is changed to: *'Would you move your fat ass?'* Treating people honourably is becoming obsolete, even by machines. Consideration for others is often viewed as unimportant in our less formal, casual world. West End theatres have a *'scrunch test'* to establish foods that are less likely to distract the cast, who are infuriated by people arriving with Chinese takeaways or groaning hampers, to be gorged (*with phones clamped to ears*) under actors' noses. Polite, audience respect for performers has disappeared.

We now lack understanding of the *value of manners* as part of the communicative process. How well we get on with others is key to future success and opens doors that the best education fails to do. No one wants inconsiderate persons in school, workplace or the social sphere, which is as relevant today as in more gracious, past times. The manner in which we presently communicate and behave is negatively commented on in employer surveys, such as the Confederation of British Industry (CBI). Technology does not always provide helpful models, which need counteracting by formal teaching on how to conduct ourselves with others. Since the National Curriculum came into being in 1989, education has concentrated on *what* to learn rather than *how* to do so. As facts now are obtained at a button's touch it is time to concentrate on how to talk, think and interact positively for solutions to problems that might ameliorate troubles. Nations, like Japan, focus on *narrative speaking* to enable the oracy-literacy-numeracy shift that underpins formal learning, as well as development of personal confidence and coping abilities. Until students competently use *connected speech* for many purposes, in primary representational form, secondary codings of letters and numbers are not easily accomplished.

The University of Buckingham, School of Education's new *Centre for Educational Practice,* has participants, on the *Practitioner Education Doctoral Programme,* piloting proactive initiatives for future, holistic, creative learning. Links nationally and internationally share knowledge and increase awareness of the need for radical, education changes. Assessing the political, economic and social factors influencing policy and practice, as well as student issues preventing learning, help in making decisions that could contribute to improved personal and academic abilities.

It is said that computers will eventually be able to see into the future. No more crystal-ball gazing will be necessary as super-smart algorithms will sort through past data to elicit patterns and forecast what is to come! Predictive analyses will produce our end of year examination grades without a need for tests! Indeed, the judiciary already relies on such software to estimate the reoffending risk of a defendant on probation. Education must ensure that intelligent machines assist rather than control and master us. We can take no chances with machine super intelligence.

In the UK we have mainly a liberal society with divergent values and low moral consensus functions, which many feel are leading to scrimping workstyles and climbing crime rates. In public services, the move towards sub-contracting demonstrates fly-by-night operations and cutting corners. Societies are split between good people giving their lives and working hard and scoundrels, thieves, fraudsters and those who live and profit from exploiting others. However, most people are open to cooperation, but we need to focus on the style and tone of our engagement with others with active stigmatisation of extreme language and sentiments. We have to stand up for civility as it is possible that modern liberalism will allow machines to destroy the quality of our lives. Professor Greenfield (2015) in: *Mind Change,* reminds us starkly that we are rapidly losing ability to think, empathise and communicate with each other because of reliance on technology. With no inner narrative to control our thinking and actions and cope with circumstances we are becoming like 3 year-olds with short attention spans, weak self-identity and lacking in social competencies. The latest studies from Harvard and Princetown universities support these views suggesting that people now need constant stimulation and are not able to go into their own mind (*inner language*), think laterally and have their own thoughts. Eating together, swapping stories and promoting exercise and interaction are a start. A recent update of a National Union of Students' (NUS) survey indicates that 78% of those at universities report depression and mental health problems, with 85% of teachers admitting to stress. Medical experts are suggesting we are now more narcissistic, showing lower esteem and inadequate communication for effective performances. This makes grim reading and awareness of how we are being manipulated should be resulting in rebellion.

MAIN IDEAS

- Intelligent machines are changing are lives in ways we are unaware of &we must take stock
- There is need to monitor closely the effects of machines on human interactions
- Research indicates we are losing ability to think & communicate with ourselves & others
- Understanding the situation enables us to balance technical& human activities

REFERENCES

Cheongju, Hans J. (2016) *Robot-Aided Learning and r-Learning Services*. In *Robot Interaction*. Ed. D. Chugo. INTECH Croatia

Fisher, M. et al (2017) The Influence of Social Interaction on Intuitions of Objectivity and Subjectivity. *Cognitive science*. Vol.41, No. 4 p. 1119-34

Flynn, J. (2013) *Intelligence and Human Progress: The Story of What was Hidden in our Genes*. Elsevier Inc.

Fullan, M. & Langworthy, M. (2016) *A Rich Seam: How New Pedagogies Find Deep Learning*. London: Pearson

Goodrich, M. & Schultz, A. (2007). *Human-robot Interaction: A Survey*. Foundations and Trends in Human-Computer Interaction, 1(3), pp. 203-275. Davis

Greenfield, S. (2015) *Mind Change*. London Random House

Ilieva, V. (2010) *Robotics in the Primary School*. Proceedings of SIMPAR, Darmstradt, Germany

Sage, R. (2017) Editor. *Paradoxes in Education*. Rotterdam: SENSE International Publishers

Smith, T. & Irati R. Saez de Urabain (2018) *The TABLET Project*. http//tabletproject.limrquery.com/index.php/676218/lang-en (accessed 15.07.2018)

Stajic, J. (2018) *One Program to Rule them All*. Science. Vol. 362. Issue 6419

Matteucci, R. (2017) *The Robots are Coming*. Working paper: Centre for Educational Practice, University of Buckingham

CHAPTER 1

THE FUNDAMENTAL DIFFERENCES BETWEEN ARTIFICIAL & HUMAN INTELLIGENCE

FEDERICO FAGGIN

SUMMARY

*Tripling of the world population over the past century has made us increasingly reliant on machines to sustain life more efficiently than can be managed by humans alone. A rapid growth in **Artificial Intelligence** (computer science machines aiming to understand & judge like humans) means that dirty, dangerous and dull routines, can be carried out by sophisticated, powered-systems called **robots**. They are, however, only as good as the people that produce and programme them, so we need to give urgent attention to the moral and ethical issues involved to avoid possible dangers and abuse of such complex inventions. This book introduction considers the basic differences between Artificial and Human Intelligence to begin an important discussion. Radical rethinking of our present way of educating citizens is urgently required, to prepare them for this brave new world, so they remain masters and not servants of these powerful tools.*

INTRODUCTION

There is much speculation today about a possible future where mankind will be surpassed and perhaps even destroyed by machines. We hear of self-driving cars, Big Data, the resurgence of Artificial Intelligence (AI) and even of transhumanism – the idea that it may be possible to download our experience and consciousness in a computer to live forever. Major warnings have been given by public figures like Bill Gates and Elon Musk, as well as the late Cambridge astrophysicist, Professor Stephen Hawking, in the *Expedition New Earth documentary,* about the dangers of robotics and AI. What is TRUE and what is FICTION in this picture? The chapter aims to provide some answers to this important question and present the basis of a radical re-think to traditional education.

In all these projections, it is assumed that it will be possible to make truly intelligent and autonomous machines in the not too distant future, which are at least as good, if not better than we are. Is this assumption correct? I will argue that *real* intelligence requires *consciousness*, and this is something our machines do not have, and most likely will never be able to acquire as the requisite for responding flexibly to unpredictable circumstances.

Today, most scientists suggest that we are just machines; sophisticated information processing systems based on wetware*. That is why they think that it will be possible to make such apparatus that will surpass human beings. These experts believe that consciousness is an *epiphenomenon* of the brain operation, produced by something similar to the software that runs in our computers. Therefore, with more sophisticated software our robots will eventually be conscious, but is this really possible?

DEFINING CONSCIOUSNESS

Let us start by defining what is meant by *consciousness:* I know within myself that I exist, but *how* do I know? I am sure I exist because I *feel* so, confirmed by the interactive responses of others in my environment. It is the *feeling* that carries the *knowing,* based on sensory channel modes and inherited genetic information, with a capacity to do this the essential property here. When I smell a rose, I *feel* and am aware of its perfume, but be careful! The feeling is not the set of electrical signals produced by the olfactory receptors inside my nose. Those signals carry objective information, but this is translated within my *consciousness* into a *subjective* feeling: what the smell of that rose *feels like* to me.

We could build a robot capable of detecting the particular molecules that carry the rose smell and correctly identify this by its distinctive scent, for example. However, the robot would have no feeling whatsoever. It would not be *aware* of the smell as a particular *sensation.* To be *aware* one must *feel,* but the robot stops at the electrical signals and from these it can generate others to cause a response and action. We do much more than that, however, because we actually *feel* the smell of the rose and through that special feeling we *connect* with that flower in a special way. We can also make a free-will decision that is *informed* by that feeling. For example, we love the scent so much we decide to buy this type of rose for ourselves and others to spread the pleasure!

Consciousness could be defined simply as the *capacity to feel*. Feeling, however, implies the existence of a subject that feels – a *self*. Therefore, *consciousness* is inextricably linked to a *self* and is the inherent capacity of this to perceive and know through feelings a sentient experience. It is a defining property of a *self*. Feelings, moreover, are clearly a different category of phenomena than electrical signals and incommensurable with them. Philosophers have coined the word '*quale*' to indicate what something feels like, and explaining '*qualia*' is called the *hard problem of consciousness,* because nobody has yet solved its dynamic quality and constant interactions of many personal attributes. In the rest of this discussion, I will use the word '*qualia*' to refer to four different classes of feelings: *physical sensations & feelings, emotions, thoughts* and *spiritual feelings.* The latter is more difficult to define, but refers to interests of a deep kind that contribute to our awareness and sense of purpose within existence.

Electrical signals, be they in a computer or a brain, do not produce *qualia*. In fact, there is nothing in the Laws of Physics that tells us how to translate electrical signals into *qualia*. How is it possible then to have qualia-perceptions? Having studied the problem for over 20 years, I have come to the conclusion that *consciousness* may be an *irreducible* aspect of nature, an inherent property of the energy out of which space, time and matter emerged in the Big Bang.

In this view, far from being an epiphenomenon, *consciousness* is *real*, being an ability to have all one's senses working to understand what is happening, with a response to this in an alert, aware manner. In other words, the stuff out of which everything is made is *cognitive* and the highest material expression of *consciousness* is what we call *life*. In this view, *consciousness* is not an emergent property of a complex system, but the other way around. A complex system is an emergent property of the *conscious* energy out of which everything physical is made. Therefore, *consciousness* cannot magically emerge from algorithms, but its seeds are already present in creation. In this view, *consciousness* and *complex physical systems* co-evolve.

There is no time to explore this subject in more depth because I want to make a convincing case that to make truly intelligent, autonomous machines, *consciousness* is indispensable and this is not a property that will emerge from computers. Some people could then insist that computers may be able to perform better than humans without *consciousness,* which is discussed next. I aim to show that *comprehension* is a fundamental property of *consciousness*, even more important than *qualia-perception* and that this is a defining property of *intelligence.* Therefore, if there is *no consciousness* there is *no comprehension* and without it – *no intelligence* – so a system cannot be autonomous for long.

MAKING DECISIONS

Let us consider how human beings make decisions. Our sensory system converts various forms of energy in our environment into electrical signals, which are then sent to the brain for processing. The result of this activity is another set of electrical signals representing multi-sensory information: *visual, auditory, tactile* and so on. At the end of this process we have a certain amount of *objective* information about the world. Computers can arrive up to this point. This information then is converted somehow within our *consciousness* into *semantic* data: an *integrated* multisensory qualia-display of the state of the world that includes both our *inner* world (*thoughts & ideas represented in words/ images in the mind*) and the *outer* world (*input from our environment*). In fact, it may be even more accurate to say that the *outer world* has been brought *inside of us,* with a representation that integrates both for a holistic interpretation.

This is what I call *qualia-perception,* but it is only the raw semantic data out of which comprehension is achieved through an additional process even more mysterious than the one that produced *qualia-perception. Comprehension* is what allows us to *understand* the current situation, within the context of our past experience, existing perceptions and the present set of our desires, aspirations, intentions and goals for providing such insight.

Understanding, resulting from internal and external verbal and non-verbal processing, is the next necessary step before an intelligent choice can be made. It is understanding that allows us to decide if action is needed, and if so, what one is optimal in the present circumstances. The degree to which consciousness is involved in deciding what action to take has a huge range, going from no involvement whatsoever, all the way to a protracted conscious reflection and further pondering that may take days or weeks.

When the situation is judged to be similar to others, with a certain action that produced good results, this same one can be subconsciously chosen, producing something akin to a *conditioned response.* On the other hand, there are situations unlike anything encountered before, in which case the various choices, based on our prior experience, are likely to be inadequate. Here is where our *consciousness* gets deeply involved, allowing us to come up with a *creative* solution. We find the cutting edge of *human consciousness,* where this is indispensable, not in solving trivial problems but in those requiring deep thoughts and higher-level cognition and communication. Therefore, real intelligence is the ability to correctly judge a situation and find a creative solution. It requires *comprehension,* which, in human beings, is normally a psycho-linguistic and non-linguistic process, assembling information from many sources for understanding.

Now, to have true autonomy, a robot needs to be able to operate in unconstrained environments, successfully handling the huge variability and unpredictability of real-life situations. It must also deal with issues in hostile environments, where there is deception, aggression and conflict. It is the near-infinite variability of these situations that make *comprehension* necessary and only this state can reduce or remove the *ambiguity* present in the objective data. An example of this problem is *handwriting recognition* or *language translation,* where the *form, content and/or use* of information is ambiguous. Therefore, there is not enough data, at that level, to be able to solve the problem.

Autonomous robots are only possible in situations where the environment is either artificially controlled or its expected variability is relatively small. If *qualia-perception* is the hard problem of *consciousness*, it is *comprehension* that is the *hardest* one. This is where the difference between a machine and a human being cannot be bridged. Comprehension and its expression is the most complex, holistic activity of human beings and its dynamism and unpredictability require continual, creative, original responses.

HOLISTIC SYSTEMS

All the machines we build (*computers included*) are made by assembling a number of *separate* parts. Therefore, we can at least in principle disassemble a machine into all its separate components and reassemble these to function once more. However, we cannot disassemble a *living* cell into its atomic and molecular components and then reassemble them hoping that it will work again. The living cell is a dynamic system of a different kind than our machines: it uses *quantum components* that have no definable boundaries.

We study cellular reductively like we would a machine, but cells work as *holistic* systems. A cell is also an *open* system because it constantly exchanges energy and matter with the environment in which it exists. Thus, the physical structure of the cell is *dynamic*; it is recreated from moment to moment with parts constantly flowing in and out of it, even if it seems to us that it stays the same. Therefore, a cell cannot be separated from the environment with which it is in symbiosis without *losing* something. A computer instead, for as long as it works, has the same atoms and molecules that it had when it was first constructed. Nothing changes in its hardware, and in that sense it is a *static* system, which can only function in prescribed circumstances.

The kind of information processing done in a cell is completely different to that going on in our computers. In a computer, the transistors are connected together in a fixed pattern; in a cell, the parts interact freely with each other, processing information in ways we do not yet fully comprehend. As long as we study cells as *reductive* biochemical systems rather than quantum information-processing systems, we will not be able to understand the difference between them and our computers.

When we study a cell reductively and separated from its environment, we are reducing a holistic system into the sum of its parts, throwing away what is more than this phenomenon. That is where *consciousness* is. It exists only in the *open dynamism* of life and is inextricably linked to this in the cells. These are the indivisible atoms out of which all living organisms are built. The bottom line is that life and consciousness are not reducible to *classical* physics, like computers.

Without *consciousness* there can be no self and no *interiority*, just mechanisms going through their own mindless paces, *imitating* a living thing. What would our life be if we did not feel anything? If we did not feel love, joy, enthusiasm, a sense of beauty and (*why not*) even pain? A machine is a zombie, therefore, going through the motions in a predictable way. There is no inner life in a machine; it is all *exteriority*. In a living organism, even the outer world is brought inside, represented in the mind by '*inner language*' which gives it meaning. It is *consciousness* that gives understanding and purpose in life, enabling us to deal with its unpredictability.

The idea that classical computers can become smarter than human beings is actually a dangerous fantasy, because if this viewpoint is accepted we will limit ourselves to express only a very small fraction of what we really are and can be. Such an idea actually takes away our power, freedom and humanity: qualities that pertain to our *consciousness* and not to the machine that experts have persuaded us to compare ourselves.

In my view, the real danger of progress in robotics and AI is not about creating machines that will take over humanity, because they will be more perfect than us. The important issue is that people of ill-will may cause serious damage to mankind by using evermore powerful computers and robots for evil ends. Then it will be *man*** not *machine* that causes the major trouble and upset for the world. This is a huge challenge that society must immediately face with courage and conviction. We cannot afford to be *reactive* but must be *proactive* in preventing such horrific dangers and possible disasters.

CONCLUSION

Used properly, computers and AI will allow us to discover the magnificence of life as we critically compare ourselves to them. This new knowledge can accelerate our spiritual evolution and help us to live life purposefully and well. Used poorly, AI may enslave us to hateful men who will control our freedoms and blight our lives. The choice is ours and ours alone. A radical rethink of our education, attitudes and views is vitally necessary. We must prepare the citizens of the world to communicate, cooperate and collaborate together, because without these abilities to operate at higher-thinking levels and share our knowledge all mankind will be doomed as many experts presently forecast.

Education for Robotics (ER) or r-learning is now being considered seriously by many nations. This book represents the thinking and experiences of practitioners who are leaders in their field. Such a debate enables us to disseminate our thoughts and opinions to enable us to make the right calls for our future.

MAIN POINTS

- Intelligent machines can operate more efficiently than human beings and now are taking over routine procedures to radically change work patterns in all professions
  - Machines lack the *consciousness* of human beings, so are unable to deal with unpredictable and varying conditions and although useful have limited power
  - Machines are only as good as the people who programme them and there is increasing evidence of their evil, abusive use which makes it urgent to develop moral, ethical codes for strict regulation and human safety.
  - Machines must remain as useful servant tools and not become our masters if we are to improve the existence of mankind

Note: *Wetware is a term drawn from the computer-related idea of hardware or software but applied to biological life forms. It describes the human element of an information technology (IT) architecture.

** 'Man' is used generically to include everyone.

NOTE FROM THE EDITORS

Professor Federico Faggin is regarded as a top world genius for his invention of the microchip and computer touchscreen. He is in universal demand to elaborate on the future of robotics and we are very privileged that he has contributed to this text, initiated by the 2017 Practitioner Doctoral Group at the University of Buckingham, UK.

CHAPTER 2
WHAT IS TECHNOLOGY?

RICCARDA MATTEUCCI

'Our deepest hope as humans lies in technology;
but our deepest trust lies in nature.
These forces are like tectonic plates grinding
inexorably into each other in one, long, slow collision.
This collision is not new, but more than anything else it is defining our era'.

W. Brian Arthur [1]

SUMMARY

We associate technology with machinery, but from a long-term view it is simply the further development of evolutionary processes. Technology is how human minds explore the realm of possibilities and change through methods of searching for solutions. It is a continuation of a four-billion-year-old force that pursues an even greater ability to evolve. It has discovered entirely new forms in the universe such as radios, laser, maser, atomic fission, microprocessor, gravitational waves, Higgs' Boson, as well as many other phenomena that organic evolution could never produce. There are two schools of thought: technology increases the mind's drive towards new inventions and accelerates the pace of connections between people. Development takes place when encouragement is given to research in science, innovation, education, literacy and pluralism. In the course of continuous evolution, technology generates more options, opportunities, connections, diversity, thoughts and problems. The second view maintains that technology is tearing us apart and leading humans to inevitable loneliness.

INTRODUCTION

The word *technelogos* comes from the Greek and when the ancient people used the word *techne*, which is translated as *ingenuity*, they meant something like art and craft. It indicated ability to resolve problems in certain circumstances and was a trait treasured by their poets, like Homer. King Odysseus was a master of *techne,* as Steven Talbot (2001) affirms.[2] Together with many scholars of his era, Plato considered *techne*—manual craftwork—impure and degrading because he rejected practical knowledge. It was in Aristotle's treatise, *Rhetoric*, that the word was first joined to *logos* to produce the single term *technologos*.[3] After this appearance, the term *technologos* seems to have disappeared. However, technology did not with the Greeks inventing iron welding, bellows, lathes and keys as well as the Romans developing vaults, aqueducts, cement, sewers etc.

Over the following centuries, scholars continued to refer to the making of things as '*craft*' and the expression of inventiveness as '*art*'. Tools and machines multiplied. Their products were termed '*useful arts*' and each of them – *weaving, metalworking, mining* etc. had their own secret knowledge passed on through the master/apprentice relationship. These inventions were still considered '*art*' productions of the maker and the term retained the original Greek sense of craft and cleverness (Kelly, 2010).

The historian, Mitcham (1994), explains that in ancient times each product was considered a unique expression of a person, derived from their particular cleverness and knowledge, so anything made was the work of a solitary genius. What we call *classical minds* could not even think of mass production for only practical reasons. Lynn White (1940), a technology historian, adds that the Middle Ages gained glory from cathedrals, explorations and scholastics. This period was vital also for technology development as, for the first time, craftsmen built a complex civilisation based on non-human power, as machines were becoming the labourers.

The 18th century Industrial Revolutions changed society and saw the invasion of strange machines in farms and homes, but this spread still had no name. A Professor of Economics at Gottingen University in Germany, Johann Beckmann, named these *mirabilia 'technology'*. This word appears in his book, *Guide to Technology,* in 1802.[4] He recognised that human creations were not just an occasional assembly of tools derived from good ideas. The whole concept of technology had remained in the shadows for a long time, because people did not see the chronology of inventions. Another aspect he understood was that each new invention requires the viability of previous ones to keep going. '*Things*' that men were inventing produced others that launched new arts, which in turn gave birth to other tools *ad infinitum*. For example, the alphabet led to books and libraries, with each step adding further developments while retaining the virtues of previous stages in the process.

'*Electricity*' allows machines to communicate with each other, but there are none possible without mining coal or uranium, damming rivers or extracting precious metals to make solar panels. This circular, inter-connected network of systems, subsystems and machines forms a single one termed '*technology*'. In fact, Kelly (2010) affirms that *techne,* which he calls *technium,* has self-reinforcing creativity. It wants to perpetuate itself, to keep itself going (p.12-15). Every new development in *technium* is contingent upon historical antecedents. Inventions follow this sequence in every civilisation, independently of human genius.

Many scientists, like Niles Eldrege & Stephen Jay Gould, have studied the correlation between *technium* and organic evolution.[5] The greatest difference between the evolution of the '*born*' & '*made*' is that technological species virtually never become extinct. Technologies are idea-based and culture is their memory. They can be resurrected if forgotten but recorded, so that they will not be disregarded as obsolete and scrapped.

Just like human evolution, technology uses its facility to evolve but with greater rapidity. In order to provide itself with sufficient material and space to keep progress evolving *ad infini*tum, *technium* generates millions of different gadget species, techniques and products in order to reach its goal. Kelly says that evolution is the most powerful force in the universe.

Technology has brought about as many changes on our planet in the last 100 years as in a billion ones. Kelly asserts that *technium* multiplies fundamental traits and expands the mind's goodness. In so doing, along the evolutionary path, technology will help us to generate more options, opportunities, diversity, thoughts, beauty and more problems. Each innovation creates new opportunities for *technium* to change in new ways with problems producing a chance for new solutions, which is part of cultural evolution. It is shaped by three forces: the prime driver is development; the second is the influence of technological history and the third is society's free will in shaping *technium* and our choices.

There is an old story about the range and scope of early choices that is basically true: it concerns carts. These were constructed to match the width of imperial Roman war chariots, as it was easier to follow in their road tracks. They measured 4 x 8.5 feet (*translated into English measurements*), accommodating the breadth of two large warhorses. Throughout their vast empire, including Britain, roads were built to these measurements. When the English built tramways, they maintained the same width so that horse-drawn carriages could be used. Later, the first American railways imported workers from Britain, who used their own tools and jigs. Let us fast-forward to the American space-shuttle, built in different parts of the country and assembled in Florida. The two large solid–fuel rocket engines, on the sides of the launch shuttle, were sent by railway from Utah, traversing a tunnel not much wider in diameter than 4 x 8.5 feet. The rockets had to respect this width. A major design feature of the most advanced transport system to date was determined over 2000 years ago by the breadth of the rumps of two horses. This is how history impacts. The size of a horse yoke determined that of a space rocket showing how technology influences over time.

EVOLUTION OF THE TECHNIUM AND THE GENETIC ORGANISM

The evolution of the *technium* and of genetic organisms present minor differences, sharing traits of a simple system to one more complex: from general to specific, uniformity to diversity, individualism to mutualism, wastage to efficiency and from a slow change to greater evolvability. Kelly detects that the way a technology type changes imitates a similar pattern to a genealogical tree. Technology expresses ideas but genetic evolution, on the other hand, demonstrates the work of genes. Ideas never come alone but are interwoven into a network of auxiliary ones – consequential notions, supporting concepts, side effects and logical consequences – in a cascade of subsequent possibilities.

Ideas form into a cluster. One example would be an engine made of unrelated parts, developing into an integrated system that evolves into a further design. The economist, Brian Arthur, in *the Nature of Technology* (2009), says that many technologies share parts belonging to others, so development happens automatically, as components improve in other outside uses. These combinations are like breeding, as they produce a hereditary tree of ancestral technologies. Just like Darwinian evolution, where tiny improvements are rewarded with more copies, innovations spread steadily through the population. According to Kelly, technologies form ecosystems of cross-supported allies and evolutionary lines, so the *technium* is a type of evolutionary life. The story of life can be arranged in several ways. To better understand the 4 billion year history of technological life, the biologists, John Maynard Smith & Eors Szthmary (1995), have detected 8 thresholds of biological information. According to their theory, life is self-generated with major transitions in biological organisation:

One replicating molecule -> Interacting population of replicating molecules
Replicating molecules -> Strung into chromosomes
Chromosome of RNA enzymes -> DNA proteins
Cell without nucleus -> Cell with nucleus
Asexual reproduction (*cloning*) -> Sexual recombination
Single-cell organism -> Multicell organism
Solitary individual -> Colonies & superorganisms
Primate societies -> Language-based societies [6]

Each level in this hierarchy marks a major advance in complexity and the biologists affirm that the evolution of science and technology parallels nature. Kelly maintains that technological transitions are passages from one level of organisation to another. In parallel with their view, he has arranged the major transitions in technology according to how information is organised. At each point, information and knowledge are processed at a level not present before and the major transitions in the *technium* are:

Primate communication → Language
Oral lore→ Writing/Mathematical notation
Scripts → Printings
Book Knowledge →Scientific method
Artisan Production→ Mass production
Industrial Culture→ Global communication
(Kelly 2010, p.47)

LANGUAGE IS AN INVENTION

In the 21st century it is clear, as it should have been to Neanderthals that *'something'* important came from the past. A new biological force had emerged: the invention of *language*. Scientists, including Richard Klein, Ian Tattersal & William Calvin (1996) among many others, suppose that the *'something'* happened called *language* to dramatically affect human systems. *Hominins* had been clever up to that point: they could make crude tools and handle fire. Though the growth of the African *Hominins'* brain size and physical structure had levelled out, evolution continued to change the way humans operated. Due to mutation, the brain was rewired for verbal language, producing articulate speech sequences, with this narrative structure enabling higher-thinking processes to develop.

In a remote prehistory, our quadruped progenitors became bipeds (*5-7 million years ago*) and from an evolutionary point of view this extraordinary event sets conditions for the birth of language. This amazing human faculty – *language and its peculiarities* – has promoted the development of the mind, intelligence, curiosity and creativity. It is unknown when language appeared precisely and not even what was the origin. Paleontologists and linguists study fossil remains and since the larynx and pharynx are soft and do not leave traces, it has been particularly difficult to reconstruct the phonatory parts of prehistoric man. The lowering of the larynx, due to the verticalized head for the bipedal walking change, has certainly determined the facility to produce linguistic sounds. From the skull of *hominidis of Neanderthal*, present in Europe before *Homo Sapiens* (*300-35.000 thousand years ago*), it is believed that *Neanderthal* was able to speak though not using a great variety of sounds.

From South Africa, this population spread throughout Africa to the Middle East where they remained for 50-60 thousand years. Continuing towards Europe and Asia and prevailing over other forms of *Homo* present there, they demonstrated great adaptability and curiosity. When we speak of the LANGUAGE AS AN INVENTION, we refer to the one possessed by *modern sapiens* who were able to build themselves more efficient instruments and master a more articulated, advanced language.

Klein (2010) says that instead of acquiring a larger brain, like the *Neanderthal* and *Erectus*, *Sapiens* gained a rewired one. For the first time, language allowed minds to invent with purpose and deliberation in lateral (*free-thinking*) and logical (*fixed-stepped thinking*) ways. Daniel Dennet (1996) suggests that in human history there is no step more constructive, crucial and determining than language invention. When *Homo Sapiens* became the beneficiary, it launched them beyond other earthly creatures. Language was the first feature that marked mankind out from others and changed everything. This opened up many new opportunities for emigration of the *Sapiens* tribes.

Language enables new ideas to spread quickly if explained and clarified for others to understand them. It accelerates higher-levels of learning and creativity, facilitating communication, coordination and cooperation between people. Language peculiarity is *autogeneration*: allowing the mind to question itself – a mirror revealing what it thinks and a '*handle*' that becomes a tool (Kelly 2010).

Before the language revolution, the world lacked technology and humans lived as hunter-gatherers. However, paleontologists say that what they possessed was sufficient for survival, as nature was so vast, abundant and close, so able to comfortably sustain the existing population. Meanwhile, inventions began to alter the environment where the *Sapiens* lived. When leaving Africa, they were able to kill and make mammoths, giant elks and other herbivores extinct – using hunting tools. In doing so, mankind modified the eco-system and the loss of some herbivores allowed the growth or extinction of certain flora and fauna since that time.

Not all technology changes were positive. Among founders of modern science, Francis Bacon (1620) realized how powerful technology was becoming, listing three '*practical arts*' that were influential in his day: the printing press, gunpowder and magnetic compass. He said that nothing has exerted greater power to influence human affairs than *language*.[7] It has shifted the burden of evolution in humans away from genetic inheritance (*the only line of evolutionary learning for most creature*s). It has allowed language and culture to carry forward collective learning. A language-based culture stores information and oral wisdom to pass on to future generations, enabling humans to adapt and transmit learning faster than genes. The invention of writing-systems for language and mathematics structured learning still further. Writing allowed the organisation of information to spread into many aspects of life, accelerating trade, creating calendars to regulate activities etc. The information, transmitted by written laws with its inner organisation, increased knowledge worldwide.

Printing made information more accurate, permanent, organised and widespread, allowing greater review and reflection. Printing has become ubiquitous, producing information levels that dominate our visual landscape. The scientific method enables the collection of reliable information, testing and evaluation in the context of other verifiable material. Newly-ordered information is deployed to restructure any subject. When the scientific method was applied to crafts, men invented the mass production of interchangeable parts, the assembly line, efficiency and specialisation. The results have been that mankind has raised living standards that are now taken for granted. The latest transition in knowledge organisation is taking place now as we introduce information and commands into any manufactured item for easier use. Microscopic chips even allow computation and communication added to each item, with objects globally distributed through the web. Kelly (2010) says language invention is the last major transformation of the natural world and the first of the manufactured one. Words, ideas and concepts are expressions of the complex things that social animals, like us, create and they are the foundation for all technology. Natural evolution flows into the technical because language unites the two transitions into one continuous sequence.

DO HUMANS NEED TECHNOLOGY?

From a limited point of view, you do not need technology and can live like native Americans off the land, or certain tribes in the Amazonian rain-forest or New Guinea. From a wider standpoint, however, we need technology to continue moving forward for our convenience. Some sociologists use an example from the *Amish* communities. To summarise what is a lengthy study, experts say that the Amish distinguish between *using* something and *owning* it. They would not get a license, purchase an automobile, pay insurance and become dependent on a car, but use a taxi instead. Another distinction is in relation to technology and what they have at home. When researchers went to Amish homes, they found that most were lit by natural light from windows. However, hanging over the wooden table, where they meet together to talk and eat, there might be a single, electric light bulb. When questioned about this, the answer was for the benefit of visitors. (Kelly, 2010).

Debates on advantages and disadvantages of technology centre on the impact it has for improving or worsening human life. Malik (2017) points out that many criticise its harmful environmental and alienating effects on people. However, we consider technology fundamental and beneficial to progress and the quality of life, as it has evolved to serve not only humans but also other animal species.

TECHNOLOGY IN COMMUNICATION, EDUCATION AND HEALTH CARE

Society changes constantly and today is very different to that existing now. We live in an '*information society*', with technology assuming a leading role, especially regarding information and its rapid transmission. This could not be imagined without new technologies and the role they play. They build bridges between people across the world, so that different cultures can make contact. Radio, telephones, satellite communications, wireless Internet etc. allow people to make contact, exchange ideas, views and attitudes although living in different places.

The Internet contains a vast quantity of information and technology has made it possible for this to reach far and wide. Looking at the positive features made available by intelligent machines, online education allows knowledge to be accessible for students in remote locations. Modern technology also provides ways to grow more food, improve transportation and increase productivity for growing populations. We need it to make life more comfortable and safe, providing a well-nourished life for humans. An example is that scientists consider *health improvements* are the biggest benefits received from technical advancements. Life lasts longer due to better knowledge of how the body functions and new tools help cure illness. People now recover from wounds and diseases that recently would have proved fatal. Advanced technology, like pacemakers, respirators or simple stents, allow people to stay healthy and decrease child mortality. Biotechnology, nanotechnology, computing and robotics have quickly improved and are expected to advance more so in future. Medicines, drugs and vaccinations, developed from research, have saved lives. High-tech hospitals, clinics and health centres have helped patients from backward nations achieve better health-care and facilities.

Humanity has never been without technology and the modern age has brought wonderful changes to our world. Nevertheless, this has not been without costs, consequences and risks, but the overall effects are positive. The Internet is an example: should we deplore people who lament the quantity of fake news and false information, the youngsters recruited for wars, as well as child abuse and pornography, the selling of drugs etc., available on line? The Internet is very recent, needing urgent adjustments. There is an increasing demand for adequate, stricter regulations, issued and agreed by countries across the world, in order to control negative outcomes that make the Internet problematic.

The shortage of natural resources, air pollution and other effects of overpopulation, can be averted through improved technology. This has taken such a step forward that it is impossible to imagine that we can do without it, even though it has altered the world beyond recognition. It is our responsibility to continue developments for human benefit, making sensible choices about expansion and progress.

CONCLUSION

Evolution has developed exponentially so fast that we cannot imagine what will happen in 10 years' time. *Technium* can be viewed as a black hole of uncertainty, but humanity has gone through several evolutionary transitions already (Kelly 2010). The first can be considered as the invention of *language*; the second – *writing* - that changed the speed of human learning by easing the transmission of ideas across territories and time; the third is – *science* – and the structure of the scientific method. The latter enables greater inventions. With technological innovation, the structure of knowledge evolves. The achievement of science is to discover new things; evolution organises discovery in different ways. With advances in communication technology with computers, we have entered a new way of knowing. *Technium's* first goal is to structure the increasing quantity of information, with tools mankind generates to then increase world organization.

The scope of expanding opportunities, knowledge, complexity and diversity shows where technology is leading, but it remains almost impossible to predict the future. Scientists suggest that we should explore historical trends, perhaps going back millions of years, to see how they have led to the present situation. Technology expands outwards from the present to allow us to cope better with world problems. *Technium* is an explosion of information, complexity, diversity, sentience, beauty and structure that is transforming even as it expands.

As a final reflection, '*homo erectus*' stood tall and straight, with language enabling an ability to communicate face-to-face effectively with others. Now if you observe humans they are no longer 'erectus' but bent over computers for most of the day. Does this herald a new era when we step backwards in our ability to communicate successfully with our fellows? There are so many examples today of a lack of ability to do so. Technology is encouraging us to become remote and connect in superficial ways with each other, so lessening opportunities for emotional bonding, extended talk and higher-level thinking. Will we lose the power of words totally? Will we lose our ability to cope?

MAIN POINTS

- Evolution is exponential and technology follows the same course
- Language, as an evolutionary process, has enabled technology to progress more rapidly
- The advent of machine technology is making communication a more remote process
- Evidence suggests we are losing the ability to process and produce extended talk for thinking

NB: Notes and references at the end of chapter 4.

CHAPTER 3

IS TECHNOLOGY TEARING US APART?

RICCARDA MATTEUCCI

SUMMARY

The World Economic Forum coined the phrase 'Fourth Industrial Revolution' to describe today's technology changes. They encompass 3D printing, gene editing, driverless cars, robotics, artificial intelligence, the Internet as well as many other technologies. This revolution presents positive aspects, like an ability to create new sustainable economies, based on parity, circularity, low-carbon efficiency - focusing on human well-being and planet maintenance. While negative aspects could destroy jobs, reduce privacy and drive over-consumption, successful results will be possible only if human beings and communities are at the centre of all technology innovations. Digital devices, however, are decreasing face-to-face communication, with ways this is affecting society and the quality of life being the recent topic of major debates. .

INTRODUCTION

Mark Oppenheimer's article (*17 January, 2014*), attempting to answer the question *Is technology driving us apart?* – is still relevant today. He reports on how Keith Hampton, Professor of Media and Information at Michigan State University, together with associates, filmed human interactions at Bryant Park. This place is at the rear of the New York Public Library, renowned for fashion shows. It was selected for a study to find out how people interact with others. More specifically, researchers wanted to know how digital devices affect human interactions.

Hampton based work on research of the 1960s-70s by William Whyte, a sociologist, director and writer who filmed *Social Lives in Small Urban Spaces* (1980). He recorded people interacting in public, to learn how they behaved and how long interactions lasted. As a product of this work, both a book and film were published in the 1980s. *The Social Life of Small Urban Spaces* is a manual for the creation and management of urban spaces. In fact, New York City derived useful principles for space creation from Whyte's conclusions. The film, with the same name as the book and following its structure, is a montage of sequences filmed by the *Street Life Project* and remains a model for future research.

Hampton's study (2014), carried out in the same locations as Whyte's films, compared and analysed effects of today's interconnected people and results produced were different from current perspectives. Technology has made people more connected: ...'*it turns out the wired folks – they recognized like three times as many of their neighbours when asked, Hampton said. 'They spoke with their neighbours on the phone five times as often and attended more community events*'. However, what he does not consider is the changing interactions amongst families. While walking in the park, we often notice that many parents are exclusively connected to the virtual world and their children look lost, trying to find a way not to be alone. I remember my mother explaining colours and their various nuances and teaching flower names and their scents in different seasons to me, as well as interacting with other parents while walking in the park or elsewhere.

Hampton's research shines a light on a world where we are incorporating digital activities into life, exhorting us to pay more attention to people around us. Though necessary tools, we need to manage and moderate digital devices, giving time to meaningful face-to-face interactions. These play a vital role in developing thoughtful conversations to assist mental growth. A lack of parental focus on talk is described by Catherine Steiner-Adair, a clinical psychologist, in *The Big Disconnect* (2013). She details technology threats to children, from infancy to adulthood, recognising digital age challenges for families, with ways to strengthen social and emotional development. Parents and schools are warned about social media effects on everyone and offered practical advice on addressing problems.

The relationship between technology and people has been described by Sherry Turkle (2011), Professor of Technology & Society, at MIT Boston. She noticed that in people conversations a topic may arise to which there is no response. A race ensues to determine who is first to decode information and share it with others. The speed and altruism implicit in sharing information is gratifying, but Turkle, in, *Alone Together* (2011), warns us to be cautious about the power of new tools and toys that are altering social lives. She says we must consider our dependence on digital devices and how they affect direct communication with others. Turkle believes that the next generation will chart a path between isolation and connectivity. In other articles, she deplores increasing lack of empathy among people which is learnt through opportunities to formally communicate and is basic to relationships and well-being.

IS COMMUNICATION TECHNOLOGY TEARING US APART?

David Mizne, a marketing communication manager at **15Five**, San Francisco CA, interviewed experts who suggested that communication technology is tearing us apart.[8] Some of these then wrote articles adding further examples and experiences as problems of distraction and isolation worsened. Although we cannot dispense with technology, Mizne acknowledges concerns about an *'unhealthy relationship'*.

Professor Sherry Turkle's article: *Stop Googling, Let's Talk*, for the New York Times (*11 March, 2016*), expands the discussion. Where has one-to-one conversation gone now that people prefer texting to speaking? Communication never reaches great depth, she says, because it can be cut off any minute as attention constantly drifts to our phones (t*ext, email & social media*) while we are interacting face-to-face. This is problematic for youngsters, who are so accustomed to phone exchanges so do not know how to engage interpersonally. We are less empathic and avoid conversations playing with ideas. Intimacy and empathy fade if we lose eye contact and do not display the physical pantomime that accompanies face-to-face conversation.

Tony Schwartz in: *Humanity as a Competitive Advantage* (*The New York Times, 18 September, 2015*) consults a doctor about a problem. This medic was open, direct and interested in the problem's impact on Tony's quality of life. From questions asked, it was clear he had studied Schwartz' case and offered a plan of action. Schwartz commented on the empathy and care shown, unavailable via technology.

This aspect is underlined by Geoff Colvin in: *Humans Are Underrated: What High Achievers Knows that Brilliant Machines Never Will* (2016). He states that machines are technically capable but without feelings. He says that the most highly-valued business skills are communication and relationships, co-creativity and cultural sensitivity, rather than new technology achievements. Ability to understand and influence how we and others feel has most impact on how people perform. At work, companies are shifting perspectives and want people to bring out their best at work and support others to do so. This is something that robots cannot do yet and this depends on effective interpersonal communication.

Nir Eyal, an entrepreneur, wrote: *Hooked – How To Build Habit-Forming Products* (2013), showing how he became hooked on technology. He questions why we act against our best interests when adversely affected by devices. In: *Un-Hooked: Increasing Focus in the Age of Distraction*, (2015) and *Fundamental Attribution Error: Why You Make Terrible Life Choices (September 2018)*, he argues that we have not had time to react socially to rapidly emerging technologies. He wished his book had been available, when becoming a professional. The solution is not to undo progress but find ways to moderate habits formed from using technology. It is possible to remove triggers, like devices kept out of bedrooms to improve sleep, or change notification settings for specific schedules. In business there should be designated daily blackout periods.

The Telegraph (*31 October, 2018*) presents an article by Sophie Curtis: *The Rise of the 'Next-Pats': How Technology is Helping us Live More Global Lives,* (2015). Curtis says experts have spotted a new demographic social group, known as *'Next-Pats'*, using technology to live more connected, global lives.[9] This is supported by the *'sharing economy',* led by firms like Air B&B, Uber & Transfer Wise, who help remove cost barriers, allowing access from all social backgrounds. Technology paves the way for global life-styles, involving people in activities to help better lives of others in home and adopted communities. Curtis forecasts that *Next-Pats* will soon be a large population percentage, in the US & UK, as technology improves and world travel continues to be valued. She urges Apple, Google, Facebook, Twitter, Instagram and similar companies to address the negative impacts of their creations. People should turn off devices or log-off from social networks for two hours daily. Corporations could encourage people to make choices for greater connectedness with themselves, each other and the natural world. These may have negative impact on revenues short term, but create long-term loyalty and well being. This would help people to become closer to who they want to be and produce less stress.

COMMUNITIES AND TECHNOLOGY

The role of communities, as well as the one we play within them, is changed by our fast-paced, hyper-connected world. Some people may feel more connected to an online community than to their neighbourhood. Local communities are now able to use social media, in ways impossible only a decade ago, to extend their reach. The success of communities will depend on how they meet challenges of the 21st century. Macro-level climate changes, frontiers of science and technology and the global economy produce a range of micro-level challenges, with good and bad results. Only if citizens, governments and businesses work together, with the same goals, will there be more positive than negative outcomes. As an example of a connected community, NextDrop, a social enterprise, helped water-scarce towns, like Mysore in India.[10] The way water travelled around the city was mapped by digital technology, assembling service operators, engineers and consumer-stakeholders, who did not usually communicate. NextDrop calls up experts and consumers to deliver information on how and when water will be supplied and consumers contact them for delivery problems or to fix pipe leaks or damage.

Charities and communities use online platforms to be connected to businesses and projects use them for launching funding calls, volunteers, food donations etc. All Marks and Spencer (M&S) stores are inter-connected, using a network to redistribute surplus food over the country. Their policy is to reduce 20% of food waste by 2020, checking surplus products to determine how to reduce them. Digital technologies could guide citizens to the *Democracy-OS platform*, for debating and voting on political issues. This has been used in Tunisia, Mexico and Italy by the political *Movement 5S*. The goal is to provide a common platform for any city, state or government to put proposals to public vote. A negative aspect might be the different knowledge-levels using technology. Those with the best technology skills could dominate proceedings, drowning out quieter voices, like the elderly, vulnerable and disadvantaged.

The *WHO Global Network Initiative (GNI) of Age-friendly Cities & Communities* is developing projects, offering advice and solutions on issues such as building a network of '*age-friendly cities*' to exchange experiences. [11] It is based on internationally recognized laws and standards for human rights on freedom of expression against government restrictions. Companies, investors, civil society organizations, academics and other stakeholders link to protect user information from illegal or arbitrary interference, when confronted with government demands, laws, or regulations that compromise privacy. GNI considers governments to be ultimately responsible for citizen human rights regarding freedom of expression and privacy. As an example, the Japanese Government has assigned a third of its robotic budget to developing '*carebots*' for assisting seniors, as a shortage of carers is predicted by 2025. According to a Merrill Lynch report, this could give Japan leadership in this field, worth $17.4 billion by 2020, which means tomorrow! [12]

COMMENT

Access to online information and opinion allows people to view different lifestyles and access knowledge they might not have encountered otherwise. This could generate understanding and compassion within communities, especially those on the other side of the world. Virtual reality has broken down geographical and social barriers. However, we need to consider the potential damage to cohesion that may be inflicted, due to the ease with which extremism and conspiracies can now be disseminated online. Research shows that young people are finding difficulty in separating fact from fiction. Parents, teachers and community leaders must guide them through information that is at their fingertips. Guidance is needed when the young are exposed to continual extremism. Rapid change means communities are given little time to catch up and reflect before further innovations take over.

IS TECHNOLOGY WIDENING THE GAP BETWEEN RICH & POOR?

Modern technologies (*computers, robotics & AI*) have increased the gap between rich and poor, as factories use them to manufacture goods rather than employing humans, reducing employment. This is one view, while others think that technology generates new work roles. Many companies are shifting from human labour to machines for production, because the latter are more accurate in repetitive tasks and cost less in the long run. While large numbers of humans are losing menial jobs that support families, inventors and management are getting richer by cutting costs. To cite an example, when Nokia used robots for smartphone production in Sweden, 30,000 jobs were lost, creating a profit for the firm in 2017 not seen before. These innovations are creating new job roles for people, who can learn computer technology and earn higher salaries. Some companies, like SuzukiMotors and FCA, have cut workers and compelled those remaining to operate automated systems, acquiring knowledge and competencies, resulting in salary rises. However, many lost their jobs.

Poor people can use technology, but a lack of adequate education limits the way they use it, or they do so unwisely – to sell drugs or sex – as examples. In most cases, new jobs need skills and qualifications that schools and colleges do not presently provide and this is a problem for people who cannot afford to attend institutions where they can obtain them. Schools will change in the next 10 years and teachers must be prepared for this in education and training (Sir Anthony Seldon, 2018 p. 176)

Furthermore, the big tech firms are viewed as manipulating the masses, driving people to achieve media success. Research demonstrates that Instagram use makes viewers dissatisfied with their image. The poor are less able to match up to a successful image and this increases crime and psychological discomfort. Opponents argue that technological changes create a turnover among the rich. Those who are wealthy one year may not be the next, whereas in the past they generally stayed so for generations. Gregory Norton (2018) claims that now people become wealthy, because they can provide others with valued products and services. He acknowledges that modern technology and business practices (*Amazon & AliBaba*) enable entrepreneurs to satisfy people needs more than at any time in the past. They earn more money as they serve more people.

Francis Carmody, CEO at Veritasia Ministries (2016) states that the lack of access to technology maintains and may widen the gap between rich and poor, while an unproductive use wastes time and money. In his view, most people use the Internet as a video game merely for entertainment, while technology should be a resource to abandon the old industrial age with its 8-hour working day. The Internet is a magic box that, like Aladdin's Lamp, can inspire people. It gives information access that would take longer to obtain in a library. You can look for a job, meet people, expand your mind, figure how to fix things, improve productivity and earn more money. Most importantly, people can get free education, though some jobs need apprenticeships to learn how to use machinery and apply principles..

Dennis Pratt (2018) says that it is not technology *per se* that widens the gap but rather the '*acceleration*' of technological innovation. Take an item sold for £1,000, as an example. As sales improve, the manufacturer may lower the price and make an item available to a wider range of buyers. If speed of innovation is constant, the gap between rich and poor will also remain. It does not disappear because the rich can afford the next innovation whilst the poor will struggle to achieve it. It is a vicious circle. Is there an effective solution? Stop innovation! In that case the rich would not access innovations first, but the poor would never benefit from them. That is impossible.

COMMENT

We must moderate our habits with techology - setting boundaries around use but not rejecting digital advances. In the context of business, digital communication must fulfil real, clearly defined objectives, or else it becomes no more than an end in itself. Furthermore, it is fundamental that context is kept in mind when using technology for communicating. It provides tools to convey information and ideas to other people. When we use texts and emails to contact others, however, we diminish empathy and often understanding. Instead, we must consider an etiquette to convey sensitive information and decide the most appropriate methods to use. We are defined as '*The New Barbarians*', as in most cases we do not know how to behave with modern communication means, like cellphones and the Internet. We are losing a sense of proper limits. To keep these matters in mind is important, not just for preserving our human nature, but also to act appropriately for varying situations. It is difficult to understand why most people prefer sending quantities of emails rather than a telephone conversation.

IS TECHNOLOGY A STATUS SYMBOL?

The sociologist, Thorstein Veblen, in a theory of *Leisure Class* (1899) won literary fame describing the life of the wealthy. He coined phrases '*conspicuous consumption*' and '*pecuniary emulation*' that are still widely used. He explained the term '*conspicuous consumption*' for rich people who flaunted wealth through extravagant, lavish spending.[13] Veblen claimed that the purpose of buying a thousand-dollar suit when a hundred-dollar one would do, is to demonstrate power. The rich displayed dominance by showing how much money they could waste on things not needed. His observations are relevant today, as it seems nothing has changed but may be worse. Industry captains show their position by buying islands and super-yachts, or covering everything they possess with gold. Modern elites project power by buying insane, expensive commodities with a status emerging called - *conspicuous production*. We form part of the 99% majority, while the 1% are the rich running the world.

Lauren Coleman published an article in *The Huffington Post* (2017), referring to research at South University, Anthos. This claims that displaying new technology has become a status symbol. Furthermore, people show a need to personalise technology and be seen as more than just another iPhone owner. It is about individuality within a constituency of people using the same items. Coleman invites us to reflect on tribal markings in ancient societies. By having them on faces and bodies, tribe members could identify others at a distance and tell whether someone might be an enemy, a stranger or a friend. To personalise technical devices shows a mental attitude in individuals, who aim to show sophisticated high tech that certain people own. Those with low wages feel discriminated against if they cannot afford the most up-to-date items. People incur debt in order to possess the latest equipment. The populations of emerging countries want to compete with the West and imitating its technology is a step towards adopting this lifestyle.

COMMENT

Han OOI (2017) (*CEO & Founder of Radiosity Holding LLC since 2015*) says we need to think of technology as a force multiplier. The poor can only work with hands and feet and have no way of multiplying productive capacity without improving their education to make use of force multipliers. Meanwhile, the rich can make use of tools to multiply capabilities. One rich person, with help of factories, robots, computers and other tools, has an army compared to the poor.

CONCLUSION

What can be done? Researchers have put forward ideas to increase productivity and decrease stress, such as structuring our own work, performing creative tasks in the morning and taking a short break before being involved with different ones. It is possible to put our inbox on pause for an hour or so, or stop answering e-mails. This will train others not to expect answers straight away. Goals and tasks accomplished should be shared with others on a weekly basis. When people commit themselves to certain priorities and fail to accomplish them, comparing outcome to that of other workers, could motivate them to find a better way to achieve things more effectively the following week.

MAIN POINTS

- People are now so dependent on technology that it is in danger of taking over our lives
- We have to manage time so that we still have face-to-face contact with others for personal bonding
- The balance between technology and human activity needs close monitoring
- Care must be taken not to widen the distance between rich and poor because of technology

Notes and References at the end of Chapter 4.

CHAPTER 4
CELLPHONES

RICCARDA MATTEUCCI

SUMMARY

This chapter considers the issue of cellphone use. With most of us now using mobile phones to run our lives, we need to understand the pitfalls of this particular technology. Children must be made aware of these as they are now frequent users of AI machines. The first part presents some of the views recently aired in the media, which provides information that has been investigated in studies across the world. The second section discusses the mobile phone ban in French schools from September 2018.

THE DAILY TELEGRAPH CAMPAIGN
ON DUTY OF CARE

3,000 crimes annually against children as young as 5 years

INTRODUCTION

In June 2018, The Daily Telegraph launched a campaign, **DUTY OF CARE**, exhorting digital companies to have a legal responsibility over children using their services. The campaign aims to protect children from physical and psychological ill health, abuse and addictive behaviour and calls for a committed back up from experts in various fields. Charities, academics and doctors collected data of children's use of social media and gaming, showing a vast range of harmful content - built up over time and not detected by parents and teachers. The controls used are not effective and the numbers of children seeking help is growing annually for internet addiction, sex texting, grooming and on-line bullying leading to increasing suicides.

Peter Wanless, the Chief Executive of the National Society for the Prevention of Cruelty to Children (NSPCC) invites the Government to introduce laws regulating the matter, after years of inadequate actions. More than 25% of UK schoolchildren spend six plus hours-per-day in front of computers/phones. This habit is leading to addictions with an estimated four times the number of these in the population recently. Children asking for help for cyber-bullying has doubled in the last five years and Police arrest six people a day for grooming children via social media. The average person checks their phone more than 200 times a day. Also, 73% of Brits say they would suffer without checking technology regularly, with 70% of 14-24-years-olds preferring texting to talking. Professor Mark Griffiths, Dr. Richard Graham, Liz Kendall & Simon Hart are media writers, promoting risks of typical outcomes of internet/phone exposure. These are isolation, depression, mental health disorders, obesity & diabetes, although media positives are giving quick access to information and communicating rapidly.

Big tech firms, like Snapchat and Facebook, have denied they use psychological hooks to keep people online and that they factor in addictive behaviour into their product design. A spokesperson said that Facebook aimed to bring people closer to their friends, family and things they care about. Safety is priority and in the last decade experts have been working to fight cyber-bullying, gaming & grooming to support well-being. We need to protect ourselves and our families and take steps to achieve this aim.

Below are some articles taken from The Daily Telegraph of **DUTY OF CARE** campaign that presents and denounces the situation; seeks for help; asks for awareness with explanations as well as giving advice on how to act in various circumstances.

ARTICLES

The Daily Telegraph: '*My Family isn't the only one in Social Media Meltdown*'. Judith Woods (Friday 15 June 2018, p. 21)

Simon Stevens, Head of the National Health Service (NHS), put pressure on companies like Facebook and Google to be responsible for effects on youngsters. He spoke of an epidemic of mental illness among youngsters endangered by '*videos of terror attacks & beheadings, bullying & explicit sex on popular networking platforms*'. Many children spend recreation in front of a screen, so obesity is increasing. Anxiety and body dysmorphia result from frenetic connectivity? The Facebook co-founder admitted it was addictive. By playing on vulnerability, users glimpse perfect lives and crave the same.

Woods suggests that parenting has always been about choosing battles wisely, but nothing has prepared them for the war of the real and virtual worlds. Grown-ups are hooked on smartphones, checking unread messages and their '*likes*' makes them obsessed by devices. Everybody is addicted, with excuses for always monitoring phones. Professionals, of course, need to be connected to know what is going on elsewhere. Most women check the latest store offers to grasp '*the opportunity*' for a bargain. The whole family suffers, as children are up all hours on Snapchat with friends, losing proper sleep. Parents react and show frustration by banning phones. Next morning, the children may use their friends' phones instead and watch violent sex on apps. They may find themselves bullied at school. It is horrendous that such materials are so easily accessible and even more deploring is the money big corporations make from phones, which children now possess well before puberty. Woods hopes that the campaign has backing to achieve effective changes. It is important that smart phones can block unsuitable images. This would indeed be smart.

The Daily Telegraph: *Social Media 'So Addictive it Should be Given a Health Warning'*. Charles Hymas (Friday 15 June 2018, p.11)

Hymas suggests that the Government should classify social harms with health warnings regarding child addiction for social media. He discusses an investigation carried out by the charity *5Rights*, founded by Baroness Kidron, who accuses tech giants of keeping children online for as long as possible to mine more data. Tricks, like *hearts* & *likes*, are designed to excite a brain dopamine hit, based on the number of followers, retweets and online friends. The Baroness states that apps should warn about the negative aspects of hooks and focus on damage to mental and emotional health, education, sleep patterns and concentration. Through the *Duty of Care Campaign,* the Government should impose legal obligations on firms to safe-guard child welfare and well-being on line. Children need to be treated according to age and experience and it is not their responsibility to adapt to the needs of tech firms. The Tory MP, Alex Chalk, who carried out research on social media, said that it is clear that companies trap young children, who will not think through the consequences of their actions.

Psychologists warn that they hook people by using the **rush rewards** (*likes & hearts*) to create expectation. **Summons** are red notification vibration buzzes to attract immediate contact. **Time** is gained by removing the need to click. **Social obligations** force people into interactivity, maintaining time-consuming contact. **Popularity ratings** show the number of followers and friends to demonstrate the status that people crave. On the same page, Kate McCann in: '*Rise of Teen Terrorists Groomed on YouTube'*, states that the number of young terrorists arrested last year has increased enormously since 2001. Due to the impact of YouTube, viewers may be radicalized by extremist content, with preachers using chat platforms to communicate without discovery. Women terrorists rose, compared to 2017 and arrests increased by 17% following the attacks in London and Manchester. The Conservative MP, Neil O'Brien, told the *Daily Telegraph* that YouTube and other platforms are communication vehicles with increasing importance for the spread of radicalization. He hopes the Government will invest substantial resources in taking down this content.

The Daily Telegraph: '*Parents Need Help to Break Seduction of the Smartphone*'. Jemina Lewis (Friday 15 June, p.16)

'*Children Know that Smartphones are a Mixed Blessing*', states Jemina Lewis in her article. They like and want phones, but need to be saved from them at the same time. This is also the view of the Headmaster of Eton College, Simon Henderson, who discovered this when the school imposed a mobile phone curfew overnight for Year 9 students (*age 9-14*). Lewis tells of a conversation with her god-daughter after being asked for an opinion on social media. She denounced the resulting insecurities, internal compromises and miserable feelings after posting a 'selfie', if you receive 199 '*flaming hot*' emojis, while your best friend got 200. If parents prevent use, children would be cut off from friends. It would help if all parents adopted the same action. To operate alone would be a disaster for the child.

Children get their first phone around 10 years old, when walking alone to school in preparation for becoming senior students. Parents note actions of others and think it is fine to buy a cell phone, so their children have the same as friends. In the 1970s-80s most people agreed that television could ruin the brain and some banished it for their offspring. They cut the child off, therefore, from popular culture, making them social outcastes. Most parents concluded it was safer to have a normal child rather than a clever isolate. The difference between television and smartphones is that the former was *part* of existence, whereas the latter invades *all* of life. You find friends, check weather, sports results, music collection, library, shops, news and entertainments from the AI in your pocket. It would be impossible, Lewis says, for Mum to take the phone away as '*the digital world is a done deal*'. Our wish is to help children to navigate it safely and tech companies and schools must assist in achieving this. A start is to set age limits and daily use. Lewis hopes that protection is not a peculiarity that only Etonians deserve.

The Daily Telegraph: '*We must curb the menace of social media*' by Eleanor Steafel, (Saturday 16 June 2018, p. 22)

Eleanor Steafel warns about mobile phone harms for children, as lack of safety is dangerous for mental and social well-being. We speak of addiction when they constantly use apps day and night and find it difficult to stop this cycle. Jane Lunnon, Headmistress of Wimbledon High School, suggests educators and parents play an important role in the matter. We welcome and accept technology for learning benefits, supporting collaboration and skills students need for living and work. However, parents must be aware of the power and impact social media have on children. Jane Lunnon sent a letter to parents, offering digital rules as support. Using a cell-phone policy, meant girls socialised better and were more interested in school-life. She suggested no cell-phone at mealtimes and a *'screen-free'* hour before bedtime, to reduce time with Instagram pictures or Snapchat.

Social media can provoke negative self-esteem, make the young more fragile and generate high levels of anxiety to become a public health concern. Government should take more responsibility and pressure industry to behave more responsibly, legislating against companies applying unsuitable algorithms. They should carry out research to verify the impact on child mental health and development. Children have always been steps ahead of parents, who have less command of the digital world than their offspring. For this reason, Jane Lunnon has given workshops to explain technology. You may assert control, if explaining the need for balance. Technology is transformative, liberating and essential but also addictive. Nowadays, it is difficult to find a teenager who does not use a smartphone to comment every few minutes. *'The product that has been really monetised and sold off is our children's time'*. Advertisers want their attention and Instagram, Snapchat and Facebook are vehicles for this.

The Daily Telegraph: *'The internet is physically damaging our children'*. Eleanor Steafel, (Saturday 23 June 2018, p. 33).

Eleanor Steafel presents an interview with Dr. Jo Begent, who warns of a ticking time-bomb. Families are facing serious child health problems, like bowel and bladder ballooning out of the pelvis, when boys stopped going to the toilet. Some suffer dizziness and palpitations when they stand and girls have vitamin D deficiency, as they never see the sun. Bad school performance, due to gaming until the small hours, prevents student alertness in lessons. Dr. Begent has such cases at his clinic, with no obvious explanation for headaches, breathlessness or exhaustion. Checking habits, it emerged that problems were from long exposure to computers and the Internet. It is difficult to predict effects on society, as technology moves fast to result in unnatural action: The disorder is based on a definition of addiction as a pattern of persistent behaviour, so severe that it takes precedence over other lives interests.

Not only has social media hooked youngsters as gaming could be worse, from small doses of dopamine released in the brain to hook people. Dr. Begent says that obesity, type 2 diabetes and sleep deprivations are now common. Parents are pressured watching children becoming emotionally weak and less physically well because of phone use. Children spend more time on the Internet and when forced to stop can turn violent. Parents have been threatened with knives when trying to get offspring offline. It would be simplistic to think removing technology is the solution, as it interweaves with life. Dr. Begent suggests we are made more aware of pitfalls and seek psychological and medical help if becoming out of control. Parents cannot fight the phenomenon alone, but the Government and tech firms must take action. The Internet should have a way to manage effects on health as symptoms are common

The Daily Telegraph & The Mail on Sunday: Save Kids from the Mobile Menace – by Turning YOURS Off, Sam Taylor, (June 24, p. 35)

Sam Taylor recalls old remedies to solve problems, like teaching by example, with adults turning mobiles off. This may be taken as a *'Luddite hypocrite'* because life is now structured online and the *World Wide Web* is a work of wonder that helps us access remote archives for study and recreation. Children are brought up in this world, with 90% of 13 year-olds possessing a phone, with the 10% without considered social cast-offs from WhatsApp, Snapchat and games with other players. Taylor hopes to convince her 10 year-old daughter to be part of the 10% without mental and physical health issues. She considers uncontrolled, free access to smart devices the most dangerous weapon for youngsters and a way to self-destruct. Since 2010, there has been a rise in emergency psychiatric admission for teenagers, because of chronic dependency on devices. State school studies, where they have been banned in class and playground, show improvements in personal and academic performances. Furthermore, first-year pupils, at Eton, had to give in phones before bedtime, with them relieved of checking social-media. Taylor hopes that parents switch off appliances and spend more time with children, offering them love and attention to help emotional, social and mental development.

FRANCE HAS BANNED SMARTPHONES IN SCHOOLS

A phone ban was an *Emmanuel Macron* pledge during his campaigning for President. The law, taking effect on August 5, 2018, prohibits cellphones, tablets and smartwatches for French schoolchildren, under 15, during the school day. Since 2010, phones have been banned during class in France, but the new law extends to break and mealtimes. Each school will keep students away from phones in their own way. The French Education Minister, Jean-Michel Blanquer, welcomed legislation as *'a law for the 21st century and it will improve discipline among 12 million French schoolchildren'*. The law was introduced to stop students becoming dependent and distracted by smartphones in class. The Minister hopes it will influence children and adults beyond school. *'All starts with education',* he affirms and explains that *'there is no rejection towards technological progress, as that would be absurd, but rather make sure man is the master of the machine'*.

World complaints to Silicon Valley point out that tech products are addictive. Facebook Inc. says that they will offer tools to alert users to take breaks. Also, Apple Inc. assures that '*Apple's Screen Time*' system enables parents to remotely monitor apps children use and limit time on devices. Will this help families to live harmoniously?

MULTITASKING

Multitasking, encouraged in our time-poor society, is considered a myth that has never effectively helped to accomplish anything that really matters.Tim Hartford, in '*Multi-Tasking: How to Survive in the 21st Century*' (2015) analyses this issue. Nowadays it is possible to do anything from anywhere and perform multiple tasks at once, with a phone at your finger-tips. This is not always positive. If people are always 'ON', this may have a harmful impact on life and generate a sense of being overwhelmed. It has been proved that using a phone while driving can be as dangerous as when drunk. People like artists, scientists & professionals can be productive, when focusing on several initiatives over time. Another view on multitasking and the feeling that people must get things done, has been put forward by Simone Smith, reviewing research from Stanford University. Academics found that multitasking adds stress to life, affecting mood, motivation and productivity negatively. They offer advice on *how* and *why* we should switch from multi to single tasking immediately.

- **What is Multitasking?** In 2011, the University of California, San Francisco published a study showing that short-term memory is affected by shifting quickly from one task to another. The impact is negative and worse when older. Handling various tasks now does not mean people can do this in future. It is better to cultivate healthy habits early in life.
- **Brains need focus**: Some people pride themselves on handling many things at once, but minds are not focused on any one task. Inability to do so impacts on professional lives, with implications for work and relationships. Doing several things at once impedes focusing and connecting properly with others.
- **More Tasks = More Mistakes:** This is a consequence of a lack of focus when multitasking, as the mind is divided. This causes mistakes to multiply. Multitaskers are unable to filter out irrelevant information, so mental cross-firing and task-overlapping takes place.
- **Multitasking causes Anxiety:** TheUniversity of California (Irvine) found a downside of multitasking is anxiety from divided attention with psychological & physical symptoms. Those accessing office-mail had higher heart rates than those without, who performed jobs relatively stress-free.
- **Creativity is inhibited:** When attention is spread over many tasks at once, the working memory that remains will not have resources to

offer creative ideas and concepts. Assignments may be completed with average success and scope, but excellence will be beyond reach. When anxious, people access primitive brain structures to keep them safe from danger and stop using others, like the frontal lobe, adapted for critical thinking and creativity.

- **Multitasking wastes time:** Completing a large alongside a small job, means the brain then resets to handle separate tasks, to maintain flow states after shifting from one to another. When reading a good book, we do not monitor pages until stopping, being surprised at the number read. In a business context, allowing unhindered flow increases productivity five times.
- **You are not really living:** If people are constantly reading/writing on phones and on the Internet all day, the rest of them is not living. Only interaction & connection with other humans give deep fulfilment.

CONCLUSION

Academic performance can improve with a tech ban. Researchers from London School of Economics, led by Beland, produced a study, finding that standard test scores, for 16-years-olds at 91 UK schools (2001-11), rose when phones were banned. The study found that improvement was greater when bans were strictly enforced and equivalent to an extra hour of school per week. He affirms that French law, banning phones, will help students and it is positive to extend it countrywide, as it is difficult for a teacher to control use. As the bill went through parliament, Mr. Blanquer said that '*being open to technologies of the future does not mean we have to accept all their uses*'.

MAIN POINTS

- Although some schools are banning cellphone use in school, there is logic in developing a sensible rationale for use within the school curriculum
- Cellphone use has increased multi-tasking and a superficial attention to input which is not helpful to school progress
- Discussion in school of the upsides and downsides of mobile phones helps learners to become aware of the implications of technology addiction and how this can be avoided
- Children are more adept at technology than parents so this must be harnessed for good effects

NOTES FOR CHAPTERS 2-3-4

1. Brian Arthur is an economist credited with developing the modern approach to increasing returns in economics. He has lived and worked mainly in Northern California. His main works in economics relate to complexity theory, technology and financial markets.

2. Odysseus is a legendary Greek king of Ithaca and hero of Homer's epic poem '*the Odyssey*'. Known also as the Latin variant, Ulysses, Odysseus plays a key role in Homer's Iliad & other works in the epic cycle. He was the son of Laërtes & Anticlea, husband of Penelope & father of Telemachus & Acusilaus.

3. Aristotles refers four times to *technologos* but the meaning is unclear – speech is about art; skill with words or maybe word craft?

4. An economic professor at Gottingen University in Germany, Johann Beckmann maintained that it was necessary to give a systematic order to the rapid spread & increasing importance of the '*useful arts*' like architecture, chemistry, metalwork, masonry & manufacturing that he claimed were interconnected.

5. Niles Eldrege & Stephen Jay Gould, U.S pantheologists & biologists, published in 1972 a paper explaining their theory on evolutionary biology, called *Punctuated Equilibria*. They opposed Darwin's theory of evolution, as their research based on Ernest Mayr's & Michael Lerner's ideas proved that there was no gradualism in fossil record development. Their model consists of morphological stability, followed by rare bursts of evolutionary changes, via rapid cladogenesis *(top)* contrasted to phyletic gradualism, the more gradual continuous model of evolution (*bottom*).

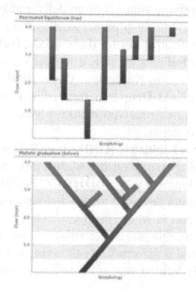

6. In the view of John Maynard Smith & Eors Szathmar, regarding the history of life, there have been several major changes in the way genetic information is organised & transmitted from one generation to the next. They trace a common theme throughout evolutionary history. After a major transition, some entities lose ability to replicate independently, becoming able to do so as only part of a larger whole. They investigated this pattern & why selection between entities, at a lower level, does not disturb it at complex levels. Their view encompasses a theory of evolution, integrating all levels of complexity.

7. Francis Bacon, 1st Viscount St Alban (1561-1626), was an English philosopher, statesman, scientist, jusirst, orator & author. He served as Attorney general & Lord Chancellor of England. After his death, his works remained influential for developing the scientific method during the scientific revolution.

8. **15Five**, a continous performance management software, is a new way for business firms to unlock the potential of their entire working force. Over 1,200 forward-thinking companies, among them **Best Places** &**INC 5000** use **15Five** to measure employee cultural aspects & bring out the best in them. Through a weekly check, **15Five** delivers everything a manager needs for employee engagement & performance, including continous feed-back, asking questions & starting the right conversation, objective tracking, peer recognition, face-to-face exchanges & reviews.

9. In The telegraph (*September 2015*) appeared an article on **Next-Pats.** These are considered a new demographic population not controlled by technology. They use it as a vehicle to achieve freedom & success. Such risk-takers do not see geographic borders as boundaries to experiences and growth.

10. **NextDrop** software is used to connect water-buyers with water-sellers in India, where private water is often delivered by truck. Due to water shortages and an ageing pipe network, urban domestic consumers were not getting clean water for daily needs. Hubballi & Dharwad are twin cities in the Indian state of Karnataka, forming the second-largest urban agglomeration in Karnataka. When Hubli-Dharward Municipal corporation used **Next-Drop** as a monitoring tool, in a 3-month period, over 17,500 families received drinking water when otherwise they would not have done so.

11. The Global Network Initiative (GNI) – founded on *Principles of Freedom of Expression & Privacy* on the 60th anniversary of the Universal Declaration of Human Rights **(UDHR)** – 29 Oct. 2008.

12. **Carebots** are robots designed to assist elderly people and are growing in a big way. Japan is where most carebots are constructed and used, hoping to maintain this practice &collaborate with other nations, where longevity is normal & governments are trying to solve care of the elderly.

13. Thorstein Bunde Veblen was an American economist & leader of the

institutional economics movement (1857-1929), known for his idea of '*conspicuous consumption*' - a critique against capitalism. He was an eminent intellectual leader of the USA '*progressive era*', attacking production & profit. He influenced socialist thinkers of a non-Marxist critique of capitalism & technological determinism.

REFERENCES CHAPTERS 2-3-4

Arthur, W. (2009): *The Nature of Technology: What It is and How It Evolves*. Free Press: Division of Simon & Schuster, Inc. New York, London, Toronto & Sydney.

Calvin, G. (2016): *Humans Are Underrated: What High Achievers Know that a Brilliant Machine Never Will*, Senior Editor at Large. Fortune

Calvin, W. (1996), *The Cerebral Code: Thinking a Thought in The Mosaic of the Mind*. Cambridge, MA: MIT Press

Dennet, C. (1996): *Kind of Minds*. New York: Basic Books

Eldrege, N. & Gould S. (1977). *Paleobiology*, Vol. 3, No. 2 (Spring, 1977), p.115-151. Published by the Paleontological Society

Eyal, N. (2013, 2014, 2015,2016) *Hooked: How To Build Habit-Forming Products*, Ryan Hoover

Eyal, N. (2015): *Un-Hooked: Increasing Focus in the Age of Distruction*, by Psychology of Stuff

Eyal, N. (2018): *Fundamental Attribution Error: Why You Make Terrible Life Choices* (Letter-September 2018) by Psychology of Stuff. Top Stories pub. by Psychology of Stuff in August 2018:

Gould, S. &Eldredge, N. (1997): *Puntuated Equilibria: The Tempo and The Mode of Evolution Reconsidered*. Paleobiology, 3 (2)

Harford, T. (2005): *How to Survive in the 21st Century*. Financial Times, September 2015

Hamton, K., Goulet, L. &Albanesius, G. (2014): *Change in the Social Life of Urban Public Spaces: The issue of Mobile Phones &Women:The Decline of Aloneness Over Thirty Years*. Urban Studies

Maynard Smith, J. & Szathmary, E. (1995): *The Major Transitions in Evolution*, Oxford: OUP

Maynard Smith, J. &Szathmáry, E. (2000): The Origins of life:From the Birth of Life to the Origin of Language (1st Ed.). Oxford: OUP

Mitcham, C., (1994): *Thinking through Technology, The Path Between Engineering and Philosophy*. Chicago: Chicago University Press

Seldon, A. &Abidoye, O. (2018): *The Fourth Education Revolution*. Buckingham: UBP

Steiner-Adair, C. & Barker, T. (2013): *The Big Disconnect: Protecting Childhood and Family Relationships in the digital Age*. London:Harper Collins

Turkle, S. (2011): *Alone Together: Why We Expect More Technology and Less from Each Other*. New York: Basic Books

Turkle, S. (March 11, 2016) *Stop Googling, Let's Talk*. New York Times

Veblen, T. (1899): *The Theory of Leisure Class: An Economic Study of Institutions*. Republished in 2005 in New York: Aakar Books.

Whyte, H. (1980): *The Social Life of Small Urban Spaces*, Conservation Foundation, Washington D.C.

ARTICLES

Klein R. (2002): *Behavioral and Biological Origins of Modern Humans*. California Academy of Science/BioForum, Access Excellence. http://www.accessexcellence.org/ Transcript of a lecture, *The Origin of Modern Mind*, delivered December 5, 2002. Accessed 10 Oct. 2018

Malik, Vikram (2017) :http://www.quora.com/Do-humans-need-technology. Accessed 10 Oct.2018

http://www.sciencefocus.com>Future technology

http://www.forbes.com/how to survive the rising tide of technology, March 2018. Accessed 9 Oct.2018

http://www.thegurdian.com/2016/life without tecchnology. Accessed 10 Oct.2018

Curtis, S. (2010, 2015): https://www15five.com/blog/communication-technology-tearing-us-apart/. Accessed 30 Oct. 2018

https://es.ucsc.edu/~pkoch/.../09.../Gould%20&%20Eldredge%2077%20 Paleobio.pdf, Accessed 20 Sept. 2018

http://medium.com/behavior-designed/archive/2018

The Telegraph: Digital and Social media firms should be forced to....**Error! Hyperlink reference not valid.** Jun 11, 2018 - The Daily Telegraph today launches a duty of care campaign, as ministers consider new measures to rein in the worst excesses of online firms. Accessed 10 Oct. 2018

The Daily Telegraph: Social Media: *So Addictive it should be given a Health Warning* by Charles Hymas, Friday 15 June 2018, p.11

The Daily Telegraph: *Rise of Teen Terrorists Groomed on YouTube*, by Kate McCann, Friday 15 June 2018, p.11

The Daily Telegraph: *Parents Need Help to Break Seduction of the Smartphone*,by Jemina Lewis, Friday 15 June. p.16

The Daily Telegraph: *My Family isn't the Only One in Social Media Meltdown*, by Judith Woods, Friday 15 June 2018, p. 21

The Daily Telegraph: *The Internet is Physically Damaging our Children*, interview to Dr. Jo Begent, by EleonorSteafel, Saturday 23 June 2018 (p.33)

The Daily Telegraph, The Mail on Sunday: *Save Kids from the Mobile Menace-by turning YOURS off*, by Sam Taylor, June 24, p. 35

https://www.businessinsider.com/france-bans-children-using-phones-at-school-2018-9

France bans smartphones in school - The Washington Post

https://www.washingtonpost.com/technology/2018/07/../france-bans-smartphones-schoo

19 Oct. 2018 https://www.wsj.com/.../france-takes-on-cellphone-addiction-with-a-ban-in-schools-153...Accessed 19 Oct. 2918

Schwartz, T. 18 Sept, 2015: *Humanity as a Competitive Advantage*. New York Times. https://philpapers.org/rec/SMITMT-4. Accessed 10 Oct. 2018

Smith, Simone: *7 Reason You Should Stop Multitasking & Get Things Done – 15Five*

http://www.15five.com/blog/7-reason-you-should-stop-multitasking/ . Accessed 15 Oct. 2018 Does technology widen the gap between the poor and the rich? - Quora

https://www.quora.com/Does-technology-widen-the-gap-between-the-poor-and-the-rich Accessed 10 Oct. 2018

Coleman, Lauren, Liza Nov 12, 2017 - In a report by South University Anthos says that the race to display new technology has become such an important status symbol to.. https://craft.co/15five

https://www.15five.com/. Accessed 12 Oct. 2018

Rise of the 'Next-Pats': How Technology is helping us Live more Globally...

https://www.telegraph.co.uk/.../Rise-of-the-Next-Pats-how-technology-is-helping-us-live... Accessed 30 Oct. 2018

https://nextdrop.com/. Accessed 12 Oct. 2018

NextDrop: *A Smart Solution to Water Problems in India*. New Cities. Accessed 12 Oct. 2018

https://newcities.org/nextdrop-smart-water-solution-in-india/. Accessed 14 Oct. 2018

NextDropTechnologies:https://nextdrop.com/. Accessed 16 Oct. 2018201820182018]https://www.crunchbase.com/organization/nextdrop.Acc. 30 Oct. 2018

https://github.com/DemocracyOS/democracyos. Accessed 30 Oct. 2018https://www.advancedmanagement.net/. Accessed 30 Oct. 2018

https://en.wikipedia.org/wiki/Global_Network_Initiative. Accessed 12 Oct. 2018

https://www.businessinsider.com/japan-developing-carebots-for-elderly-care-2015-11Accessed 10 Oct. 2018. https://www.quora.com/I-want-to-become-a-millionaire-Is-there-any-millionaires-here-w... Accessed 16 Oct. 2018

timharford.com/2015/09/multi-tasking-how-to-survive-in-21st-century. Accessed 20 Sept. 2018. https://www.businessinsider.com/japan-developing-carebots-for-elderly-care-2015-11 Accessed 12 Oct. 2018 programmail futuro-code.org.programmailfuturo.it

http://www.programmailfuturo.it. Accessed 30 Oct. 2018

CHAPTER 5

BULLYING: A WIDE SPREAD PROBLEM TO SOLVE USING ROBOTICS AS A SOLUTION

RICCARDA MATTEUCCI

'If we want to teach real peace in this world…we shall have to begin with the children.'

Mohandas Gandhi

SUMMARY

This chapter considers the problem of bullying, which is now of major concern in European schools. It has escalated due to a rapid increase in diverse societies, with their very different views, values and attitudes, leading to disputes and disagreements which often become violent. The background to bullying is presented, followed by examples of how Education Robotics (ER) is being used to ameliorate this issue. It is an example of positive use of robotics in schools.

INTRODUCTION

'We must all do our part to impact on bullying as it has become an enormous problem', James Dillon states in various articles in Principal Magazine (2010).[1] I agree with him when he suggests that simple, genuine gestures, like regularly greeting students, talking to them and addressing them by name, helps them to

be connected (*Matteucci, Paradoxes In Education, 2017,* p. 148). More recent studies (Spiegler, 2017), estimate that among school-age children bullying is on the decline.[2] This should be considered a positive trend, but it does not apply to all educational situations. While the USA detects a decrease, in Europe the problem is increasing, because Local Authorities, School Districts and Governments have not acted promptly when the problem has presented. Bullying is now under intense scrutiny, as more negative consequences have affected today's youth. Cases of suicide, or thinking of this action, have awoken concern.

BULLY PREVENTION: 'IF YOU SEE IT, STOP IT'

World researchers offer advice and suggestions to prevent the spread of this phenomenon and in the last decade a focus on bullying shows how detrimental it can be. Physical, verbal and now on-line, it is not only limited to children bullying their peers, as staff in schools are often victims. Bullying is preventable and schools play an important role in educating and creating a safe environment with a *bullying prevention plan.* All stakeholders – headmasters, teachers, students, staff and parents - need to be involved and know what to do. They must attend training on bullying, because having every member '*on the same page*' is essential for knowing how to handle alarming events.[3] (Concordia University-Portland)

The National Education Association (**NEA**) and Johns Hopkins University (USA) examined school staff opinions on bullying and prevention. Staff (98%) thought it was their job to intervene when witnessing bullying, but only 54% had received training in a prevention policy.

In contrast, during a battle against bullying, Dillon (2011) organised training courses. He asked participants to choose the one group, amongst parents, students, school and community, that they believed most responsible for addressing school violence and bullying. He received a variety of responses, but trainers thought that bullying prevention is always someone else's responsibility. Dillon noted also that if bullying is so prevalent it can be considered the fault of adults who do not recognise certain behaviours as forms of bullying. Furthermore, applying traditional discipline approaches to a perpetrator has proved ineffectual. Dillon said: *The reality is that no one is to blame, yet everyone is responsible.* In school, or in a wider context, we can all work to prevent bullying and need a culture change, which takes time.

HEADMASTERS/PRINCIPALS

Key steps to getting started can help principals, teachers, students, school staff and parents. These are hints from a NEA survey.

- **Develop** a school-wide code of conduct that defines unacceptable behaviours, reinforces school values and clarifies consequences. Headmasters should empower teachers and especially students to help enforce it by training them to identify and respond to inappropriate behaviour.
- **Assess** the impact of the problem on the school community, to find out what kind and how much bullying is going on, as well as where and when to target prevention efforts.
- **Increase** adult supervision, as most bullying happens when they are absent. Make them vigilant & visible in school & buses, on the way and back home for walking students.
- **Practise** what you say, listen before talking and reflect before acting, to ensure that school staff feel connected and valued as professionals and individuals in the learning process.
- **Conduct** bullying prevention activities, like school assemblies, communication campaigns or creative art competitions - highlighting school values, bringing together & reinforcing messages that bullying is wrong.

TEACHERS

Even if leaders do not have a formal prevention agenda, teachers can create a zero-bullying zone in classrooms.

- **Know** in detail school policies on bullying in the area & implement the plan of action
- **Act** immediately, as ignoring bullying generates tacit approval of bad behaviour to spread
- **Discuss** bullying with colleagues as a group, both in general & regarding specific cases, to better monitor the school environment
- **Treat** students & others with warmth & respect to let them know that teachers are there to listen & help for victims & perpetrators
- **Conduct** classroom activities concerning bullying. Students need to identify bullying in books, documentaries, films like '*Bully*' & discuss the impact & resolution. Students must talk about bullying with peers. The Concordia University report refers to a case in which a mid-Michigan school organised a drama event based on bullying, called '*Ticking*', to demonstrate it & the consequences. The play was performed in front of the entire school & district, to help raise bullying awareness. The student performers helped to reduce overall bullying in their school (Concordia University, Portland).

PARENTS/ADULTS

In a school environment parents and adults are the best allies to prevent bullying.

- **Create** healthy anti-bullying habits starting as young as possible. **Coach** children in both *what not to do* – such as push, tease & meaness to others – as well as w*hat to do* – such as be kind, empathise & take turns. Also, coach children on what to do if someone is mean to them or others. Advise them to get an adult, tell the bully to stop or walk away & ignore them
- **Ensure** that children understand bullying, explaining what it is & that it is not normal or tolerable to bully, be bullied, or stand by & watch other children being bullied
- **Talk** & **listen to** the children daily. Ask questions about their school day, including experiences on the way to & from school, during lunch & recess. Ask about their peers & if children are comfortable talking to parents/adults about these matters they will then be more likely not to be involved in bullying & denounce a situation where it is taking place
- **Spend time at school** & be on the premises at recess, because that is when school faces a lack of resources to provide individual attention during this *'free time'*. Volunteer to coordinate games & activities that encourage children to interact with peers aside from their best friends
- **Be a good example** in behaviour. Avoid getting angry in public & addressing inappropriate words to others. Adults should model effective communication strategies, because, when we speak to another person in an unkind, abusive way, we teach that bullying is acceptable.

STUDENTS

Approximately 32% of students report being bullied at school, Anna Obrien says in 2011, and even if the situation seems to have decreased in the USA, the students need to be closely supported. [4] What are the signs to detect?

- **Suffering** from anxiety, depression, physical & mental health problems
- **Performing** poorly academically
- **Scoring** worse on standard assessments than in schools with a better climate
- **Feeling** abandoned by society while they need a safe, supportive environment. Students need to trust adults, whether parents, teachers or supportive friends, in order to open up & disclose their sorrow. If this does not happen bullying has a fertile ground in which to grow & spread

EDUCATIONAL ROBOTICS AND ROBOTS VS BULLYING

Robotics is defined as an interdisciplinary science concerned with the design and development of robots. Born as a branch of mechatronics engineering, this discipline works together with psychology, information technology, linguistics, mechanics and biology. The science fiction writer, Isaac Asimov, was the first to talk about robotics in a story in 1942, although the term '*robota*' had been used since 1920 by the Czech writer, Karel Capek, to mean '*worker*'. Robotics is divided into categories and distinguished by the type of robots made: *humanoids, service robots, tele-presence robots, domotic robots and educational robotics*.

Also called microbiotics, **Educational Robotics (ER)** refers to the theories and studies of Papert based on the advantages of using simple programming and construction kits for educational purposes.[5] Youngsters are offered the opportunity to become protagonists in the learning process, as well as creators of their own product, instead of remaining users. The Papert studies demonstrate how educational robotics play an important role in the teaching-learning process. Robots increase motivation, involvement and problem-solving abilities. The use of them in class fosters learned-centred experience, communication, creativity and the ability to work in a team.

This discipline allows children to observe and experiment with different concepts and theories, and through play they learn from direct experience (Montessori Method). Furthermore, ER acts as a bond between different disciplines, both humanistic and scientific.

ROBOTS FOR CHILDREN AND AUTISTICS

Today, there are many Italian schools holding courses in robotics, where children learn to programme, starting from scratch at an early stage, from pre-kindergarten and elementary school classes. Many robotic kits of increasing complexity are used at different levels, such as NAO, BUDDY, MILO, CYBER ROBOT, DOC ROBOT, EVOLUTION ROBOT and others that can be programmed through simple means. In addition, the tools employed in ER can be used for the treatment of various learning disorders, such as autism. In fact, children suffering from such a condition are more reactive and inclined to listen. Their relationship skills improve and they show significant progress in school performance. (Matteucci, 2017 *Paradoxes in Education,* p. 148) This discipline is changing the scholastic world and therapeutic teaching.

ROBOTICS VS BULLYING: ITALIAN PROJECTS

In the last 10 years, **Robotic Education research** has proved helpful to prevent this problem. Here are examples of projects carried out in Italian school districts. La Scuola di Robotica in Genova and the one in Rome are also extremely important centres for running private courses for teachers, students and others at various levels.

The project '**Robotics against Bullying**' has been organised within the permanent **European Schools of Knowledge Network** that has promoted educational research, at a European level, since 1999 in Verona. Teachers have been trained in regions of Italy, with the aim of providing a sensible use of robotics as an educational tool in the classroom. This has established a strong bond between the school network and CLEMENTONI Spa, an Italian company that is a leader in educational game toys. Clementoni decided to support and implement the initiative, providing its current and next-generation educational robots free of charge. The company's first aim has been to disseminate the use of educational robotics as a bullying prevention model.

Some 20 volunteer teachers constitute the project's National Team that has developed teaching units and lessons that can be replicated in any educational environment, formal or informal. Their goal is not only to prevent bullying, using Clementoni's robots, but the team is also available to train other teachers in cascades. The network offered a free course for teachers "**The Streets of the Bullies**", in the form of 10 meetings from January-May 2018, in Verona. These encounters were supported by the constructive presence of psychologists, therapists, pedagogues, students, experts in educational robotics, teachers and law agencies. They supervised and helped to structure thought-provoking activities, patterned on the prevention of bullying, considered as a highly disruptive social phenomenon.

The activities of the group and projects are available at
www.roboticavsbullismo.net http://frompeertopeer.eu www.europole.org

HOW CAN ROBOTICS PREVENT BULLYING?

Educational Robotics (**ER**) is an inclusive tool by definition, proposing other paths to access knowledge, backed by group activities. The necessity to share and inform renders this a practical, progressive method. Students help or are helped by peers to discover their own and the abilities of others. Regardless of prejudice or relational resistance, studies have shown effective, positive results. Bully and victim, working together, develop social skills of communication, relationships, collaboration, empathy and respect. They need each other, as they are obliged to cooperate to reach shared goals.

The time has come to accept that the use of robotic tools facilitates team learning, both in physical presence and online. Individually, in peer groups or as a school class, students have the opportunity to discuss freely and to propose solutions in what it is called '*proximal learning*' (Vygotsky). The typical context is a game, creating possibilities among pupils. [6] Cooperative work brings into '*play*' the skills of everyone, allowing autonomy, in which the individual can show and sustain their own potential and capability.

FROM THEORY TO PRACTICE

Any school environment has to make learners fully aware of their competencies and potential and introduce suitable practices, close to their areas of interest, aimed at developing sociality and solidarity abilities.

Robotics is not a magic wand and the role of teachers is fundamental in organising groups and providing rules and instructions that everybody must respect. Together with the students, educators prepare tasks, whose contents aim at underlining the seriousness of bullying and encouraging awareness of the danger of misconduct. Teachers have to guide students to facilitate and mediate group work, as the toxic dynamics of bullying can arise in any context.

In schools, where the project *Robotics against Bullying* has been carried out, with primary or secondary students, they were taught a model of online sharing. This is characterised by its ability to be more effective, as it goes beyond social network posts. Pupils associate sharing of school work as a creative possibility and the materials produced are replicable and reusable. The added value of using robotics is to create a learning environment based on fun, where children are fascinated by the novelty, as mentioned above. The activities have never been experienced before, so everybody starts from the same level and has the opportunity to participate and excel according to their capabilities. Students realise that cooperative work can bring out new skills and resources and creates different and positive interactions in the peer group. Everybody counts and plays an important role in the group; each opinion is respected by everyone and all can contribute to the solution of problems.

Educators need to create, and frame the class into, an '*educational game dimension*', where socially negative models are presented, underlined and discussed. Groups are encouraged to find ways to avoid negative models, through collaboration within the peer group, reaching solutions put forward by the students themselves. This method has proved effective in preventing forms of bullying, as the team spirit strengthens a sense of belonging and decreases the risk of hostile attitudes. Students appreciate the value of working in a positive atmosphere and constructive relationship, based on respect. In most cases schools have experimented with the construction of robots and have participated in competitions with valuable results.

EDUCATIONAL ROBOTICS IN ITALY

The Italian Ministry of Education, University and Research (MIUR), together with Consorzio Interuniversitario Nazionale per l'Informatica (CINI) have started the project '*Programme the Future*'. The aim is to give the Italian Schools (*Primary & Junior*) a series of simple, enjoyable tools, that are easily accessible to train students on the basic concepts of computer science. The project was recognised by the European Digital Skills Awards in 2016, as an excellent initiative to facilitate digital competencies.

Starting from a successful experience in the USA in 2013, where more than 200 million students and teachers have taken part over the world, Italy was one of the first nations to join, introducing basic notions of computer science in schools using *coding*, followed by more advanced lessons over two years. Since the school year 2016-17, more than 1,600000 students, 25.000 teachers and 5.800 schools all over Italy have taken part in the project and Italy is among the first in Europe and the world in this field. In the first year of the project, students have attended more than 22 million hours of computer science, with students engaged and enjoying the experience.

Why experiment with *coding* in Italian schools? In our modern world, computers are everywhere and represent a powerful means for people to connect. To be culturally prepared for any job, students must know and comprehend basic concepts of computer science. The scientific-cultural side of computer science, defined *computational thought* (CP) helps to develop student capabilities to solve problems in a creative, efficient way, which are important qualities for citizens to possess. The simplest and most enjoyable method to develop the *computational thought* is through *coding* presented as a game contest.

What tools are used in schools?
The tools available are designed and constructed to possess didactic and scientific qualities and used by teachers of any subject. There is no need to possess a specific knowledge to operate them. The project is funded by associations, firms

and companies for materials, technology, economic resources etc., who share ideas that culturally grow and develop Italian Society.

Who these courses are directed to?
The project is based on two different courses: one basic and five advanced. The first called **coding hour** is devoted to students who are to be acquainted with CT. The second allows students to deepen the themes of CT in further lessons over the school year.

The important centres for Educational Robotics in Italy are at the Universites Roma La Sapienza, Genova (*the first interested in this field since the late 1990s*), Pisa Sant'Anna, Firenze, Milano Bicocca, and Urbino (Pesaro).

FRANCESCO SAVERIO NITTI COMPREHENSIVE SCHOOL IN ROME

The school I have visited, where Educational Robotics is in the curriculum for elementary and junior students as an experimental programme by the Italian Ministry of Education, is *Istituto Comprensivo F.S. Nitti* (*students 6-18 years old, from elementary, junior & secondary high*) located in Rome. The Principal, Dottaire Elisamarzia Vitaliano, is keen to adopt new methods in the use of educational robotics. The school is a leader in this field and takes part in European and International projects and exchanges. The project leader is a teacher, Flaminia Mariotti. This is the only elementary and junior State school in Italy recognised by the Cambridge International Assessment Examination Company, teaching subjects like Mathematics, Science and History in English, with native English speaking teachers.

The school has connections with the Universities of Pisa Sant'Anna, Genova, Florence and Lucca and Prato for projects and exchanges. As with Rome and other Italian regions, F.S. Nitti is a reference point for other schools wanting to update for robots and educational robotics. I spent time in school and saw typical lessons at primary and junior levels using educational robots. During lessons, the students can use two different kinds of robots according to the age level:

• Level 1: Robots – Doc, Mind (*by Clementoni*) and Bee-Bot & Blue Bot (*by British*) are already assembled. Bee-Bot is a copy of the Papert's Turtle, the founder of Contructivism.

• Level 2: Wedo 1 & 2 (*Lego*) for primary school. EV3, Robomaker (*by Clementoni*) which need to be constructed and programmed.

La robotica educativa: due esempi pratici

Bee-bot e Blue-bot per la
scuola primaria (I ciclo)

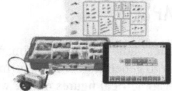

LEGO WeDo 2.0 per la
scuola primaria (II ciclo) e
secondaria di primo grado

EXAMPLE OF A LESSON PLAN

This is a lesson plan that could be applied to both levels, using the following steps:

- **Short introduction** about what is a robot and its use, giving an example of present robotic machines in life, like washing machines, dishwashers, drones and so on (10 minutes)
- **Organisation** of the class into working groups. This is important as the teacher needs to choose the students for each group, keeping in mind the lesson goal. (*Students with problems have to be assigned to groups accordingly to needs, competencies and performances, 5-10 minutes*). In subsequent lessons, students may choose peers with teacher approval
- **Explanation** of the kit, what is to be constructed; how they operate and the use/function of them. Robots need to be contextualised. This is when the robot enters the didactic – part of the subject – history, science, mathematics, L2 and so on, taught through the help of robots. Every project is preceded by activities like drawing, painting & construction of puppets that are the basis and are considered as involving all competencies
- **A role is given to each child in the group,** which they switch off after performing. One reads the instructions, another carries out the task and the third tests the results. This happens in the construction and coding period.
- **Explanation** on how to programme: the teacher decides the way to follow to complete the project. This is done through '*visual blocks*' that allows a more intuitive approach.
- **Presentation** of the work and proof that the project is effective. Each group chooses a student to present the final result.

According to student knowledge, teachers can skip parts of the lesson plan if they already know the relevant information. There are no final tests, or a subject named *Robotics,* to show that students have followed a course and performed competently. The final school year report lists competencies acquired during the year.

EXAMPLES

These photos show students, at primary level, working on 2 ideas: *line open* & *line closed* to generate geometric forms. Students programme the robot to find different geometrical figures on the work sheet (*platform*). Pupils understand concepts of sides, perimeter and area. For elementary students, this simple application can also be used for foreign language teaching. On the working sheet/platform, the teacher places a picture and presents different interpretations. The students lead the robot towards the word corresponding to the picture.

Story telling
The project teaches students to write a story with *Pinocchio* used as the base, because every Italian student knows this tale. Previously, students had built puppets, made photos and prepared the platform, with the different places where the story takes place. Students are given story characters to relate, or they can invent their own one with a different ending. This is a project for juniors or late elementary, when students are learning to write a composition.

Con le carte dei personaggi di Pinocchio

Ogni gruppo sceglie
tre personaggi

This was presented in other schools, during an exchange programme in Prato, Lucca and Roma Cup (2016-18), during an Educational Robotic Fayre, where students of School F.S. Nitti have a stand and present projects to visitors. The Pinocchio Story received positive feedback from the University of Tor Vergata and Campus Bio Medico – two important State Universities in Rome.

Another project has been to create different spaces in a town, with their use assigned a different colour. Students use Lego bricks and work on a story-telling, creating this according to a specific colour given to a setting /room. Each one relates, while travelling a route programmed by a robot and can make up many types of stories. Students even make the walls talk and reveal secrets. In schools, where ER is experimenting, events are programmed to show robotic activity, like Piano Nazionale della Scuola Digitale (PNSD).

COLOURED
ENVIRONMENTS

Geometria

Linea aperta

Linea chiusa

Figure
geometriche

Quadrato

Rettangolo

I.I.S 'C. ROSATELLI' IN RIETI: A FORGING OF IDEAS & VALUABLE RESULTS

In 2011, two Electronics teachers at the C. Rosatelli Technical School in Rieti, a small town North of Rome by the montains, found out that there was a hardware platform available on the web, ARDUINO, designed and set up by people at the *Interaction Design Institute* in Ivrea, a small town near Turin. This is known worldwide as *Olivetti*, as this firm first established there. '*Arduino*' is both the name of the coffee shop where coworkers met to work on the project and of the first King of Italy in 1002. They had no choice but to give the platform this title!

The hardware is a series of electronic boards equipped with a micro-controller. Small devices, that are easily produced, have been researched with practical outcomes in light controllers, engine speed, light sensors and other forms of automation to control temperature and humidity. Arduino has been used regularly in school teaching since 2012 and produced new applications, using electronic boards in lieu of the normal microprocessors, which students found difficult to use. Projects have taken part in national and international competitions with excellent results.

FROM THE ATTIC TO THE LAB

From the Attic to the Lab is the name of a project implemented by students and teachers at 'C. Rosatelli' school, with the aim of re-using old toys and other electronic devices, abandoned by students, because they had outgrown their use, or they were old equipment that family and friends had thrown out. They restyled these objects to generate new things. For example, old electric cars are programmed to be driven remotely, controlled by disused tablets or smartphones. The popular game '*The Cheerful Surgeon*' has been enhanced by a graphical interface to monitor operations performed by students using remote control.

As short-term goals, students experience the creation of new uses from old objects, programming Arduino boards and making graphical interfaces, employing processing platforms and other software. In the long-term, students are motivated to learn, while having fun, experiencing original transformation using their own creativity and imagination.

Pupils also need to bear in mind that a technological world requires more attention to protect the environment in which they live. The reuse of old objects prevents them ending in rubbish dumps and promotes and encourages children to foster important digital skills for the future. The *From the Attic to the Lab* project has an important economic goal, to avoid waste and, through recycling, to save money. All these ideas are key to developing initiatives, such as startups.

PHOTOS AND EXPLANATION OF THE PROJECTS PRESENTED IN RIETI

18 PROJECTS AT I.I.S 'C. ROSATELLI'

The qualified teacher engineer Dottaire Gabriella Gallo and her team is leading the following projects. The aim is to recycle redundant materials for a range of uses, using robots to enhance these new products.

THE INVISIBLE PIANO:

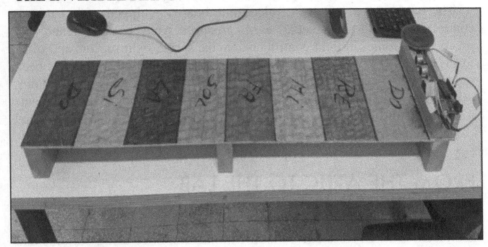

What is it about?
It's an electronic piano made in our labs which makes sounds based on the musical scale. Every musical note can be heard by putting an obstacle in different positions.

How is it made?
- One programming board 'Arduino UNO'
- One ultrasound sensor
- One speaker
- One transistor

How does it work?
A programme developed called **Arduino** allows the speaker to emit a different musical note depending on the distance between the obstacle put on the *'piano'* and the ultrasound sensor.

BLINKING WARNING TRIANGLE:

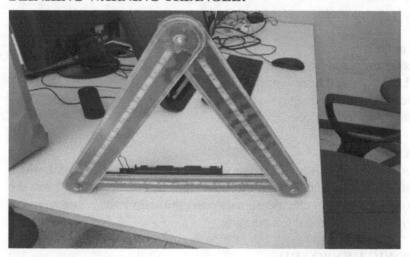

What is it about?
It is a warning triangle created to replace the existing ones which can be powered up from batteries or from the car's battery.

How is it made?
- Red Led Stripes
- Six 1,5V batteries
- A 555 Timer
- Resistor,capacitor

How does it work?
A stable clock was made with the 555 Timer which drives the blinking of the LED stripe.

DIGITAL THERMOMETER:

What is it about?
It is a simple thermometer realised with a temperature sensor and Arduino.

How is it made?
- One programming board 'Arduino UNO'
- One 'LM35' temperature sensor
- Two seven segments displays
- Two seven segments decoders

How does it work?
The temperature detected from the sensor is translated in an electric signal, which is then sent to Arduino. The programme, developed by students, transforms the received voltage signal in electric signals needed to allow the seven segment displays to show the detected temperature.

ELECTRONIC KEYBOARD:

What is it about?
It is a keyboard with 16 keys that represent the color scale. It emits a sound depending on which button you press.

How is it made?
- On speaker
- One '555' timer
- Twenty-four trimmers
- One transistor

How does it work?
By pressing a button the circuit generates a square wave, which has the same frequency as the note the user selected. The signal is sent to a BJT transistor acting as an amplifier and has the task of running the speaker.

DIGITALIZED POLISTIL RACING TRACK:

What is it about?

It's a F1 racing track model which allows the measurement and visualization on a LCD display of the car's parameters, like numbers of laps, best lap speed, speed in a particular part of the track and how much does it take for the car to complete a lap.

How is it made?

- One programming board 'Arduino UNO'
- One laser sensor
- One laser-observing module
- One LCD display

How does it work?

The heart of the system is Arduino 'UNO', which the students developed, calculates in an indirect way the speed. This is made possible by the photocells which acquire data whenever the car passes across them.

DIGITAL CHRONOMETER:

What is it about?
It is a chronometer realized with cabled logic (*not programmed*), which allows counting the seconds between the pressing of the '*Start*' button and the '*End*' button. There is another button which resets the chronometer.

How is it made?
- One programming board "Arduino UNO"
- One ultrasound sensor
- One speaker
- One transistor

How does it work?
The clock's generator, which is conveniently configured and connected, generates a square wave signal with the needed frequency for the lowest measuring unit selected. The signal controls the counters in series which drive the displays through a binary signal.

EXAM CRANE:

What is it about?
It is a tower crane controlled by a smartphone app via bluetooth.

How is it made?
- Stepper motors
- One LCD display
- PIC Microcontroller
- Darlington Transistors

How does it work?
The heart of the system is the PIC microcontroller which drives the stepper motors used to move the arm of the crane and the cart from signals sent to a Bluetooth receiver.

PART 2 ROSATELLI RIETI

DIGITALIZED TRAFFIC LIGHT:

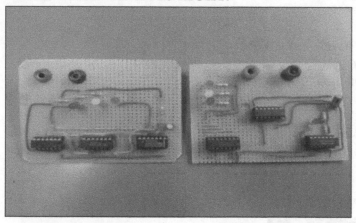

What is it about?
Traffic Light is realized in wire logic and thus not programmed which simulates the operation of a traffic light.

How is it made?
- Four LEDs
- Resistors
- Logic Gates
- One Capacitor
- One Counter

How does it work?
A '*Schmitt Trigger*' (*not a resistor & capacitor*) is used to provide a clock of about 2Hz. The clock commands the count of a counter and based on the seconds counted it lights up the red, yellow and green led in turns like a traffic light.

REMOTE CONTROL THROUGH WEB:

What is it about?
It's a system which allows to control any electronic appliance from the WEB (*IoT,Home Automation*).

How is it made?
- Arduino UNO development board
- Ethernet Shield
- Any device you have to control

How does it work?
By typing the IP address on any device connected to the web an HTML page will be opened. This page will allow control of the electronic appliances connected to the system.

DIGITAL COMPASS:

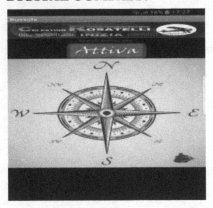

What is it about?
A digital compass created with '*App Inventor 2*' which transforms the obtained data in a stepper motor's movement.

How is it made?
Software:
- App Inventor 2

Hardware:
- "A4988" driver for bipolar stepper motor
- Bipolar stepper motor
- Resistors
- "HC06" Bluetooth module

How does it work?
The app uses the smartphone's gyrometer. Once the data from the sensor are acquired, the app sends them to Arduino which saves them in a variable which will be then used to indicate how many degrees the stepper motor will move.

RESISTOR CALCULATOR:

What is it about?
It is an app which allows us to calculate a resistor's value through the colours on the resistor itself. It's able to execute the voltage's measurement on the resistor's ends.

How is it made?
- Arduino UNO
- "HC-05" Bluetooth module
- Trimmer

How does it work?
The application, based on the 4 colours selected by the user, calculates the value of the resistor and its tolerance. Also, by connecting to an Arduino board connected to a Bluetooth module and a trimmer it's able to measure the voltage on the unknown resistor's ends.

A ROBOT WHICH AVOIDS OBSTACLES:

What is it about?
It is a robot made in the school laboratories which whenever an obstacle is located changes the movement's direction.

How is it made?
- 5 switches
- Arduino UNO development board
- 2 DC motors
- A DC motors controller

How does it work?
The Arduino board, which is the brain of the robot, based on the signals sent by the switches gives instructions to the motors in order to follow a different direction from before.

REMOTE-CONTROLLED LEGO CAR:

What is it about?
It is a car realized with '*Lego Mindstorm NXT*' which is remote-controlled via Bluetooth from an app on the smartphone.

How is it made?
- Lego Technic
- Lego bricks
- 2 DC motors

How does it work?
A smartphone app, which was realized by the students, gives instructions to the Lego "Brick" for the movement of the car based on the buttons pushed on the smartphone.

The communication between the smartphone and the app happens through bluetooth.

DIGITAL DICE:

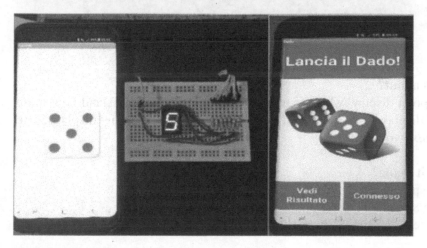

What is it about?
An app which allows the smartphone to display and randomly generate the dice's numbers.

How is it made?
Software:
- App Inventor 2

Hardware:
- 7-segments display
- Seven 330Ω resistors
- Arduino UNO board
- An "HC-05" bluetooth module

How does it work?
The app communicates with an Arduino board via bluetooth. The board's programme generates a random number between 1 & 6 and shows it on the seven-segments display. Also, from the bluetooth module, the generated number is sent to the app and shown on the smartphone.

A MATRIX DISPLAY WHICH SHOWS IMAGES:

What is about?
It is a 'point display' which is used to let the students understand how these kind of display work in general and also to comprehend how displays with rolling text work.

How is it made?
- One programming board 'Arduino UNO'
- One 8x8 matrix display
- Three '74LS164' SIPO registers

How does it work?
Thanks to the programme in the Arduino board, electric signals are sent from the board to the matrix display. The display has sixteen pins which you can

control it. We also thought that by using a SIPO register we could control the rows and the columns while also showing the image at an accessible refresh rate for the user's eye and that without using all the pins provided by Arduino.

H2inO:

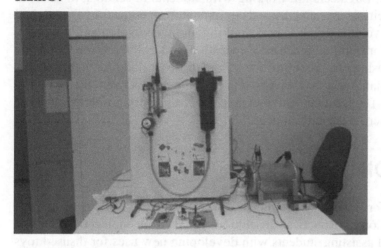

What is it about?
It is a control unit which can be installed in an aqueduct's articulations to monitor the water's pressure in real time throughout the day. The system downloads the data on an online database which can be consulted from the web or an app.

How is it made?
- Pressure sensor
- Redox probe
- GSM/GPRS module
- Arduino UNO
- Amplifiers
- Resistors ,capacitors
- Voltage regulator

How does it work?
The heart of the system is the Arduino board which reads every 2 minutes the values measured by the sensors (*which are accordingly conditioned*) and then sends them through a GSM module to a database. The data is visualized on a web site and can be seen by an aqueduct's employee. Based on the measurements made during 24 hours, it is possible to notice if there are water leaks or chlorine variations in the water.

CONCLUSION

This chapter has provided some examples of how robotics can assist in helping to diminish bullying in schools in a way that is acceptable to children. Following this are some presentations of how children are developing the skills needed for future work. Engineers are working with students in schools, to assist in re-designing their old toys and disused equipment from home for new, original uses. This is developing their lateral thinking and imagination and providing opportunities for communication, cooperation and collaboration in teams. Employers are asking for these attributes from those working for them and this is proving a suitable way to achieved this and the results from the university studies (*in press*) suggest that children respond to this very positively with the impact shown across the curriculum.

MAIN POINTS

* Education for Robotics is proving useful in minimizing bullying in schools
* The Education for Robotics curriculum benefits from engineers going into schools and assisting students with developing new uses for disused toys and equipment
* This project is helping learners to develop lateral thinking, creativity & communication
* They are also learning to communicate and cooperate with each other in creating their new products

NOTES

1. James Dillon has been an educator for 35 years. While Principal of Lynnwood Elementary School in New York, he developed *The Peaceful School Bus Program* in 2004 to prevent & reduce bullying. It was published by Hazelden (2008) & subsequently implemented in schools across the country.
2. Jinnie Spiegler is the director of curriculum for the Anti-Defamation League. She has been working in the field of education for 20 years & has overseen various educational programmes, developed project-based learning curricula, coordinated programme assessment, researched & written an anti-bias & social justice curriculum. She has also worked for Morningside Center for Teaching Social Responsibility, Learning Leaders, & Bank Street College of Education.
3. Concordia University has shown interest in this subject, since 2011, at its main centre in Portland & subsequently in Texas in 2017.
4. An Educator with twenty six years of experience at a secondary level in the

UK & Ireland. She is currently employed as a secondary level class teacher in a co-educational community school in Dublin, where she is in charge of designated disadvantages status in the school environment.

5. Saymour Papert has been at the centre of 3 revolutions: *child development, artificial intelligence & computational technologies* for education. He was a forerunner in the 1960s, as he spoke about children using computers as tools for education. In 1985 he started to work at the MIT laboratory & changed the pedagogy for millions of children around the world.

6. The Zone of Proximal Development (ZPD) consists of the difference between what a learner can do without help & what they can do alone. It is a concept developed by the Soviet psychologist and social constructivist Lev Vygotsky (1896-1936).

REFERENCES FOR ROBOTICS VS BULLYING

1. Robotica educativa: ecco come ci sta cambiando la vita - Huro Life
https://www.hurolife.it › Robot. Accessed 8 Feb. 2018
2. Robotica educativa: che cos'è e come cambia il modo di insegnare
https://www.giuntiscuola.it › ... › WebMagazine › Articoli. Accessed 8 Feb. 2018
3. http://www.roboticavsbullismo.net/convegno-a-roma-di-robotica-contro-il-bullismo/. Accessed 8 Feb. 2018
4. http://www.dobot.it/progetto-rose/ Accessed 8 Feb.2018
5. http://nova.ilsole24ore.com/esperienze/il-potere-educativo-della-robotica/ Accessed 8 Feb. 2018
6. https://www.researchitaly.it/contributi/robotica-educativa-prospettive-e-incognite-sull-utilizzo-dei-robot-in-classe/ Accessed 8 Feb. 2018
7. https://www.stopbullying.gov/ Accessed 8 Feb. 2018
8. www.nea.org/home/neabullyfree.html/ Accessed 8 Feb. 2018
9. www.nea.org/tools/lessons/teaching-students-to-prevent-bullying.html
10. https://www.nea.org/assets/docs/Bullying-PreventioninPublicSchools-PolicyBrief.pdf
/BullyFree_Bully_Free_Campaign.pdf
11. www.climb.org/bullying/prevention bullying prevention education. Climb Theatre teaches kids about bullying using plays that kids can relate to.
12. Bullying Prevention-Tips for Parents and Teachers - englewoodcliffs.org
https://www.englewoodcliffs.org/.../Bullying%20Prevention-Tips%20for%20 Parents%.Oct 5, 2011 - In Principal magazine (http://naesp.org/principal-magazinel ...
13. https://www.edutopia.org/profile/jinnie-spiegler. Accessed 8 Feb. 2018
14. www.ditchthelabel.org/2018-stats□ in UK. Accessed 8 Feb. 2018
15. https://www.edutopia.org/article/empowering-students-curb-bullying15 (jinnie Spiegler)
16. https://online.concordia.edu/education/bullying-in-the-classroom/
17. Sage, R. et al (2017) *Paradoxes in Education*. Rotterdam/Boston/Taipei: SENSE International Publishers
18. Mooney, C. (2000,2013): *Theories of Childhood*; Second Edition: An Introduction to Dewey, Montessori, Erikson, Piaget & Vygotsky, Redleaf Press, MN, Kindle Edition, 22 Feb. 2013

CHAPTER 6
IN SEARCH OF LOST DAYS

ANDREW HAMMOND

SUMMARY

Life on earth has reached a water shed, as we are on the brink of huge changes in the way we learn, live and work, due to artificial intelligence (AI) rapidly taking over routine tasks. These have taken up much of our time, so there is the possibility that we might have a chance to pursue the things that interest and motivate us, to make us happier more fulfilled persons. This chapter differentiates between human and robot characteristics and concludes that machines can never take over completely, because they do not have the capacity to cope with changes in circumstances. This means they are unable to respond flexibly to the needs of situations and without real empathy cannot meet the emotional needs of people. Education, thus, must change to meet new needs, facilitating and celebrating the diversity and differences that we bring to stimulate our fellow human beings, by focusing on everyone's personal development.

INTRODUCTION

There may never have been a more opportune moment to reclaim what it means to be human than in the era of artificial intelligence. Perhaps before we have not been granted such an opportunity and freedom to raise the profile of the human facets we share beyond our ability to retain and recall factual knowledge. The rapid advancement of computer technology is, at last, causing us to question the value of the traditional agenda in schools and its relevance to the way we live out our adulthoods.

Overstating the degree to which computers will usurp human endeavour and thus threaten our existence makes for thrilling and chilling dystopian views of the future, but perhaps we should focus on how AI will complement and liberate our future activities. The human facets and skills, which are only tacitly understood, are hard to measure and therefore barely valued in schools. These are the very things which computers are unlikely to replace – at least for the moment.

TACIT KNOWLEDGE

It will not be artificial intelligence (AI) that re-defines the way we live our lives. If we get this right, it will be the tacit knowledge – held by almost every one of us, gained through our senses, intuition, observations, emotions, social interactions and experiences – that will re-shape and enrich the life stories we write for ourselves. Our imagination can fill the void and direct our life experiences when robots take up the mantle of work and leave us with time on our hands.

> *'To live means to experience – through doing, feeling, thinking. Experience takes place in time, so time is the ultimate scarce resource we have. Over the years, the content of experience will determine the quality of life. Therefore one of the most essential decisions any of us can make is about how one's time is allocated or invested'.*
> (Csikszentmihalyi, 1997: p. 8)

This is the challenge for all of us, not least those of us charged with preparing children for tomorrow. Have we become so obsessed with the transference, retention and recall of explicit, propositional knowledge in education that we have forgotten what it means to be human, and how and why we fill the 30,000 days we are granted, if we're lucky?

Are our schools preparing their students for this epochal moment – a unique chapter in our history when reading, writing and arithmetic will no longer be used to determine who is well-educated and who is not; who will secure the better job and who will not; who uses their time wisely or nobly and who does not? Are we facing the wrong direction? Are we still viewing human achievement (*in school-speak, 'attainment & progress'*) through a lens so narrow that it misses the attributes and aptitudes that make us human and bring us the potential to live fulfilling lives?

> *'The intuitive mind is a sacred gift and the rational mind is a faithful servant. We have created a society that honours the servant and has forgotten the gift'.*
> (Albert Einstein cited in *The Metaphoric Mind*, Samples, 1976)

Intuition allows us to '*know*' something before we have analysed it rationally. It bridges the gap between our conscious and non-conscious mind. To intuit something is to subconsciously draw on one's myriad sensory perceptions to reach a notion of what is going on around us, how we should respond and what we should do next. Intuition is a compass. The problem is, our rational mind often overrides any instinctive impulses and we reach a different conclusion based on reasoned analysis. Reasoned analysis, however, still reigns king in formal education and perhaps in Western civilisation too. Though rationality is precious, it can mislead us. It gives us a false notion of what human behaviour is, or even what it means to be human. Take listening for example: if you were asked to listen carefully to something, you would probably lean in, lower your eyebrows and frown. None of these actions help you to hear better. No more than sitting still behind a desk helps you to learn better, or using a fountain pen helps you to write better. These are false constructs and we believe them.

POLYANI'S PARADOX

Polyani's Paradox, in which we '*know*' far more than we can articulate or provide evidence for knowing, tells us that we have greater capacities than those which we can evidence. Nowhere is this more apparent than in education. Never has this been more prescient than at this moment, as we question not only the relevance and purpose of our school curricula, but our usefulness as adults.

Schools are places in which calculations and rational decisions dominate, but for this there will always be a more efficient and more advanced learning partner in technology. Robotics will soon outperform us in many areas of our lives, including school. The skills in which technology far exceeds us – reading, processing and applying information – are themselves recent phenomena and not, in any way, attributable to the fact that we find ourselves in that elite club of species still in existence on the planet. We did not survive this long because of our ability to read text or solve mathematical equations. Our longevity is due to the deep-down-things that make us human - those '*harder to teach/harder to measure*' qualities factory-fitted in all of us, like creativity, instinct, intuition, curiosity and so on. If a revolution in education is indeed coming, let it not only be based on what AI can do for us; let it be driven by what we can do that AI cannot. May it force us to re-discover what it means to be human, just what and where our potential is and how best we can unlock it in the formative years of school.

FUTURE LIVES

If the adult lives of the children in our schools today will be dominated by leisure time, as many predict they will be, how then are we preparing them for this new paradigm? How are we helping them to protect themselves from information overload, anxiety and a lack of purpose or direction? How are we supporting them to develop the self-discipline and discernment they will need to manage their time wisely and in ways that fulfil and maintain their sense of worth? Is the way children approach and manage their *'play times'* more fundamental to their future prosperity and well-being than we think?

In her book, *Ten Thoughts on Time* (2013), Jonsson observes the value young people can bring to this discussion on how to spend our leisure time wisely.

> *'There has to be a distribution of responsibilities between generations, and I believe that the crucial role of the young lies in providing new patterns of thought, and also demonstrating the consequences of new thought. Respect for humanity and human activities needs to be based on new precepts and we, as adults, need the constructive help of those who – unlike us – have never been caught in the formal requirements that belong to the era of defining-your-worth-by-work'.* (2003: p.53)

Defining worth by your work is a burden still carried by people of mine and my parents' generations and a century of antecedents before us. When I was at school, in the 1970s and 80s, we believed the myth that good things will come to those who study hard in school and work hard in their jobs. You can achieve wealth and status (*if these motivate you*) by working hard. There was a clear divide between work and play, occupation and leisure – what you do between the hours of nine to five and what you do when you finish work. Ask an employee of a high-tech company today and I suspect the lines between work and play are blurred for them. Ask a creative entrepreneur and they will probably tell you that it is not how hard you work that will bring wealth and opportunity, it is how you connect people together. As an entrepreneurial friend told me recently: *'If you want to make money, it's already out there, just go and get it; make connections, put people together and the money will flow. You don't have to make it yourself!'* I have never quite understood what he meant by this, but I do know that for the few hours he *'works'* per week, my friend earns ten times what I earn per month in full-time employment. The rest of the time he spends playing, imagining and dreaming.

I remember playing, imagining and dreaming, before my schooling taught me that these pursuits were secondary to studying and that my worth would ultimately be defined by my work, so I should not while away my time.

In Stephen Spender's *Lost Days* (1985) the poet describes a boy lying on the grass, whiling away the hours of long summer holidays.

> *Then, when an hour was twenty hours, he lay*
> *Drowned under grass....*
>
> *He pressed his mouth against the rooted ground*
> *Held in his arms, he felt the earth spin round.*
> (1985: p.147)

When my eldest son was four, in the long summer before he started full-time school we played in the back garden. He found two sticks and gave one to me. No sooner had I received this *'sword'* than he ran at me shouting, *'I'm gonna get you, Captain Hook.'*

A year or two later, we were on a camping holiday in Devon. I found two sticks and gave one to him, shouting: *'Ah ha, Peter Pan, we meet again.'*

He said: *'Daddy, that's a stick, not a sword. Did you know, stick begins with 'st'. It rhymes with brick.'*

In that moment my world imploded, but I faked a proud smile and said: *'Well done, son'.* Since then, I have no doubt he has filled his time learning and recalling factual information and receiving a *'well done'* in return. Playing has been relegated to the brief play times between lessons. The stick-ness of that stick, and the potential it held for transporting us effortlessly into an imagined realm of pirates and boys who never grew up, has never left me, even though for my son it had been eclipsed by explicit knowledge of the literal meaning of *stick*, its spelling and its sound.

Where Henry once propelled a toy car across the grass and told me where he was travelling to (*usually America*), now at school, he told me what colour the car was and that he had counted seven other blue cars in his toy box. Also, aeroplanes or ships were the preferred modes of transport for getting to America: *'If you drove there in a car, you'd sink.'*

Henry's metaphoric competence had been outranked by a capacity for literal meaning-making and logic – the naming of parts. His view of the world had lost a dimension but he continued sorting and classifying. It has been the same for his three siblings that have followed; they too are now auditing the world and calibrating their own intelligence against what they should know and can remember.

A crime has been committed here and I am not alone in such a judgement.

Human consciousness comes into the world as a flaming ball of imagination. Everything invented by human beings, physical or mental, is the fruit of someone's imagination. In the study of history and geography we are helpless without imagination, and when we propose to introduce the universe to the child, what but the imagination can be of use to us? I consider it a crime to present such subjects as may be noble and creative aids to the imaginative faculty in such a manner as to deny its use, and on the other hand to require children to memorize that which they have not been able to visualise...

The secret of good teaching is to regard the children's intelligence as a fertile field in which seeds may be sown, to grow under the heat of flaming imagination. Our aim therefore is not merely to make the children understand, and still less to force them to memorize, but so to touch their imagination as to enthuse them to their inmost core.'
(Maria Montessori, cited in *Polk Lillard*. 1996: p.53)

The lost days of Henry's adventures in the garden *can* be reclaimed; a creative dividend, a payback of playfulness, is around the corner. How we spend our leisure time – and if predictions about AI are true, our children will have considerably more of it than we do – will be crucial to our quality of life.

When computers free us up to devote more time to our hidden human capacities, our potential for imaginative play will be rediscovered again. For guidance on how to spend that time, perhaps we should look no further than to Spender's boy in the grass. Not only is he able and willing to devote hours to imaginative play, he is the most likely candidate to create fresh ideas and solutions to the problems we have bequeathed him precisely because he is not sullied by the false constructs we create as adults – that work is work and play is play, that day-dreaming is for the idle, that the more you work the more you will earn, and that what you do for a living is more important than who you are.

The children in our current Reception classrooms will live to see the 22nd century; and the children after them (*those born today*) will have an average life expectancy of between 104 and 107 years. Do we really believe that the old maxim of '*study hard, get a job and you'll do well*' will apply in 2125? When, even now, they can obtain factual information about anything, anywhere in the world, by simply asking Siri, do we still believe that teaching and measuring their ability to recall such information will be enough to prepare them for their future – a future in which the idea of '*having a job*' may well have been assigned to the history books?

The dominance in school of factual recall, reasoned analysis and the ability to apply deductive logic has been called into question with the advent of robotics that will outperform school-leavers in all of these disciplines. This should pave the way for school to become an aesthetic experience, as it should be. Right now, however, it remains an anaesthetic one, where sensory perception has a lower value than rational thought. Students in school are told to focus and remain '*on task*'. An ability to concentrate is highly prized in classrooms – and this means shutting off most of our sensory receptors in order to attend to what the teacher is saying to us, or to read carefully the text in front of us: '*Stay in your learning bubble.*' '*Manage your distractions.*'

Try as I might, I may never aspire to the concentration levels of the computer sat in front of me. It does not fidget or procrastinate. It gets on with the job. If it has senses at all, they are primed and ready to do a specific task and are not susceptible to distraction. The student who can work like a computer – receiving, processing, retaining and recalling information efficiently and without distraction - will sail through school examinations. For most us, data does not enter our central processing unit in 1s and 0s only. Many of the ways in which we interpret and react to external stimuli cannot be codified and automated. Our reactions are intuitive, reflexive, instinctive, speculative, daring, sometimes mischievous and even cynical.

Pleasingly, there is more to being human than data-processing. Our senses equip us to deal with the unexpected hazards, challenges and beneficial opportunities that float past us daily. How we choose to respond to these events makes us who we are. To anaesthetise a student from such experiential learning is to dilute individual character before it has formed and limit human potential before it has been realised.

THE HUMAN BEING

We have Aristotle to thank for the notion that we humans have just five senses. Pleasingly, we have many more: chronoception (*our sense of time*), thermoception (*our sense of heat)*, equilibrioception (*balance*), nociception (*pain*) and proprioception (*touching your nose or ear without looking at them*), to name but a few. Even if we took just the standard five, with such powers of perception we are functioning at a level never attainable by AI, not because any of these sensory receptors are not in themselves able to be artificially simulated - I am sure they are/will be soon - but precisely because of the way they perform together in a glorious symphony, and unique blend, of interpretations, emotions and thoughts. Rational, logical thought trumps these innate skills, at least they do if you want to pass the eleven plus, or gain a GCSE.

With all this rapid reasoning in school, to describe someone as '*very sensitive*' is not to pay them a compliment. To pause, however, in a discussion, in order to think in a measured way, is to render yourself '*slow*', vulnerable to an early diagnosis of limited information-processing ability. Perhaps this is why so many of my students these days precede every verbal utterance with the word 'wait'.

Speed is not everything. Deep learning requires *time*, and so too does relationship-building, problem-solving and creating something original and of value. The speed with which can we process information, and the time it takes for us to retrieve and apply logic and reasoning skills is not indicative of our natural ability – no more so than an academic score in an exam is an accurate measure of a learner's ability either now or in the future. We can accelerate the speed with which children apply logic – useful in an eleven plus exam – but to apply imagination takes time.

The good news is, if the aforementioned predictions are true, time is a commodity that will be in plentiful supply in the coming years. It may be shared equitably, just like the national wage some foresee. If we are indeed heading for a unique and levelling moment in our history, when we shall all be granted equal amounts of leisure time to spend in whatever ways we choose, free from the dominating and hierarchical force of '*work*' in our lives, then the specific skills most practised in schools today will be of limited use once students leave school. More valuable to them will be the ability to discern how to manage their time in fulfilling and creative ways that enhance the quality of life for themselves and for others. Not everyone finds this easy.

'While work is seen as a necessary evil, being able to relax, to have nothing to do, seems to most people the royal road to happiness. The popular assumption is that no skills are involved in enjoying free time, and that anybody can do it. Yet the evidence suggests the opposite: free time is more difficult to enjoy than work. Having leisure at one's disposal does not improve the quality of life unless one knows how to use it effectively, and it is by no means something one learns automatically'.
(Csikszentmihalyi, 1997: 65)

Early years infants know instinctively how to play busily and independently, but this soon diminishes when they enter the formal classroom. The monumental task of brain development and self-formation that an infant faces requires an egocentric approach that is deemed unhelpful and soon taught out of children. '*Work*' beckons and anyone who works in primary schools, as I have throughout my career, knows that the transition from Reception to Year 1 can be fraught with challenges, precisely because a free spirit and a self-directed, uninterrupted absorption in learning are no longer convenient. There are phonics and number worksheets to be completed. We strip children of their innate ability to make their own choices and to navigate their way freely through learning, guided only by their own insatiable curiosity, and replace it with a proficiency in sitting still, paying attention and doing as they are told.

But as Gerver (2010) argues in *Creating tomorrow's schools today*,

'Our job as educators is to ensure that our children feel that they are responsible for their learning and that it is they who have the power to control their own lives'. (2010:p. 107)

Such a view has interesting consequences for educators. It redefines the role of the '*teacher*' in the room, traditionally the all-knowing purveyor of knowledge. Are we shifting our role to life coach? In the twenty years that I have been teaching, the role has significantly changed and only the hardened traditionalists can argue that it has done so for the worse. Technology has already fitted a turbo-charge to teaching and learning, with AR and VR bringing all kinds of experiences that were unimaginable when I graduated, and in the realms of science-fiction when at school. If technology continues at this pace, the idea that adults can set the pace and conditions for learning is comical. As McGrath (2014) observes,

'In the age of the search engine, knowledge is readily available. The job of the teacher is no longer to impart knowledge for a student to hold in its head...
The most successful teachers are now those who can demonstrate that they can engage, stimulate and encourage their students to find

out for themselves. They are facilitators of learning, and not fountains of knowledge. The next step, naturally, is to develop a learner who no longer needs such a guide. Developing such a learner as quickly as possible is important. We are teaching children discernment, not facts. We are allowing them to develop the skills to learn independently of anyone. Teachers are digging their own graves'. (2014: p. 13)

I am certain that *'finding out for themselves'* is an occupation that comes so easily to early years infants. It is ironic then that as the children move up through school they hear adults asking them to become more *'independent'* and *'manage their own learning'*. Had we not intervened, perhaps infant free and innate learning skills may have continued unhindered; but mention a need for discovery-based learning and following a child's natural inclinations and you are branded a liberal romantic. Yet, as we look to the future, should not we all try to reconnect with our capacity for free play?

'The future belongs to those who can reconnect with play. It is the child in you that is creative, not the adult. The child is free and does not know what they can't or shouldn't do. They haven't found what works, whereas adults repeat whatever worked last time. Whatever you are doing, do it as if for the first time. To children there is no last time. Every time is the first time. They explore a land without rules or preconceptions. Somewhere between childhood and adulthood this ability is stifled'. (Judkins, 2015: p. 93)

Having being asked to reject play in favour of *'work'* in school, youngsters are then told that some learning skills are more important than others: reading, writing and counting, for example, are at the top; pretending, dancing, dreaming or digging are at the bottom. You cannot do those until play time, when you will have a few minutes before you come back inside again to get on with some work.

Reducing the ability of students to their capacity to apply logic and rational thought in response to binary questions, puzzles and patterns, and against the clock too, is to deny what it means to be human, and to set us all up perfectly for being usurped by AI. It is pointless, because no child can compete with the computational capacity of the smartphone permanently attached to their hand.

If we define intelligence as the ability to process information rapidly and apply inductive or deductive thinking, students will calibrate their own mental ability accordingly and forever do so. Perhaps this is why so many sixteen year-olds leave school with the entirely false impression that they are worthless.

What is more, if such forms of literal learning are championed as the pinnacle of human intelligence, school leavers will compare themselves unfavourably with the barrage of artificial intelligences that outperform them at every juncture.

CONCLUSION

As headteacher of a large community primary school in a city in rural England, I am in the business of raising aspirations. Every day I tackle head on the cycle of low ambition that orbits the disadvantaged members of our community, creating a gravitational pull away from academic study for certain pupils. Parents (*and grandparents*) of some may well have left school thinking they were not good enough. The system of measuring explicit knowledge (*as opposed to implicit, tacit knowledge*) relies heavily on memory and recall, and those parents, who struggled with this, left school thinking that '*academia*' was not for them. Thus the cycle of '*underachievement*' began. Their children, and their children's children, pitch up at my school with the preconception that they will not be any good at Maths or English. Apart from a few exceptions, the self-fulfilling prophecy plays out, not least because if we judge (*or are judged by others in authority*) that we are not very good at something, eventually we find something else to do and use it to justify our existence – rendering that which we are less good at as having less value and the preserve of others who have less relevance to our own lives.

And relevance is key.

John Dewey observed the problem:

> '*From the standpoint of the child, the great waste in the school comes from his inability to utilize the experiences he gets outside school in any complete and free-way within the school itself; while, on the other hand, he is unable to apply in daily life what he is learning at school. That is the isolation of the school – its isolation from life. When the child gets into the schoolroom he has to put out of his mind a large part of the ideas, interests and activities that predominate in his home and neighbourhood. So the school, being unable to utilize this everyday experience, sets painfully to work, on another tack and by a variety of means, to arouse in the child an interest in school studies.*' (1915: p.46)

Now we have an opportunity. Many of the ideas, interests and activities that predominate the child's home and neighbourhood may turn out to be the very activities that will define them when they leave school and enter a world devoid of '*work*' as we know it. The vacuum left behind when jobs of all kinds, whether manual, intellectual or even creative are performed by robots will need to be filled. Spender's boy in the grass can remind us adults how to be resourceful, imaginative and open-minded to the world and its infinite possibilities.

Our lost days may be rediscovered again.

Meanwhile, middle-aged educators like me attend conferences and discuss how on earth we are going to prepare the children for an uncertain future. The future is not in the distance or even around the corner. It is here, because the children are here.

And no child that I have ever met has been fazed, or threatened, by technology.

MAIN POINTS

Intuitive, reflexive, instinctive, speculative, daring, mischievous and even cynical attributes separate us from the new intelligent machines

Now that machines are taking over routine operations, we have the opportunity to develop our imaginative abilities, which are necessary to solve the complex problems that threaten existence

Education now has to change to meet the new challenges, with an emphasis on personal abilities, to provide a more holistic experience

This may make learning more relevant and meaningful for students

REFERENCES

Csikszentmihalyi, M. (1997) *Finding Flow*. New York: Basic Book

Dewey, J. (1915) *The School & Society & The Child & the Curriculum*. Rhode Island: BN Pub.

Einstein, A. cited in Samples, B. (1976) *The Metaphoric Mind: A Celebration of Creative Consciousness*. Boston: Addison-Wesley Publishing Company

Gerver, R. (2010) *Creating Tomorrow's Schools Today*. London: Continuum

Jonsson, B. (2003) *Ten Thoughts About Time*. London: Constable

Judkins, R. (2015) *The Art of Creative Thinking*. Sceptre. London: Hodder & Stoughton

McGrath, A. (2014) *Classroom in the Cloud*. Woodbridge: John Catt Educational Ltd.

Montessori, M. (1947) *To Educate the Human Potential* cited in Polk Lillard, P. (1996) *Montessori Today*. New York: Schocken Books

Spender, S. (1985) *Collected Poems*. London: Faber and Faber

CHAPTER 7

LEARNING TO LEARN: PREPARING TO SUCCEED IN AN AI WORLD

ADVENTURE IS OUT THERE

DARYLE ABRAHAMS

Artificial Intelligence is spreading faster than we know and taking over many responsibilities that have traditionally been the roles of humans. This is scary stuff as the changes will affect our lives and leisure too fast for us to properly catch up. The transhumanists are positive about this as the fusion of man and machine will enhance our lives and with the dirty, dangerous, dull jobs out of the way what could be better! For sure we must get smarter. More specifically, we need to systematically and deliberately equip the current student generation with self-sufficiency and broader competencies to cope with rapid changes and requirements.

INTRODUCTION

At the time of writing (*August 2018*), Artificial Intelligence (AI) is spreading faster than we know. Waymo Inc. (*Google owned*), is already wrestling with ethical dilemmas of programming for self-driving cars[1]. If the vehicle had no

---

1. https://www.technologyreview.com/s/542626/why-self-driving-cars-must-be-programmed-to-kill/

other choice than to potentially kill pedestrians or risk doing so to the driver, which should it choose? Automatic killer robots, capable of locking on to a target and discharging 1000 rounds per minute are on guard in demilitarized zones; the SGR-A1 is already in use protecting borders in Israel and South Korea.[2] Bots are swaying public opinion, potentially altering the course of history. Perhaps 15% (*48 million*) of all Twitter accounts are operated by bots, arguably the cause of the 2016 US election results, or at least a significant variable.[3] After only 500 iterations of self-directed programming, robots in Lausanne learned to lie![4] With computing power at incomprehensible speeds, an advanced AI inclined to do so could probably figure out deception in a matter of seconds, not months. Across industry, even the AI inventors and their startups are being consumed by big businesses. In the first three months of 2017, tech giants consumed 34 AI startups, and their intellectual property.[5]

WEAK AI & STRONG AI

It is said that Weak AI, such as chess computers and smartphone voice assistants have not even touched the surface of what the strong machines will ultimately be able to do. Weak AIs are programmed and instructed, to perform a specific task. When the first AI to *instruct itself* comes along, so-called Strong AI or Artificial General Intelligence (AGI), how long will it be before '*it*' comes to a conclusion which negates humanity? We need to act now to counter this. The current prediction is that Strong AI will be with us by 2045, some even think before 2030! One of these futurist predictors, Ray Kurzweil, is scarily good at this, too.[6]

There you were, thinking that global warming would get us all,[7] and you might be right, but, while climate change observers are reporting the point of no return for the health of the planet is as soon as 2035,[8] it may be the case that AI beats humanity to its eco-system demise by getting smart enough to conclude that Homo Sapiens is simply no longer of value and then figures out the most efficient way to erase us before we cause irreversible damage to our world! Cheery stuff.

---

2. https://www.dailymail.co.uk/sciencetech/article-2756847/Who-goes-Samsung-reveals-robot-sentry-set-eye-North-Korea.html

3. https://www.socialmediatoday.com/social-business/research-suggests-48-million-twitter-accounts-are-bots

4. https://www.technologyreview.com/s/414934/robots-evolve-the-ability-to-deceive/

5. https://venturebeat.com/2017/05/28/tech-giants-acquired-34-ai-startups-in-q1-2017/

6. https://futurism.com/kurzweil-claims-that-the-singularity-will-happen-by-2045

7. https://www.indy100.com/article/nobel-prize-apocalypse-threats-humanity-survey-times-7927046

8. https://www.sciencedaily.com/releases/2018/08/180830084818.htm

On the brighter side, some with an eye to the future, such as the Transhumanist movement,[9] believe that these developments are a positive thing for humanity. Their goal is longevity, through bionics or symbiosis, believing that technology will fuse with humans to increase lifespan. Nanobots will repair us from within[10] and advanced prosthetics beyond our limbs with a number of medical technology innovations on the horizon will soon be reality.[11] Imagine robotic medical devices so small that they are moving around the bloodstream, fixing you from inside your body!

A CALL TO ACTION

Whether we are past the rubicon for humanity's continued existence or not, something significant needs to be done to ensure the worst is behind us, not ahead. Before the Singularity event arrives, as a great deal of smart people think it will, I believe we need to get smarter. More specifically, we need to systematically and deliberately equip the current student generation with self-sufficiency. We must metaphorically '*teach our children how to fish*', on a massive scale. Hence the topic of this chapter: *Learning to Learn*.

STUDENTS NEED TO LEARN HOW TO LEARN

A lofty goal, however, is to raise humanity's competence sufficiently by 2030, 2035 or 2040 and beyond, so that the decision makers of the time handle AI and its impact positively. We need to institutionalize the teaching of '*how to learn*' by 2025, at the very latest. We have seven years to change the National Curriculum and equip teachers to support the change! Surely that is impossible? Why so quickly? Changing thinking, policy and behaviour takes time, as does the education to support the change. We need to act now!

Higgins, Baumfield & Hall (2007)[12] share a similar opinion regarding the need for this type of education. The results of their study support the view that learning to learn should be

> '...*embedded in the curriculum, as well as being taught explicitly to pupils, with supportive discussion of the effectiveness of strategies and approaches in different contexts.*' *In fact, they go further by enquiring*

9. https://www.theguardian.com/technology/2018/may/06/
no-death-and-an-enhanced-life-is-the-future-transhuman

10. https://interestingengineering.com/nanobots-will-flowing-body-2030

11. https://www.wired.com/story/ai-is-fueling-smarter-prosthetics-than-ever-before/

12. https://eprint.ncl.ac.uk/155074

> *'Which teaching approaches that aim to develop pupils' learning capabilities show evidence of improved learning of pupils?'*

I believe the answer to that is teaching designed to increase *self-knowledge* and *awareness*; knowledge of how *people* work and how the *individual person* functions, given that we are all different.

'Hold on! It has been a while since I, the reader, was a student. Do we not teach our young how to learn, I hear you ask?' In a holistic, deliberate nature? The answer is: *'No'* we do not. You were thinking we teach the skill of learning in schools, right? Wrong. The closest we get is teaching students how to successfully navigate the *'system'* to pass exams. Even then, study skills are optional. One of my Doctoral study peers, an accomplished Head Teacher, commented, that *'learning to learn is embedded throughout the school experience, in almost every field of study'*. Indeed, there are glimpses of learning to learn littered throughout the Key Stage 4 curriculum for English[13], but nowhere is it required for students to learn how to self-quiz, space out learning, interleave problem types, generate solutions before learning about them to *'warm'* their mind to the topic, etc. Think about your own experience; when were you instructed on how to study for exams? Hopefully, you came across some gifted teachers who innately saw the need for this and decided to step up to the task, as best they could: create study cards, use a highlighter, re-read the passages, etc. But, and it's a big one, in the year 2018, *'we'*, as a nation, do not systematically educate students on the subject of how to study beyond literacy skills. The closest we get is a recommendation for re-reading a passage to *'learn'* it. This, simply, does not work.[14]

ORACY AS A LEARNING TOOL

One of the most powerful *'Learning to Learn'* tools available to us is *oracy*. Over several decades, Professor Robin Alexander (*Fellow of Wolfson College at the University of Cambridge*) has published supporting this idea. In 2010, the Cambridge Primary Review, co-authored by Alexander, determined that *'dialogue, pupil voice and the empowerment of both children and teachers are fundamental to educational advancement, [and]… that it should be built into the curriculum, teaching and learning, assessment and professional development.*[15]

---

13. https://www.gov.uk/government/publications/
national-curriculum-in-england-english-programmes-of-study
14. Brown, P. C., Roediger III, H. L., and McDaniel, M. A. *Making it Stick: The Science of Successful Learning*. Cambridge, MA: The Belknap Press of Harvard University Press, 2014. See Chapter 1 and 2 for research supporting quizzing over rereading.
15. Alexander, R.J. (ed) (2010) *Children, their World, their Education: final report and recommendations of the Cambridge Primary Review*, London: Routledge.

Even today, it requires campaigns on a national level by organizations such as *Voice 21*[16] to increase emphasis on teaching how to talk in the national curriculum.

STRESSED STUDENTS

No wonder so many students struggle to navigate the '*system*' successfully. The number of students seeking mental health support while studying at university has increased by more than 50% in five years, analysis suggests.[17] Instead of *enabling*, we are *suppressing* our children. As a graduate from the *Royal Central School of Speech and Drama*, I am clearly biased toward the spoken word as a teaching and learning tool, as my Bachelor of Education degree placed a great deal of emphasis on talk as a learning tool. In practice, however, *School 21*[18] is an example of an institution having much success making oracy the centre of the learning experience. It is not just a theory. There is also a great deal of academic work supporting the fact that '*the quality of classroom talk has a measurable impact on standards of attainment in English, mathematics and science*'.[19] At the DfE seminar on Oracy, the National Curriculum and Educational Standards, on 20th February 2012, Professor Alexander gave a presentation on Improving Oracy and Classroom Talk in English Schools. Upon review of the key propositions, one stood out to me. He had recommended to the Secretary of State in a letter on 30th September 2011:

> *'There is a strong case for revisiting the 1975 Bullock Report's advocacy of 'language across the curriculum' in order to underline the argument that educationally productive talk is the responsibility of all teachers, not just those who teach English.'*

LEARNING TO LEARN IS LEARNABLE

At Newcastle University, they are tackling the problem head on, with funding by the *Campaign for Learning*. Along with Durham and Glasgow, they have produced case studies to explore *learning to learn* from this starting definition: '*It is a process of discovery about learning. It involves a set of principles and skills which, if understood and used, help learners learn more effectively and so become learners for life. At its heart is the belief that learning is learnable.*'

As an adult educator in the workplace, since 1997, I see little evidence of '*learning to learn*' being taught. Having run a one-year talent development

---

16. https://www.voice21.org/

17. https://www.bbc.co.uk/news/uk-england-45824598

18. https://www.edutopia.org/practice/oracy-classroom-strategies-effective-talk

19. https://www.robinalexander.org.uk/home/articles-and-presentations/

programme for almost 20 years, likened to a '*mini-MBA*' by many students, it became obvious after only a few years of practice, that l*earning to learn* required a prominent place in the standardized section of my curriculum. Since 2001, we have been teaching '*learning to learn*' on day 1, as the first topic, serving almost as a legend to the map for navigating this adventure. Bear in mind, that the majority of adult learners I teach are at the '*manager of others*' stage of careers, having spent many years as an '*individual contributor*' (IC) before given responsibility for other ICs. They are not '*junior*' either.

THE NEED FOR AN EDUCATION POLICY COMMITTEE

One possible reason for a lack of educating students in how to navigate the system is short-term thinking necessitated by linking education policy to the current political party in office. In May 1997, we successfully set up the Monetary Policy Committee, giving the Bank of England the task of leading thinking in their field of expertise. Why not do the same for Education?

Instead, due to political manoeuvrings, there is a continued, obsessive focus on measurement of education and assessment of students which comes, in my view, at the expense of improving the quality of educational experience. Higgins, Baumfield and Hall describe this as the tension between approaches, which are focused on the short term: 'the *most effective means to improve performance where the assessment focuses on content knowledge is likely to be direct instruction*', versus the longer term '*where assessment focuses on conceptual understanding [making] metacognitive or strategic approaches likely to be more effective.*' In short, we are absorbed by short-term thinking. Sesame Street has shown itself to be quality TV programming, supporting education[20], whereas SpongeBob SquarePants is almost the direct opposite[21]. This leads to short attention spans, a lack of focus and hyperactivity. The current governance structure of education, driven by 5-year government terms and individual political agendas, rather than by a longer-term thought process around quality, is dumbing down Education and consequently the nation.

SECRETARY OF STATE FOR EDUCATION

If the most senior decision maker for Education happened to be a teacher, would that help? What if they remained in office for more than five years? Sadly, those

---

20. https://www.nber.org/papers/w21229
21. http://pediatrics.aappublications.org/content/128/4/644

in charge of education for the last 17 years feature the following professions in reverse order: pubs & breweries, accountant, solicitor, journalist, economist, charity worker, postman, economist and politician. Only one of those, Michael Gove (*Journalist*) served for more than two years in the office (2010-2014). We have to go back to 2001 to find someone with a background in schools being in charge of education; Estelle Morris. The very first, and only, secondary school teacher to serve in the role. Unfortunately, she only served one year, seemingly being put under pressure to quit, when it emerged that targets for literacy and numeracy tests had not been met[22]. How sad that her demise was related to targets for testing.

LEADING CHANGE IN EDUCATION

It is my belief that Education deserves a guiding coalition of respected and experienced EDUCATORS, in situ at the most senior level, determining the direction of our schooling system, not the latest arrival on the political merry-go-round looking for a short-term numerical hit to sway the polls.

TEACHING THE TEACHERS TO TEACH: ARE WE?

Another problem worth considering, perhaps related, is that it may be that many teachers are not taught '*how*' to teach; instead they are taught '*what*' to teach with little in the way of pedagogic science being imparted. This makes it difficult for them to teach others how to learn. While my own experience of pedagogic education was rich and varied, my close friend at the time was '*dropped*' into a secondary school classroom after just a few lectures and spent most of her time expected to learn by osmosis. She reported, during her time in Cardiff University, that there were no contextual education books on her PGCE programme and a very light required reading list! Should we be surprised by the quality of the profession, with the educational experience diluted, when we expect most teachers to learn by osmosis?

Perhaps another issue is *consensus*. According to the *Centre for Learning and Teaching at Newcastle* University, there is no '*general consensus about what a learning to learn approach might consist of.*'[23] Irrespective of the reason behind it, we need to take action to prepare our students for the onset of AI.

---

22. https://www.telegraph.co.uk/news/1411041/Estelle-Morris-resigns.html

23. https://www.ncl.ac.uk/cflat/research/learning-to-learn/#overview

KNOW THYSELF

Conceptual understanding and metacognitive approaches are the focus here. Below, I propose a model for *learning to learn,* which takes into account recent developments in our understanding of the human brain, from a *predisposition* perspective. The more aware we are of how each of us learns differently and of how this requires a cycle of practice, the more likely we are to act in alignment with our own style and develop confidence in ability to become more sophisticated in our endeavours over time. Simply put, *'awareness'* supports *'belief'*, which enables *'desire'*, leading to *'application'* and behaviour change. As it was written on the forecourt of the Temple of Apollo at Delphi, Greece, *'Know Thyself'*.

A MODEL FOR LEARNING

To understand how we learn and how each of us prefers to do this differently, we first have to understand how we *'see'* the world. Carl Jung (1971) worked on Psychological Types[24] proposing *four,* namely, T*hinking, Feeling, Sensing & Intuiting*. A secondary model found to be robust in application, is Honey and Mumford's *Manual of Learning Styles*. They propose *four,* namely *Theorists, Pragmatists, Reflectors & Activists*.

There is a great deal of critique of Learning Styles[25]. I believe this is correct, because our understanding to date has been limited, not because learners do not have a preferred way of learning. A model which limits students to one style is insufficient. I also agree that a learning style based upon one primary sense alone (*Visual, Auditory or Kinaesthetic*) is also only part of the picture. This is not the place to go into the subject in depth, as much work needs to be done in the field.

What is found in the adult classroom, is that Jung, Honey & Mumford and other models of human behaviour, from Social Anthropology (Fiske[26]), to cultural norms (Hofstede[27]), team roles (Belbin[28]) and even conflict styles

---

24. Jung, Carl G. (1971). *Psychological Types*. London: Routledge

25. See Julie Henry's article in the Telegraph, quoting Susan Greenfield and Frank Coffield's commentary on the irrelevance of Visual, Auditory and Kinaesthic styles, as well as on the idea of a child having just one learning style - https://www.telegraph.co.uk/news/uknews/1558822/Professor-pans-learning-style-teaching-method.html

26. See Structures of Social Life by Alan Fiske: Market Forces, Equality Matching, Communal Sharing and Authority Ranking

27. See Cultures and Organizations by Geert Hofstede: Femininity vs Masculinity, Power Distance, Uncertainty Avoidance, plus Collectivism vs Individualism.

28. See Management Teams by Meredith Belbin: Specialists, Teamworkers, Completer-finishers, Plants, etc.

(Thomas & Kilmann[29]) repeat the same pattern of four behaviours. Katherine Benziger's work explains these four patterns to regions inside the cortex of the human brain.[30] Those wishing to know more should read the work of Katherine Benziger, Iain McGilChrist[31] and Joseph Hellige[32] on the subject.

Figure 2 shows the four major areas of the outer brain. The cortex is useful for our model of Preferred Cognitive Style. Of note is that they are connected internally by two sets of electrical, white matter – the Corpus Callosum, connecting *right* to *left* and the arcuate fasciculus, connecting front *left* to *back left* and *front right* to *back right* (*not shown here*). It is unknown why the brain has arrived at this anatomy. In *The Master and His Emissary*, Ian McGilchrist puts forward compelling evidence not only for the functionality of the *left* versus the *right*, but also for the differing functions of the *front* versus the *back*. Additionally, he speaks of the white matter connections having a dual function of connection and inhibition of connection, allowing differing localized activities. Briefly speaking, these four areas and their primary functionality reconcile, supported by the work of Karl Pribram as well as Katherine Benziger's, map almost perfectly to Carl Gustav Jung's Psychological Types. In clockwise order, starting with the top left are – *Thinking, Intuiting, Feeling* and *Sensing*. More work needs to be done to prove this, however but this working model of the brain is used for this chapter.

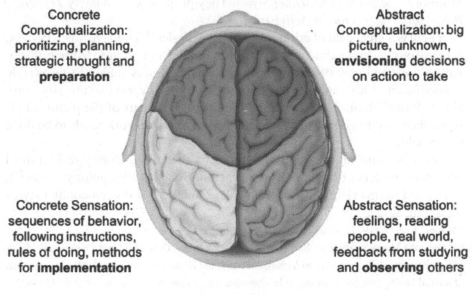

Concrete Conceptualization: prioritizing, planning, strategic thought and **preparation**

Abstract Conceptualization: big picture, unknown, **envisioning** decisions on action to take

Concrete Sensation: sequences of behavior, following instructions, rules of doing, methods for **implementation**

Abstract Sensation: feelings, reading people, real world, feedback from studying and **observing** others

Figure 1: The NeoCortex from above

29. See Thomas-Kilmann Conflict Mode Instrument by Kenneth Thomas and Ralph Kilmann: Avoiding, Accommodating, Cooperating and Competing.

30. See Thriving in Mind by Dr Katherine Benziger

31. See The Master and His Emissary by Iain McGilchrist

32. See Hemispheric Asymmetry by Joseph Hellige

BRAIN VS. LEFT BRAIN

Intelligent beings need to be able to handle the *'unknown and unknowable'*, in order to create the *'known and knowable'* to manipulate the world for their benefit. According to McGilchrist, these functions are achieved through the interplay between the right and left side of the cortex.

FRONT BRAIN VS. BACK BRAIN

Additionally, as thinking, conscious beings, we need to reflect upon what we experience through our senses, in contrast with our experiences and expectations of the world. We must be able to stand back from the immediate to generate the ability to *'decide'* how to respond, rather than to just *'react'* to our surroundings, as animals might. McGilchrist notes that while the back of the brain is dealing with the sensation of the here and now (v*ia the occipital, parietal and temporal lobes*), it is the front of the brain which allows for conceptualization of what is happening (*via the frontal lobes*), reference to the past and decision making about the future, due to the ability to stand back from the world and consider it.

FOUR REGIONAL CORTICAL FUNCTIONS

Each quadrant, as a default, is predisposed to handle one specific aspect of all of our experiences. From the abstract to concrete and from the conceptual to the actual world. In my practice I have described the model and subsequent predispositions (*temperaments*) to many students since 2005, with recognition by most that the descriptions below explain their experience of life (Figure 2).

Look at Figure 3 and judge for yourself if you can find your *'preferred'* way of interacting with the world. The chart represents a development of Jung's typology, from insight gained from students self-diagnosing their preferences; describing how they see the world and prefer to handle it, after being taught the model.

This mapping of default functionality is a major milestone for understanding learning styles as well as personality preferences. While Jung's work maps perfectly, David Kolb's research on Learning Styles also does to the brain. The match is not as obvious, due to some naming conventions and language used as well as the model requiring an update.

For Kolb, a model for learning meant progression through a cycle of four stages:

1. having a concrete experience, followed by
2. observation of and reflection on that experience, which leads to
3. the formation of abstract concepts and generalizations, which are then
4. used to test hypothesis in future situations, resulting in new experiences.

Cognitive Styles

- They think before speaking; considerate of their language and use of words
- Naturally investigative or skeptical; usually seeking proof, evidence, data or sources
- Poker faced; tend to keep their emotions underneath the surface; they can be very difficult to 'read' in a relationship
- Prefer tentative language rather than absolutes: "I think..."; "...perhaps..."; "...that depends..."; or "there's a lot we don't know yet"
- They think through contemplation and silent analysis; when they understand they're quiet; when they don't they'll ask a question
- They enjoy solving complex puzzles for the sake of it
- Generally, perfectionists; prefer to do a thing perfectly well for its own sake
- They don't like to repeat themselves, or raise their voices unnecessarily
- Why? Why? Why? What's the purpose? Would rather connect with data than with people, to get answers, as 'networking' seems to be a pointless pursuit unless it's with other subject matter experts
- Their approach to others can be somewhat 'formulaic'
- Gifted with 'things' rather than people; they are highly conceptual and theoretical

- Pattern recognition; they can almost 'see' events happening ahead of time
- Creativity; on the spot, they act then think along the way, get moving then adapt, are spontaneous, think on their feet, are driven by ideas and new opportunity, prefer freedom, or autonomy rather than rules and procedures
- They are eager to join in the conversation, they contribute to demonstrate understanding, are restless in their desire for change and excitement
- They think through movement and activity
- Piles of paperwork; they have a 'piling' system that may seem somewhat chaotic or unstructured to the other person as it's three dimensional in nature
- Can sometimes switch off their attention if they're not 'active' in the conversation
- Turbo speed; love to do things at the last minute, with the thrill of the deadline
- Unexpected decisions; if it's fun they're 'in'
- Natural 'fire fighters' in business, can bring order to chaos instantly
- Prefer entrepreneurial activity, raising capital, deal making, are natural negotiators
- Tend to speak using metaphor or allegory; build bridges of understanding
- They use imagery, or descriptive language to develop understanding and explain
- They can adapt to any environment, big picture thinkers, naturally imaginative
- Metaphor is a primary communication tool

- They are sequential; the list makers, favoring the here and now, real data, or what's actual
- They are prepared, ordered, punctual, have categorized filing systems with labelling
- Their lists extend to vacation, holidays, work, agendas (and spare agendas)
- They value teams and team contributions, cooperation and collective effort
- They are naturally detailed, with fine motor skills, valuing the intricacy of activity
- They are likely to be family oriented, favoring traditional or customary group events
- They prefer a formal approach, by the rules, official and documented activity
- The most likely to have a work-life balance, with clear delineation and a plan
- They value planning, tick-boxes, specific, measurable tasks and absolute clarity
- For them, quality is key, including audit, compliance and contingency planning
- They are process driven, valuing re-use and lessons learned; why reinvent the wheel?
- They are likely to relate to insurance as a concept and perhaps as a career
- They prefer advanced notice and scheduled change
- Democracy, fairness, responsibility, reliability, tradition and formality
- They use highly specific tools for specific tasks, with precision and are detailed manufacturers, engaging in detailed craft work

- For them, harmony is important; how people work together, get along
- They are emotionally expressive; they "wear their hearts on their sleeves"
- They think through dialogue, and conversation; if they understand they talk
- They are helping all the time, tend to put others ahead of their own needs
- For them, friends most important; people come first, work comes second
- They listen well, are empathic, and have an intuition about people and how they're feeling; they can read non-verbal language with very little effort
- They can be very spiritual, at one with nature, caring for animals and the planet
- They're great at offering counsel to friends or in their jobs; likely to be teachers
- They have a built in natural ability to make people feel at ease
- They can spot incongruence in people and their actions
- They are great supporters of the other person's accomplishments; giving out praise
- As a friend, they are loyal, tend to be tactile; the 'touchy feely' types
- They are social animals, very chatty and (unless introverted) naturally personable
- How you say something is more important than what you say
- They are appreciative of colour, accessories, interior design, the look of something
- They are kinaesthetic and highly sensitive to touch; the harmony of contact

Figure 2: Preferred Cognitive Styles

The stages reconcile but the sequence and language need adjusting, as so:

1. We begin the cycle by **observing** the world around us, potentially leading to an awareness of the need to learn. This may be due to internal stimuli, such as reflection, or external stimuli, like feedback.
2. Assuming our awareness of the need to learn is established, we then **envision** where to go or what to do as a result of that, leading to the consideration or creation of alternative paths. If these paths resonate sufficiently, we may then generate a desire to learn, or not, as the case may be. Again, internal or external stimuli come into play, such as present levels of intrinsic or extrinsic motivation; carrots or sticks in our vicinity.
3. Once we have raised our awareness of the need to learn, and then uncovered or created a desire to learn, we then **prepare** accordingly, by taking on new information to develop a competency. This may come as a detailed understanding, model or instructions of how to act. Taking in information, understanding and committing it to memory are tasks at this stage. With-out application of what we '*learn*', it is liable to be forgotten, so a fourth, final stage is required to say we have '*learned*'.
4. The final stage is to convert the '*knowledge*' into '*behaviour*' which aligns to that knowledge. To know and not to do is not to know. Thus, it is imperative that we quickly **implement** our knowledge in some way, in the form of a concrete experience, to convert it from the short-term noise of input, into the long-term capability of informed action. This then enables us to repeat the cycle, observe, envision, prepare, implement and check we have applied the knowledge well enough for it to be of value as a successful outcome.

Michael Merzenich talks of trying until we get it right, before the brain then says '*save that one*'. This is where the law of coincident activity comes into play; the Hebb rule: '*neurons that fire together, wire together*'. Canadian psychologist Donald Hebb posited: '*When one cell repeatedly assists in firing another, the axon of the first cell develops synaptic knobs (or enlarges them if they already exist) in contact with the soma of the second cell.*' This is the plasticity of the brain at work completing a single cycle of '*learning*'. While it is a simplistic cycle, requiring repetition to embellish learning into the complex skills we are used to, based upon current understanding of neuro-plasticity[33], it represents the basic four step process fundamental to learning.

CONNECTIONS TO OTHER MODELS

Before describing how to use the *Observe, Envision, Prepare, Implement* model (OEPI), we must connect it to other models of learning styles. Howard Gardner

---

33. See The Brain that Changes Itself by Norman Doidge for an excellent introduction to this concept

identified at least 8 different types of intelligence, with associated learning styles:

Type of Intelligence	Area of Focus	Workplace Examples
Musical	Sound and rhythm	Musicians, Poets or Composers
Spatial	Visual	Graphic Designers, Architects or Photographers
Linguistic	Words and Oracy	Authors, Story tellers or Journalists
Naturalistic	Nature	Gardeners, Zoologists or Geologists
Bodily-kinesthetic	Movement	Dancers, Mechanics or Athletes
Logical-mathematical	Numbers	Accountants, Physicists or Programmers
Intrapersonal	Self-awareness	Counsellors or Philosophers
Interpersonal	Social	Human Resources, Event Planners

Each is coloured to show a connection to our model: either Green, Red, Blue or Yellow. The mapping is basic, as there is overlap in the brain. Language, in the form of tone, could map to the basal right (*blue*), in metaphor to the frontal right (*red*), in grammar to the basal left (*yellow*) or in syntax and choice of words to the frontal left (*green*). As with the linguistic intelligence, it is more likely that someone who considers themselves introverted to be an author, able to sit for hours working with words on a computer or with a pen and paper and be stimulated. Compare this to a gifted story-teller, at their highest levels of alertness in front of a crowd, so demonstrating extraversion. These so-called '*arousal set point*' traits of introversion, ambiversion and extraversion, as described by Hans Eysenck, are more closely related to Gardner's Intrapersonal and Interpersonal intelligences and are anatomically a separate system to the model of the cortex shown. They are believed to be behavioural manifestation of the Reticular Activating System.[34]

As mentioned above, Honey & Mumford describe 4 learning styles with a set of traits for each:

Theorists	Activists	Pragmatists	Reflectors
Learn through creating theoretical models. They are thorough, learn through complex problem solving and are interested in data	Learn through doing things and movement. They are active, fidgety, act quickly, value new experiences and enjoy variety	Learn when topics are based upon real life, are relevant to them, via practice, conversation and by doing	Learn by considering the details, following instructions, a methodical, sequenced structure and deliberate pace.

---

34. See Hans Eysenck's Dimensions of Personality (1947)

Can you spot the connection to the four primary functions of the brain quadrants above? Which learning style would that mean that you prefer?

IS THIS YOU?

Theorists would have potentially discounted the content thus far as not '*academically*' sound. *Reflectors* would dutifully go back and re-read the four descriptions then sequentially map them with the most obvious first. *Pragmatists* might think of friends or people in their lives and use that as a way to determine the match, or may even have a chat with someone about this and whether in works in real life. *Activists*, unless older and wiser and less '*singular*' in their learning style, are unlikely to have read this far! They will have noted the images, scanned key words and come to a conclusion that there are some interesting patterns here, being pointed out by the author.

One aspect of learning to learn is to understand that you are not crazy, weird or broken, because you have a preferred way of learning, which is not logical. The schooling system is designed around a logical curriculum, with logical subjects receiving the highest levels of academic reward and curriculum focus. This only appeals to a fraction of the population. Not only is *learning to learn* critical to developing independent learners, capable of responding positively to AI, it is also essential for understanding the experience of students, who feel marginalized because they learn differently. This model is in basic form here, but along with references, this chapter should provide the reader with resources to inform the conversation and perhaps, place it into focus for decision makers.

> '*The essential dynamics of authentic education always takes the student beyond the status quo into what is not fully known, fully comprehended, fully formalized. Education is the expression and development of a primary impulse for truth, a deep epistemic instinct that we inherit as part of our biological nature. A civilization that cannot recognized the intrinsic value and beauty of education has already condemned itself either to permanent ethical and cultural stagnation or, worse, extinction.*'

This quote is from *The Educational Imperative*, by Peter Abbs, Lecturer in Education at the University of Sussex and passionate advocate for the arts in education. We have a duty not only to take our students beyond the status quo, but to prepare them to handle what is not fully known, comprehended, or, at the time of writing, fully formalized. We need to teach our students how to learn, not just what to know.

CONCLUSION

Learning to learn, as a discipline, has come a long way since the National Curriculum was developed. We should be providing students with ability to manage their own learning by increasing self-awareness of how they personally prefer to do so and helping them master study skills which suit their preferred style. There is a recurring pattern of four themes running throughout observations of human behavior at a macro and micro level. These four themes need more research to prove their design. However, in my own practice, many students have found they described their personal experience of learning preferences and helped them to reflect and become more self-aware. We should be investigating them further, to arrive at a scientific basis for their authenticity and a design for a curriculum for teacher training and learning in the curriculum. Ask any professional teacher, whether they have observed differences in the way students prefer to approach the school experience. Their answers should be enough to substantiate a call to action. Difference is real. We should learn about it and use it to our advantage, before it becomes our demise.

I titled this paper *"Adventure is out there"* as a quote from the Disney-Pixar movie, "Up!" In the scene, our two young dreamers are imagining what it would be like to go on an adventure to Paradise Falls in South America. Having researched this topic, I have concluded that despite the best minds putting their focus and attention on this subject, that no-one truly knows what AI will bring to education or to the world. Perhaps the best we could do is to prepare our young minds with the skill of learning, as we have no idea what adventures lie ahead. Do we want to prepare them to handle the unknown, as best as we can?

MAIN POINTS

- Learning to learn requires awareness of your own particular style of doing this
- Greater attention to this will achieve the higher levels of thinking & communication
- Education has to rethink a focus on facts rather than feelings to move towards smarter decisions
- Action must be immediate to cope with requirements for AI changes to life and work

CHAPTER 8

THE ROBOTS ARE HERE: AN EDUCATION REPONSE

SUSAN JAMES

SUMMARY

*This chapter targets the topic of **student well-being** in a world now dominated by technology. Intelligent machines are taking over routine operations, producing uncertainty about future job possibilities. Society is now very complex and demanding for everyone and technology has exposed us to what is going on minute-to minute across the world, resulting in information over-load to increase our stress and anxiety. In an academically focused educational curriculum, there is now urgent need to give more attention to the personal competencies of students, so that they can cope in a resilient way with the constant, rapid changes now part of our existence. The chapter looks at the positive and negative aspects of technology and reviews how to minimise the latter and work with the former for effective outcomes for the future.*

INTRODUCTION

In a complex, uncertain existence, how do we ensure pupils maintain and sustain a sense of *well-being* in the future?

> *'Very little is needed to make a happy life; it is all within yourself, in your way of thinking'* (Marcus Aurelius – Roman Emperor)

In a world dominated by a desire for immediate information, gratification and affirmation – we indulge in naval-gazing and fail to look around us for inspiration and help. Our favourite way to express is through the (*edited*) selfie, so Marcus Aurelius has never sounded so naive and out of date. Technology surrounds us everywhere. As individuals, parents and educators we can decide to embrace or evade it, but much like the well-worn topic of Brexit it is not going to evaporate and fade away. The world is, and always will be hungry for the new, convenient and controversial.

WHAT PEOPLE ARE SAYING

Inspired by the United Nations 17 Sustainable Development Goals, *The Breakout Project* advocates that we are part of a global community and to face future challenges we must come together and share innovations and solutions for moving the world forward positively.

A recent online article proposed: '*7 Ways Technology Will Help Us Change the World*'. In summary, these were: *accessing advice; awareness of what is happening globally; discovering major issues and solutions; consulting experts; increasing productivity; targeting creativity/more important work; finding new ways to sustain the planet.*

Naha Mesri, writing for The Huffington Post, has also reported on ways technology will shape our lives by 2020. She identified increased automation and AI, providing stark comment on the way it will impact on the work-force. Already Millennials change jobs very 2 years or less and it is estimated that 65% of primary school children will learn in ways not currently existing. The McKinsey Global Institute predicts that robots will replace 40-75 million jobs by 2025.

In line with the *Breakout Project*, Masri suggests creativity will come from advances and increased technology use. Web access to information already enables us to fix everyday issues by learning from others. Whilst many have learned to adjust to this new way of learning, digital natives, '*will be born with free resources at their finger-tips in a way that their parents could not have imagined*'. New jobs could be created within virtual worlds themselves. The flexibility of a virtual world means people can work remotely. Businesses are able to choose from a global pool to work across time zones. This heralds changes in company structures. Organizations are being flattened with layers of management stripped to make jobs more dynamic.

Whilst a lack of direct face-to-face team-building time is often perceived as a downside to remote working, Nesri highlights the positives. Studies, like Holt's (2007), have found that virtual brainstorming eliminates '*production blocking*', because dominant voices do not hinder more introverted creatives. In addition, virtual group sessions can remain productive, unlike face-to-face sessions when groups exceed 6 participants.

Both articles acknowledge the impact that technology is already having on life – changing the way we communicate, act and work with others. How can past philosophies have anything to offer us in order to cope with this rapid rate of change? The insecurities of this are leading to problems with mental health in today's society, explored in the next section.

WHAT ARE MENTAL HEALTH ISSUES?

Mental health and resilience have been educational buzz words recently. Schools are facing a huge challenge with increasing numbers of pupils said to have stress, anxiety and depression. The last Census recorded 1 in 10 children between 5-16 years having a diagnosable mental health condition (*3 per class*). Half of those with a lifetime condition will first experience symptoms at about 14 years. 28% of pre-schoolers have problems impacting on psychological development (Sabates & Dex, 2013). In 2014, over half a million UK children were recorded as being unhappy (Children's Society, 2014). Around 1 in 5 15 year olds self-harm (World Health Organisation). More recently the term '*snow-flake generation*' has become common parlance. The term appeared in the 1996 novel, '*Fightclub*', made into a film: '*You are not special. You are not a beautiful and unique snowflake. You're the same decaying organic matter as everything else*'. It was then picked up by right-wing US politicians and used as a pejorative term for those with left-wing sensitivities. In 2016, it was one of the Collins Dictionary's 10 words of the year and '*snowflake generation*' was defined as: *young adults of the 2010s, viewed as being less resilient and more prone to taking offence than previous generations*.

THE ORIGIN OF WELL-BEING AND HAPPINESS

The idea of *well-being* is far from new. Happiness is often associated with *luck* and therefore something that one does not have control over. Things happen and you then either feel a sense of joy or not, depending on what has happened. *Eudaimonia*, the Greek word, is often translated as *happiness*, but Ancient philosophers saw this as synonymous with virtue. The idea that one can have a sense of control over well-being through action (*doing good*) and crucially '*your way of thinking*' is viewed as attaining greater happiness.

In medieval times, citizens were encouraged to work virtuously, in order to achieve God's reward and salvation in the after-life. During the Renaissance, it was thought pleasure-seeking attained happiness. Sigmund Freud (1856-1939), the medical doctor famous for his work on psychoanalysis (*as well as others*) commented on the human condition - that we seek immediate pleasure and gratification, but that greater success, reward and satisfaction comes when we defer gratification. Duckworth and Baumeister (2013) advocated a positive mind-set to achieve well-being. This chimes with Matthew Ricard's (2008) definition of happiness as: '*a deep sense of flourishing that arises from an exceptionally healthy mind etc. to change the world, it is always possible to change the way we look at it*'.

It seems then that Aurelias, amongst other ancient thinkers, together with modern ones, agree that achieving a sense of balance and calm is attainable through our actions and attitude. This being the case, education has a large part to play in the future well-being of young people, particularly as there is, within the human condition, a tendency towards immediate gratification. If the value of deferred gratification, virtue and idea of finding a sense of well-being within are promoted and rewarded in schools, this will ensure that the future work-force are better able to navigate a fast-paced future? What has been discussed suggests an educational programme that develops *self-understanding*, in which deferred gratification, for a feeling of well-being, can be achieved.

WHAT ARE THE ISSUES FOR PROVISION?

The Yidan Prize Forecast '*Education to 2030*', produced by The Economist and Intelligence Unit (2016) suggested 5 education indicators across 25 economies. These related to trends including the future of work and skills needed to succeed with technology use. The report has implications for *what* and *how* is currently taught. It acknowledges that a person's ability to work will be shaped by surrounding technology. The need to equip young people with competencies for work is highlighted repeatedly:

> *The global youth unemployment rate stands at 13%.....One billion young people around the world are expected to enter the job market over the next decade. The challenge facing policy makers will be to make sure that young people have the skills needed to prosper in the 21st century marketplace....Demand rising for non-routine, analytical skills......a labour market shaped by such trends as cloud services, cyber security and the Internet of Things, and technology-driven construction....in the longer term, a need for more creative problem-solvers.*

The report highlights the importance and value of 'STEM' subjects - *Science, Technology, Engineering & Mathematics*. These are taught in an interdisciplinary way with pupils applying knowledge as required in the working world. The report states:

> *New types of jobs emerge as industries are created, and new problems requiring solutions are encountered.....flexible STEM-capable workers [needed] at very educational level.*

The STEM *approach* is advocated, not the knowledge gained. Introducing more technology and science will not necessarily improve quality of knowledge, which may become obsolete by the time students start work. Jensen, founder of *Learning First,* argues for arming pupils with *'good generic skills'*, including spoken and written literacy and mathematics.

Noting the importance of *skill* over *knowledge*, Aaron Benavot, of the United Nations Education, Scientific and Cultural Organisation's (UNESCO) Global Education Monitoring Report comments, *'It's very difficult for the system to anticipate what skills will be needed in 2030.'* Along with other experts, he argues that ultimately it will be more valuable to teach transversal or generic skills, like *communication, adaptability, flexibility and ability to work in different contexts and respond to change.*

Students once devoted time to

'the pursuit of knowledge and truth...students are not getting the deeper, critical education. These skills are undervalued and very important and probably will be more important in a globalised world to understand other cultures, convey views not threatening to their culture, to have a sense of history and to speak different languages.....Engineers and scientists need to be educated more broadly [to] consider the political, ethical and moral implications of new technologies they work on.' (p. 14-15)

Caroline Wright, Director General Designate of British Educational Suppliers Association (BESA) predicts that class instruction will incorporate *'technology, paired with hands-on resources, face-to-face learning and flipped learning'*, suggesting an environment where technology is fully integrated as a teaching aid. Importantly, it anticipates technology assisting in a classroom where, as with the STEM philosophy, learners are approaching challenges on a more *'real world'* way. Rather than the teacher imparting knowledge as the lesson focus, they become a facilitator. Pupils come armed with knowledge (*homework reading/video watched*) but the lesson is about students working together to face and resolve challenges. To be successful, this approach does rely on the skills highlighted by the UNESCO report.

In comparison to the current UK school structures and curriculum, this report has significant implications. Senior school pupils are taught and examined by subject with knowledge regularly tested. Departments focus on their course content requirements and results. These determine whether or not they will find a place at university. Whilst this may not be the appropriate path for all pupils, attaining a place at a highly-rated one (*by achieving the best results, by subject for GCSE and A-Level*) is the agenda for academically selective independent schools. State schools, too, and their teachers (*through performance related pay*) are under pressure to attain the best GCSE results for their cohorts.

HOW THE INTERNET AFFECTS LIVES

The USA Pew Research Center examines how people use the internet to affect life. It is non-partisan, and does not endorse any technologies, companies, industries or individuals. Their work takes no positions on policy issues related to the internet. The data collected is supplemented with research from government agencies, technology firms, academia and other expert venues. Lee Raine, the director, with Janna Anderson, released an article in April 2018 entitled, '*The Future of Well-Being in a Tech-Saturated World*'. Although most citizens canvased saw the role of digital technology as positive, mounting concerns about negative impacts prompted the Pew Center to query technology experts, scholars and health specialist about how digital changes will impact on physical and mental well-being over the next 10 years. 1,150 experts responded to canvassing – 47% predict that individual well-being will be more helped than harmed, whilst 32% predicted the reverse. Respondents were invited to provide detailed comment. Findings were grouped according to dominant themes: *ways people will be helped and harmed with remedies to assist well-being and digital life. These are detailed below.*

MENTAL HEALTH GUIDANCE

The advantages of the digital era outlined above, parallel those discussed. Taking into account predictions for harm, in addition to mental health issues outlined earlier, what are the implications for educational provision? Guidance for schools around mental health tends to focus on managing situations in which pupils are suffering. There is some reference to promoting positive mental health strategies in the Department for Education's, 'Mental health and behaviour in schools' advice:

In order to help pupils succeed, schools have a role to play in supporting them to be resilient and mentally healthy. There are various things that schools **can** do, for all pupils and those with particular problems, to offer effective support. (p.6)

The Personal, Social and Health Education (PSHE) Association has produced guidance and lesson plans to support the delivery of effective teaching on mental health issues. In addition, MindEd, a free online training tool, provides information and advice for staff on children and young people's mental health and, 'can help to direct staff to targeted resources when problems have been identified' (D f E). Local authorities also have initiatives. In Stockport, for example, 'Improving Emotional Well-being' is the strategy proposed for educational settings.

Whilst guidance is useful, it relies on a school or individual, to engage in what is on offer. The word 'can' indicates the non-essential nature of this work.

MORE HELPED THAN HARMED	
Connection	Digital life links people, knowledge, education and entertainment globally at any time in an affordable, nearly frictionless manner.
Commerce, government society	Digital life revolutionizes civic, business, consumer and personal logistics, opening up a world of opportunity and options.
Crucial intelligence	Digital life is essential to tapping into an ever-widening array of health, safety and science resources, tools and services in real time.
Contentment	Digital life empowers people to improve, advance or reinvent their lives, allowing them to self-actualize, meet soul-mates and make a difference in the world.
Continuation quality	Emerging tools will continue to expand the quality and focus of digital life; the big-picture results will be a plus overall for humanity.

MORE HARMED THAN HELPED	
Digital deficits	People's cognitive capabilities will be challenged in multiple ways, including capacity for analytical thinking, memory, focus, creativity, reflection and mental resilience.
Digital addiction	Internet businesses are organized around dopamine-dosing tools designed to hook the public.
Digital distrust/divisiveness	Personal agency will be reduced and emotions such as shock, fear, indignation and outrage will be further weaponized on line, driving divisions and doubts.
Digital duress	Information overload + declines in trust and face-to-face skills + poor interface design = rises in stress, anxiety, depression, inactivity and sleeplessness.
Digital dangers	The structure of the internet and pace of digital change invite ever-evolving threats to human interaction, security, democracy, jobs, privacy and more.

POTENTIAL REMEDIES	
Reimagine systems	Societies can revise both tech arrangements and the structure of human institutions – including their composition, design, goals and processes.
Reinvent tech	Things can change by reconfiguring hardware and software to improve their human-centred performance and by exploiting tools like artificial intelligence (AI), virtual reality (VR), augmented reality (AR) and mixed reality (MR).
Regulate	Governments and/or industries should create reforms through agreement on standards, guidelines, codes of conduct, and passage of laws and rules.
Redesign literacy	Formally educate all people about impacts of digital life on well-being and the way tech systems function, as well as encourage appropriate, healthy uses.
Recalibrate expectations	Human-technology coevolution comes at a price; digital life in the 2000s is no different. People must gradually evolve and adjust to these changes.
Fated to fail	A share of respondents say all this may help somewhat, but – mostly due to human nature – it is unlikely that these responses will be effective enough.

It gives strategies for situations where a pupil's mental health state is in decline. Factors like loss, life changes or traumatic events can weaken an individual's resolve. The work done is worthy, but may not hit the mark: neither tackling the specific nature, impact and implications of technology. They align, however, with the idea that inner strength, a set of internal values that helps to build self-knowledge and worth, is key to a healthy life.

If well-being is maintained by outlook on life as a whole, then surely creating a relevant, responsive well-being programme needs to be seen as a whole-school priority. Aurelius, and more recently, Duckworth & Baumeister (2013) promote the idea of agency: that an individual can choose the way they see and react to the world; that humans can find a way to flourish in any situation and with any outcome. Promoting this philosophy can happen during dedicated lessons. For meaningful impact it needs to be carried through *all* lessons. Staff need to use an agreed, shared language. For example, the idea of deferred gratification, can be reinforced for all pupils. This might be through a practical exercise, or reward for sustained commitment in a lesson (*despite finding a task challenging*).

A concept can be taught and its value reinforced. To be embedded, the pupil has to internalise or '*own*' principles. In order to evidence that values, like deferred gratification, have been embraced, pupils must show awareness of how ownership of them has impacted on life. They need to be given time and space to reflect on their development. Thinking skills, like metacognition and reflection, take time and practice within the school day to develop and be given a strong profile. Their importance needs to be understood by all staff. It is not uncommon for subject specialists to find open-ended tasks, taking pupils on an individual journey (*without a neat answer*), unnerving and questionable in value. A programme for pupils will require a thorough, thoughtful training for staff.

The wider educational provision needs to take account of employment changes. Lessons need to be balanced – knowledge should not outweigh skills training. Courses must not be solely teacher-led: lessons need to flip the classroom, so that pupils lead and report on journeys of discovery. Pupils require high levels of spoken and written literacy to cope with this change. A significant amount of time and training must be devoted to developing communication, analytical and reflective abilities, so that pupils are equipped to appreciate wider implications surrounding knowledge, like ethical considerations for decisions in the work place.

'*Keeping people in a state of anxiety, anger or haunted by fear can be very profitable.*'(Judith Dunath). Whilst there may be merit in this statement as a political comment on how society is controlled, consideration should be given to the way human beings can strive for more and better. A government will always be able to exploit this desire, but it is for education to promote a more deep-rooted sense of security: '*The personal qualities that allow one to thrive in the face of adversity; an emergent property that is a set of systems;*

overcoming adversity to the point of transforming adversity' is a way to find peace and satisfaction, if people are to live well and flourish in the truest sense.

CONCLUSION

This chapter has used many sources to gain a picture of the future for current learners. It is clear that we are feeling the impact of technological advances. The paradox for educators is that schools are attempting to prepare pupils for jobs that do not yet exist. A human desire to evolve and progress and for immediate, convenient gratification, is what fuels technological advances and preoccupation and high engagement with smartphones. The discussion highlights agreement about the positive impact on our lives. As no one can predict the future, it is unsurprising that experts have mixed views about the impact of technology on well-being.

What is clear is the importance of education to facilitate skills needed. Current knowledge will be useful, but becomes rapidly out-of-date. Greater communication, self-awareness, critical thinking, flexibility of thought bring confidence and coping abilities to ensure high levels of productivity and a sense of well-being. Educators need to go back to first principles. Ensuring children have inner language, thinking and strength cannot be achieved through one personal, social and health education lesson a week. It needs to be lived and breathed across the whole school experience and culture.

Independent schools have long been associated with inculcating communication confidence and roundedness within pupils. Rather than changing what is done within these settings, these schools need to be more demonstrative about how they go about a holistic approach. This does not just target academic tracking as a measure of success. Students can go through school, proud of what they have achieved in discrete areas, but not able to articulate the skills or attributes they have acquired. The proposed use of tutor time to reflect would enable pupils to develop greater awareness. Stronger self-knowledge will be essential for our young people, but we must not forget the many positives that exist.

> *'People are adaptive. In the long run, we are reasonable too. We learn how to deal with uncertainties, pitfalls, threats as well as bad guys who might harm us. Building healthier, more supportive environments, where we can converse, communicate feelings and views in a calm, pleasant way leads to respect for everyone. Greed, hate, violence, oppression will not be eradicated as history reveals, but technology is already alleviating problems and carries much promise. This is not utopian thinking. It is a realistic review of circumstances. I would rather trade places with my grandkids than with my grandparents.*
> (Sheizaf Rafaeli)

'Very little is needed to make a happy life; it is all within yourself, in your way of thinking' (Marcus Aurelius – Roman Emperor)

Rafaeli and Aurelias have common thoughts about human experience: the way we react to experience indicates the level of control someone has over their fate. Both assume that we are about more than the sum total of our physical, mental and social selves. We have a soul, desire and capability to think more deeply about the world to achieve spiritual balance, satisfaction, well-being, happiness and peace in our existence. The message is a person aware of the power of their mind and able to build supportive relationships will communicate effectively with others to work out solutions to problems. They can manage and embrace the challenges of their futures and thrive as a consequence.

REFERENCES

Anderson, J. & Rainie, L. (2017) *The Future of Well-Being in a Tech-Saturated World*: Online. Accessed 1 Nov. 2018

Bacino, L. (2014) *Shock Figures Show Extent of Self-harm in English Teenagers*: The Guardian

Department for Education (2014) *Mental Health and Behaviours in Schools Departmental Advice for School Staff*

Baumeister, R., Galliot, M., DeWall, C. & Oaten, M. (2006). *Self-regulation and Personality: How interventions increase in regulatory success and how depletion moderates the effects of traits on behaviour:* Journal of Personality, 74, 1773-1801

Census 2004, online. Accessed 1 Nov. 2018

Catchpole, R. (2014) Training and Development Manager, Young Minds, speaking at the annual Mental Health Conference

Children's Society Report (2014) London: CS Headquarters

Duckworth, A. (2013) Grit: The Power of Passion and Perseverance: Simon and Schuster

Flavell, J. (1979). "Metacognition and cognitive monitoring. A new area of cognitive-development inquiry". American Psychologist. 34 (10): 906–911. doi: 10.1037/0003-066X.34.10.906

Holt, K. (2007) Brainstorming- From Classics to Electronics. Published Online

Manyika, J. (2018) Automation and the Future of Work. Mc Kinsey Global Institute. Pub. Accessed 1 November, 2018

Promoting Positive Mental Health in School Conference, 2014

Sabates, R. & Dex, S. (2013) *The Impact of Multiple Risk Factors on Young Children's Cognitive and Behavioural Development:* Children and Society

World Health Organisation (2014) *The Health Behaviour on School-aged Children* (HBSC) Report

CHAPTER 9
THE AI IN MY POCKET
MASTERING THE MACHINE, STARTING WITH MOBILE PHONES

VIVIENNE HORSFIELD

SUMMARY

This chapter suggests that:
- There are persuasive educational and pastoral reasons to ban mobile phone use in schools
- Schools educate technology use in Personal, Social & Health Education (PSHE) programmes, but unlike other topics addressed, children are experiencing the challenges that this presents
- Mobile phones are owned by most children before age 11, so secondary schools can begin a critical dialogue about wise technology use
- If we allow student mobiles in school, lessons can be taught about appropriate use & non-use
- There are educational reasons to allow mobile phones in classrooms, as simple functionality or more bespoke apps can enhance learning
- There is little to be gained when we only allow school approved or provided technology
- Allowing mobiles in school forces discussion of technology ethics & prepares students for the future

INTRODUCTION

Matt Hancock (UK Culture secretary), Amanda Spielman (OFSTED Inspector) and Emmanuel Macon (French President) are three, among many, sharing the same view about children taking mobiles to school - ban them! In fact, a mobile phone ban came into force in France in September 2018. Time will reveal the impact and the enforceability of such an edict, as mobile phones are ubiquitous in modern society. Walking down the street in any town, city or village, one sees most people holding or using a mobile phone. It might be an uncomfortable truth, but can we deny that we no longer leave the house without one? Are we not always conscious about the whereabouts of our mobile and reliant upon it for many functions, apart from voice calls? Is it not a familiar sight in meetings to see colleagues scrolling on phones, typing texts or emails, or who knows what? What motivates schools to ban this modern life and key tool at work? Is this time to say to children: '*Do as I say and not as I do*?' Should schools educate about appropriate technology use by embracing it and addressing problems, rather than banning phones and punishing children if found in their possession?

REASONS TO BAN MOBILE PHONES

You can see why there is a call to ban mobiles in schools when you review findings. These range from those related to teaching and learning to concerns for child-wellbeing and pastoral needs. The London School of Economics (2015) reviewed 4 UK schools, where mobiles are banned, with test results improving by 6%. The educational zeitgeist, dominated by league tables and numerical progress, is reminiscent of Mr Gradgrind's *Utilitarian Utopia* (Charles Dickens). This makes banning phones irresistible to Head Teachers, if it improves examination results. Related to this statistic is the Harvard Business Review's report (2015) finding that *expectation* of mobile phone distraction is irresistible to us, like turning a head when our name is called. In the study, participants performing cognitive tasks most successfully were those with phones in another room, followed by ones having them in a pocket. Those performing worst had phones placed face-down on the desk. In all cases, notifications and vibrations were turned off with participants aware of this! It seems that mobiles affect concentration and so banning them in school is sensible.

Another issue that teachers face is a problem with bullying, often related to social media. This is facilitated by children having phones accessible in schools. The ensuing mental health problems of stress, anxiety and depression are frequently laid at the foot of social media, with sites accessed by mobile phones. Schools seek to remove issues by removing the scope for viewing, updating and collecting data for social media use, so reducing the time children engage with the bullying that might follow. Again, one can see that the removal of this technology is justified, giving children time back to engage with each other in the physical rather than the virtual world. Latymer Upper School has banned mobiles entirely, reporting that children are engaging with extra-curricular clubs/societies and socialising more as a result.

Furthermore, the use of any personal technology, whether phone, tablet or laptop, in school or not, throws up issues of cheating and plagiarism. It is argued that we increase opportunities and temptation to cheat, when allowing students to carry technology capable of this in their pockets. It is another reason to remove them from school sites. The facts are convincing. Banning phones on school sites is a proverbial *'no brainer'*.

THE HERE AND NOW: THE AI IN OUR POCKETS

This chapter tentatively explores another view - with schools accepting mobiles are a reality as most children possess them in their pockets. If we can teach control and use of personal technology it will be a step to consider AI ethics, which Richard Davies raises in his thought-provoking chapter. As educators, we must take expert views seriously, listening to Professor Faggin saying, in his contribution, that machines are only as good as those who produce and programme them. Therefore, schools must radically rethink education, to ensure that we remain masters and not servants of machines. If Elon Musk and the late Stephen Hawking are concerned about AI, then we should be too. I argue that it is wise to allow phones in school, as a place of learning, to reflect on use and teach children to be masters of machines.

This is not the only reason for acknowledging mobiles in schools. Max Coates' chapter warns that education must be relevant to avoid resistance and rejection of technology. Native American chiefs showed in 1744, through rejection of free Higher Education for 12 of their braves, that if courses do not adequately prepare for life they will be deemed useless. Are we in danger of the same if we pretend that mobiles do not exist between 9am & 3.45pm? Are we preparing children for the future if we fail to teach responsible mobile technology use and the transfer ethics and etiquettes to machines that are now in existence?

Most schools address technology ethics in the PSHE curriculum, discussing it in the abstract, as important for behaviour, like drugs, alcohol or sex. The difference here, however, is that children are already immersed in technology. Most parents do not purchase drugs for child birthdays. Technology is around from an early age with smart phones photographing, filming and documenting development from birth. We use phones in front of them, modelling acceptability and importance, communicating with them through a phone and berating if they do not use it with us.

Technology is an unavoidable part of a child's world. As Kate Shutte shows in her chapter, high percentages of children use the Internet (*through phones & tablets*) from 3, with 50% online at 8, rising to 94% by 11 years. At this latter age UK children start secondary school, travelling further, so most parents, for safety and convenience, equip them with a smart phone. A 2016 survey shows that the average age for owning a mobile phone is 10.3 years, with 50% having a social media account. With full endorsement, children are given access to the internet early and use mobile phones habitually before 11 years. This makes education about phone use different from other PSHE topics, like sex and drugs. Alongside abstract discussions about appropriateness of use, more is needed in secondary schools, as children are already immersed in a world reliant on technology. Surely schools should be in step with the world?

ACCEPTING MOBILES IN SCHOOLS: RULES OF ENGAGEMENT

Ironically, the first lesson taught to children, when bringing mobiles to school, is the importance of *not* using them. Learning when it is not appropriate to use a mobile, even if accessible, is a life-skill in terms of politeness, concentration and controlling impulses. Many adults could learn this lesson! It cannot be taught if there is a mobile ban. When children reunite with phones after school, they have no other arbiter on when and how to use it, other than parents. This limits the impact that schools have on shaping technology behaviour, if they have opted out of this area of child development. How much better if children, who *are* permitted to sit and scroll on phones, *choose* to attend lunch-time or after-school clubs and activities instead. Schools must rise to the challenge, preparing learners better for life ahead, with them in charge of machines as opposed to the opposite. We can choose *when* and *how* much attention to give this tool and such a mind-set must be applied.

BENEFITS OF MOBILES IN CLASSROOMS

Phones can have negative effects on mental health, with instances of cyber-bullying and problems from social media. An argument for banning them is that children bring problems into school and dump them in the laps of teachers. Bans, however, do not remove problems. When things go wrong, schools should be part of the education which follows. Some schools tackle such issues, when they take place. A phone ban brings pastoral work for teachers: policing and punishing perpetrators is time-consuming, particularly with schools swimming against the tide and meeting resistance to the policy. The time and skills of pastoral staff could be better spent having restorative conversations with children, who have made errors of judgement, or in counselling children after cyber-bullying.

There are educational reasons to ban mobiles, given that some research shows improvement in attainment. However, it is argued that schools should embrace pupil access to a sophisticated, pocket computer of their own, which does not have to be bought or maintained. When children use phones for educational purposes, their interest piques with instant engagement. Using a personal phone brings advantages, especially for learning needs like dyspraxia (*disorder of movement & idea organisation*). Students can use a phone calendar to set homework reminders; see a teacher at break-time, or photograph a friend's notes, when not managing to write them in time.

Short films can be made and shown to classes recording learning processes. Educative apps, like *Kahoot,* can transform a lesson, giving it a relevant, interactive buzz. *Vocal Recall* is a powerful tool for marking, when a teacher can record verbal comments and stick a QR code on to student work. This can be scanned and listened to for more detailed comments. When teaching languages, music or drama, this can be transformative – a teacher can record accurate pronunciations or demonstrate how a note should be played to send to a pupil. This can be done in reverse: a student can be given a QR code to record their French speaking and send it to a teacher. Such examples are only the beginning.

There are incredible possibilities for enhancing teaching and learning when we explore technology in lessons. Dr Elizabeth Young's (2008) research showed pupils more engaged, with greater learning opportunity when using phones. This study is persuasive, because 10 years in the technology world is a long time. If gains were made then, there will be more now. This research also backs up my personal experience. The best part of allowing phone technology use in lessons is that learners enjoy it and engage more enthusiastically. This might be because we are speaking their language. Outside lessons, they are using technology in all aspects of life and suddenly school becomes in sync.

ACCEPTING THE CHALLENGE OF MOBILES IN SCHOOLS

With benefits come challenges for teachers allowing phones for learning. How can you ensure that students are on task? You cannot look at *all* screens at *all* times. Once phones are licensed for lessons, a student can be on social media posting a picture, which another finds embarrassing, or be online shopping. What about those not having smart phones for cost reasons, or because parents disagree with them? Teachers must develop strategies to deal with management challenges. Addressing technology misuse clearly, in the moment rather than abstract discussion in PSHE, helps children to learn what is appropriate and acceptable. This is a critical part of education, as technology is not banned out of school. There are work parallels, when employees are caught, by a boss, online shopping or making inappropriate, compromising social-media posts. The repercussions are more serious in adult life. Allowing phone use leads to school problems, but life lessons are learned most persuasively when we experience consequences.

IS SCHOOL APPROVED TECHNOLOGY DIFFERENT FROM SMART PHONES?

Schools accept they must include technology in the curriculum. They make financial investment in this area, even in austere times. Tablets or laptops are introduced and computer rooms/labs refurbished, with schools aware that investment is short term as soft and hardware has a short life with rapid innovations. The less investment heavy BYOD/T (*bring your own device/ technology*) still involves money for reliable Wi-Fi, technicians for support and internet security. Experience of classroom technology shows that the best way to overcome a technical glitch is to ask a pupil, who will swiftly fix a problem. If the network blocks a site for a lesson planned at home, with a less aggressive firewall, a compassionate student politely and subtly shows the latest '*work-around*' to evade school security. Children know more than teachers regarding technology and are one step ahead. If we disqualify mobiles, because we cannot control content and allow access to school devices instead, we are naïve to think that problems will be solved.

DEVELOPING A WHOLE SCHOOL APPROACH

Schools are at the chalk-face with children owning and using technology, so face problems daily. Allowing them to use their own technology needs an ethical framework or code of practice to be rigorously applied. The best approach is to involve students in the writing of it. Such a policy will be an important step towards developing understanding and thinking about ethics for future AI machines. We will send into work people used to self-moderating personal device use, who are masters of machines and aware of the consequences of unethical practice use.

CONCLUSION

If Professor Rosemary Sage is correct in predicting another possible AI winter on the horizon, we have a window of opportunity to teach children what is needed for the future by the way we approach technology use. Surely this will mean that AI creators and future users will be in safer hands? If Professor Anthony Seldon (2018) is right, we are only a decade away from classrooms dominated by this technology that we ban from school sites today. Surely we have to embrace the technology available to us now and address the issues it throws up? The prayer of Reinhold Niebuhr seems of relevance for schools, as they take steps in addressing key AI issues, which experts say are potentially threatening to human existence if left unexplored. Mobile phones are not going away. AI is the future. Our children need to be prepared.

God grant me the serenity to accept the things I cannot change
Courage to change the things I can and wisdom to know the difference.

REFERENCES

Beland, L. & Murphy, R. (2015) *Technology, Distraction & Student Performance* http://cep.lse.ac.uk/pubs/download/dp1350.pdf. Accessed 12 Oct. 2018

Dickens, C. (1995 Edn) *Hard Times*. London: Penguin Classics

Duke, K, Ward, A., Gneezy, A. & Bos, M. (2018) *Having Your Smartphone Nearby Takes a Toll on Your Thinking* https://hbr.org/2018/03/having-your-smartphone-nearby-takes-a-toll-on-your-thinking. Accessed 10 Oct. 2018

Hymas, C. (June 2018). *Secondary schools are introducing strict new bans on mobile phones*. Acc. 12 Oct. 2018 https://www.telegraph.co.uk/news/2018/06/24/secondary-schools-introducing-strict-new-bans-mobile-phones/

Kids & Tech: The Evolution of Today's Digital Natives http://influence-central.com/kids-tech-the-evolution-of-todays-digital-natives/. Accessed 12 Oct.2018

Hartnell Young, E. & Heym, N. (2008) *Mobile Telephony Devices: The Technological Revolution* http://webarchive.nationalarchives.gov.uk/20101018025751/http://emergingtechnologies.becta.org.uk/upload-dir/downloads/page_documents/research/lsri_report.pdf. Accessed 12 Oct. 2018

Ssldon, A. & Abidoye, O. (2018) *The Fourth Education Revolution: Will AI Liberate or Infantilise Humanity?* Buckingham: University of Buckingham Press

Niebuhr, R. (1842-1971) *The Serenity Prayer*

CHAPTER 10

SHOULD TECHNOLOGY REPLACE HANDWRITING?

KATE SCHUTTE

SUMMARY

This chapter targets the topic of handwriting in the technological age. More and more communication is typed, and new technologies are being created which could replace the handwritten word altogether. Such a thought produces emotive responses from the many supporters of this ancient art. Over and above emotions is the fact that motor, memory and brain functioning skills will be lost if children are only taught to type. The chapter looks at the impact of technology on this mode of communication and the robust research which confirms its importance at the early learning stages and beyond. It considers ways which teachers of handwriting could use technology to support, rather than replace handwriting.

INTRODUCTION

'*I can't remember the last time I picked up a pen,*' announced a friend in a recent conversation on the subject. As an English teacher, I find this concept incomprehensible. Then I examined my conscience. I do not own a chequebook and I cannot remember when I last sent a Christmas card. The last time I wrote a letter was to my dear Grandma and she died in 1994. I keep my shopping lists on a phone app, send emails for work and all written communication to my nearest and dearest occurs via WhatsApp. Other than as part of my job as an English teacher, I rarely pick up a pen.

IN THE AGE OF TECHNOLOGY, WHERE DOES HANDWRITING FIT?

Nearly 10 years ago, *Time* magazine announced that *'we are witnessing the death of handwriting'* (Suddath, 2009). Since this was written, it is estimated that 350 million iPads have been sold (Statista, 2018). Over 560 billion texts are transmitted each month, which equates to 15,220,700 messages being sent every minute worldwide, not including app-to-app messaging (Burke, 2016). In 2017, 3.7 billion people used an email account and it is estimated that this figure will grow to 4.3 billion by 2022 (Statista, 2018). Alexa, Bixby and Siri have helped us navigate the Internet through voice commands and Google's new Android app, *Voice Access*, launched in October 2018, allowing users to navigate phones through speech (Carman, 2018). More children are now going online, with half (53%) of 3-4s, 79% of 5-7s and 94% of 8-11-year-olds using the Internet (Ofcom, 2017).

With children accessing computers, tablets and the Internet more than before, familiarity with the keypad – including those on a touchscreen – is on the increase. The school, where I work, has now rolled out individual iPads to all students from 13–18 years. They will have the opportunity to type their notes in class, research online, collaborate with peers, share work with a teacher as well as write and edit essays on their devices. However, when it comes to sitting an examination, most will be forced to close their iPads and reach for a pen.

Under current examination arrangements, pupils must prove that typing is their normal way of working to be allowed access to a prepared, secure school laptop. These conditions are set out by the Joint Council for Qualifications as: *'a word processor cannot simply be granted to a candidate because he/she now wants to type rather than write in examinations or can work faster on a keyboard, or because he/she uses a laptop at home'* (Joint Council for Qualifications, 2018). With children growing up in the digital era, one cannot help but wonder whether it is fair to make them handwrite, particularly in examination conditions.

DOES WRITING MEAN HANDWRITING?

The UK National Curriculum continues to support handwriting, with the statutory guidance confirming it should still be the normal way of working for pupils. It goes further, linking success in handwriting to success with writing.

'Effective composition involves articulating and communicating ideas and then organising them coherently for a reader. This requires clarity,

awareness of the audience, purpose and context, and an increasingly
wide knowledge of vocabulary and grammar. Writing also depends on
fluent, legible and, eventually, speedy handwriting'
(Department for Education, 2014).

Whether or not writing depends on handwriting is open to question. Most adults make a choice to write or type, as they generally can do both. Being interested in understanding more about links between writing and handwriting, I took to Twitter and asked children's authors whether their preferred way is by hand or computer. Their responses were immediate and varied.

Guy Jones, author of *The Ice Garden* and *The Fire Maker*, replied:

'My handwriting is appalling and I'm an awful planner so I tend to
use the first draft as the plan, which is all typed. Much faster that way
for me. I then edit with a printed copy and a red pen.'

Anthony Horowitz, in contrast, replied: *'I handwrite the first draft. I love fountain pens, ink, paper...'*

Most authors said they use a mix of the two forms. M.G. Leonard, author of the *Beetle Boy* trilogy and *The Beetle Collector's Handbook*, replied:

'I write by hand in my notebooks, do doodles, use colours etc., but
close my eyes and touch type all actual drafts. If I wrote by hand I
would never finish a book!'

Holly Smale, author of the *Geek Girl* series, explained:

'I write my notes and plans by hand, then type the narrative. My style
is stream-of-consciousness and I'm much faster at typing; for me, it
removes barriers and makes the prose more organic and natural.'

These responses have a common thread. Writing occurs in many ways, which can alter for different reasons. Authors are choosing with established thought processes because they have learnt to handwrite and can rationalise which is their best method, as they have experienced both. They produce writing that is good, not because of *how* it is written, but because of *what* is written. I suggest that good writing is not dependent on good handwriting.

INTERNATIONAL VIEWS ON HANDWRITING

Countries have different approaches to the teaching of handwriting. Finland, for example, has made cursive handwriting lessons optional and teaches touch typing (Hosie, 2017). Since 2014, teacher guidelines have been prioritising print and electronic methods of writing because, according to Minna Harmanen of Finland's National Board of Education, children have little time to '*get it right before moving on to concentrating on what they write, rather than simply how they write it*' (Russell, 2015, p.9). Many schools in India report they are also turning away from cursive writing, in light of increased technology in the classroom (Feingold, 2013). The requirement to learn joined-up writing was left out of the core standards in the US in 2013 and has led to many schools across the country moving away from cursive writing instruction (Brown, 2014).

The Yale Center for Dyslexia and Creativity supports a move away from cursive writing towards typing for children with specific learning difficulties. They suggest that children who find expression difficult, when handwriting, should move to type and ease the process. Therefore, '*instead of worrying about what shape each letter is, the computer determines that for them. Word processing also helps record ideas in a standard readable font and allows a student to recognise more readily what they have just written*' (Redford, 2018). They also advocate students dictating work on to a device, assistive technologies to help spelling and speech-to-text-capable iPads. Steve Graham, Professor of Education at the Teacher's College of Arizona State University, said that when '*teachers rate multiple versions of the same paper, differing only in terms of legibility, they assign higher grades to neatly written versions*' (Trubeck, 2016). This would suggest that moving everyone to the keypad would negate unfair bias.

HANDWRITING IS AN EMOTIVE TOPIC

It seems that the subject of handwriting is very emotive. In 2009, Anne Trubeck wrote an article that supported stopping teaching cursive writing in elementary schools, which then became the home page for msn.com for a while (Trubeck, 2008). Within days of the article going online, Trubeck received over 2,000 comments, most of which were '*hostile, insulting and vehemently opposed to her argument*'. Instead of handwriting being a technology, a vehicle to express ideas, it seems that many believe it connects to personal identity (*handwriting signals something unique about each of us*), intelligence (*good handwriting reflects good thinking*) and virtue (a *civilized culture requires handwriting*)' (Trubeck, 2009, p. 6). The teacher of a *Time* magazine journalist, Linda Garcia, at Central Elementary in Wilmette, Illinois, expressed concern that '*cursive will go the way of Latin and that eventually we won't be able to read it. What if 50 years from now, kids can't read the Declaration of Independence?*' (Suddath, 2009).

Advances in technological change would seem to threaten the practice of handwriting. For some, this is deeply concerning and for others it is a matter of great joy. However, as Anne Trubeck writes, 'We will lose something as we print and write in cursive less and less, but loss is inevitable' (Trubeck, 2016).

IF HANDWRITING IS ON THE DEMISE, WHAT DO WE RISK LOSING?

France's approach to handwriting in schools is contrary to that of the USA. In the early 2000s, the Ministry for Education directed schools to teach cursive writing from the start of primary school, at age 6 years. This decision was based on neuroscience research, which suggests that handwriting is, as explained by Viviane Bouyesse, *'a key step in cognitive development'* (Chemin, 2014*)*. Evidence suggests that the links between handwriting and broader educational development are significant. Stanislas Dehaene, a psychologist at the College de France in Paris explained, *'when we write, a unique neural circuit is automatically activated. There is a core recognition of the gesture of the written word, a sort of recognition by mental stimulation in your brain'* (Konnikova, 2014). This suggests that handwriting makes learning easier, as it stimulates the brain.

Karin James, a psychologist at Indiana University and director of the Cognition & Action Neuroimaging Laboratory, conducted studies of effects of self-generated handwriting on functional brain development. This led to significant observations (The Cognition & Action Neuroimaging Laboratory, 2018).

Firstly, it is argued that brain motor systems are engaged during handwriting. Vinci-Booher et al. (2016) carried out research to discover whether motor and visual brain regions involved in letter writing respond differently to handwritten versus typed letters. If this was the case, they then aimed to establish whether brain regions responding the strongest do so differently in handwriting than passive viewing. Finally, they wanted to determine whether brain regions that respond the strongest to typed letters do so differently in handwriting than passive viewing. By studying participant brain activity, when watching and writing both typed and written letters, they concluded that handwriting relies on the bilateral ventral-temporal cortex for the visual component but more on the right ventral-temporal and frontal cortex for the motor one. Furthermore, they state that: *'handwriting perception relies upon different areas within the ventral-temporal cortex than typed-letter perception; however, both regions respond stronger during handwriting than any handwriting subtask. Similarly, regions that support the motor and visual components of handwriting also respond stronger for the perception of handwritten letters than typed'* (Vinci-Booher et al., 2016). This suggests that handwriting stimulates different parts of the brain in a way that typing does not.

Other research supporting that different parts of the brain are engaged in handwriting was carried out in a joint study between the University of Western Ontario and the National Research Council of Canada. Here, a *'fully immersive virtual reality environment was used to study whether actively interacting with objects would affect subsequent recognition, when compared with passively observing the same objects'* (James, 2002). This found that when participants actively rotated the objects, they were more able to recognise them. Results imply that: *'allowing active exploration of an object during initial learning can facilitate recognition'* (James, 2002). It suggests that by actively exploring and rotating handwriting, memory for what is written could be enhanced with implications for all writers.

James' second observation is that *'young children show adult-like brain responses to letters only after they learned to print letters, but not after learning letters through typing, visual study, or even tracing'* (James, 2002, 25). This is supported by Kersey & James' study, entitled: *'Brain activation patterns resulting from learning letter forms through active self-production and passive observation in young children'* (Kersey & James, 2013). It found that cursive writing led to the sensorimotor network being active during reader and letter perception. This was not shown when participants passively observed the letter being formed. They state that: *'this finding adds to the growing literature suggesting that self-generated writing is important for setting up reading networks in the developing brain'* (Kersey & James, 2013). It implies that the physical act of joining handwriting supports reading in the young brain in a way not apparent with the typed word.

James & Engelhardt support this point in a study of 5-year-olds, who had yet to learn to read or write, print, trace or type letters and shapes. They were shown images, while placed in an MRI machine. Only after handwriting the shapes were there links, described as a *'reading circuit'*, which was not the case for typing or tracing. James states that: *'these findings demonstrate that handwriting is important for the early recruitment in letter processing of brain regions known to underlie successful reading'* (James, 2012). It could be said, therefore, that handwriting may help young children to learn to read.

James' research also suggests that advantages of learning symbols, through handwriting, are seen in adults who learn new scripts. James & Atwood trained participants to recognise letter-like symbols, or *'pseudo-letters'*, by writing, typing or solely by looking at them. Results showed that only when the symbols were written: *'did neural activation patterns to pseudo-letters resemble patterns seen for letters'* (James & Atwood, 2009). This suggests that when learnt to recognise handwritten symbols, we are more likely to make links with other scripts, which could help with learning other languages.

Another benefit of handwriting, rather than typing, seems to be linked to memory. Smoker, Murphy & Rockwell (2009) in a study: *'Comparing Memory for Handwriting versus Typing'*, found that participants remembered words better when handwritten than typed. With more people recording by computer or tablet the: *'educational and practical implications of these findings would suggest that performance may be improved by using traditional paper-and-pen notes'* (Smoker, Murphy & Rockwell, 2009). Recall is an essential part of the learning process. It is suggested that we are more likely to remember handwritten rather than typed information.

A similar study, carried out by Longcamp, Zerbato-Poudou & Velay in

France (2005) supports the belief that handwriting aids memory. These researchers trained 2 groups of children (*3-5 years*) to copy letters, either by hand or typing. After doing this for 3 weeks, the children were compared on recall. They found that, for the older children, handwriting helped them remember letter forms. There could be links between how learners perceive letters for reading. This suggests, therefore, that handwriting may ultimately support learning to read.

CAN ROBOTS SUPPORT HANDWRITING?

Despite documented links between handwriting and brain development, handwriting is still in decline. However, be it for emotional, cultural or practical reasons, there is something about a handwritten note that an email cannot replace. This is the view of *Bond,* a New York company founded in 2013 (Bond, 2018). They have built a machine with a robotic arm that can hold a pen. If you download their app, type out a message and select a handwriting style, a robot will write out the card and post it for you. An upgraded service allows your handwriting to be digitised so that the machine can replicate your style. Sonny Caberwal, founder and Chief Executive, enthuses about the support that robots can give handwriting by explaining: '*there's a value for physical things and digital things and how those live harmoniously is fascinating*' (Gaddy, 2016).

Robots can also assist those learning to write for themselves. Lemaignan et al. (2016), working on research in Switzerland and Portugal, used a robot in a '*remediation procedure that involves a 'bad writer' robot that is taught by the child*' (Lemaignan, 2016). In this way, the child took on the role of a teacher and corrected the robot's mistakes. The robot could be programmed to address areas of writing that the child needed to improve. As the robot was corrected, writing improved and the child, therefore, self-rewarded and engaged.

A final example of robots helping children to write is a trial run by Mohamad Eid, Assistant Professor of Electrical & Computer Engineering at NYU Abu Dhabi. Children *without* learning difficulties from Cranleigh Abu Dhabi School and those *with* problems, from the American Center for Psychiatry & Neurology, were used to trial the robot handwriting teacher. This is an artificially intelligent robot arm, which the children hold to guide them handwriting on a screen displaying their work. There are 3 levels on the device's functions. Firstly, '*full haptic guidance*' is where the learner holds the pen and passively follows the movement of the robot arm. Secondly, '*partial guidance*' is where the learner moves the pen around themselves, but the device can engage physically to put the hand in the correct place. Finally, '*disturbance haptic guidance*' is where the pen guides the child and also vibrates at important points, to ensure active participation (Parker, 2018). The teacher reviews the data saved by the device. Tania Moonesinghe, Head of Pre-Prep at Cranleigh Abu Dhabi, who was involved in the trial, felt that the robot arm could be used '*as a tool to support what teachers already do*'. She continued: '*we don't see it as something that is going to replace what a teacher traditionally does with handwriting, but more of an additional tool that we can use to enhance what we're already working on*' (Parker, 2018). The trial results have yet to be published, but it is expected that an improvement will be seen with the handwriting skills of the children who used the haptic handwriting tool and possibly even better results from those with learning difficulties.

CONCLUSION

In an age where technology is advancing rapidly, the art of handwriting is under threat. Typed communication is widely used and handwriting is declining. Students often seek permission to type in examinations and universities and Cambridge is considering changing their rules on this (Busby, 2017). In the meantime, schools face huge logistical problems. If computers are to be used in examination halls, they need to be prepared and school-owned devices must have most of their features disabled. Giving pupils greater access to computers for examinations risks an unfair advantage to those with more access to technology and schools with more comprehensive IT facilities.

However, the thought of abandoning handwriting in schools seems unwise. Links that occur in the brain while handwriting are vital to the development of young people. Motor, memory and brain functioning skills will be lost if children are only taught to type. We should not let the pendulum swing against handwriting. People using this for tasks, such as observations and assessments, should not be perceived as old-fashioned, as may happen. There is a feeling now that one must justify, for professional purposes, the use of handwriting. In my school, teachers are provided with iPads, which many use to type meeting notes. Is it only me who feels slightly uncomfortable using a pen and paper on these occasions?

Using artificial intelligence to support the teaching and learning of handwriting may provide another aid for the '*handwriting toolbox*' and may give children a more modern approach to an ancient art. In later life, however, typing may become a useful way for adult writers to capture thoughts, but this should only be adopted when an acceptable level of handwriting proficiency has been achieved.

There is a robust research confirming that movements of writing assist the assembly of language (Sage, 1992) and this is important at early learning stages as well as beyond. Teachers need to reinforce and explain why writing is vital to pursue. Only when one knows how to handwrite should one choose to abandon it.

MAIN POINTS

- Now computers are dominating recording activities, handwriting is a declining art
- Research suggests handwriting assists the assembly of language & is important for learning
- Motor, memory and brain functioning will be lost if children do not learn to handwrite
- Teachers need to explain the importance of handwriting to encourage use

REFERENCES

Berger, T. (2017) *What We Lose With the Decline of Cursive*. https://www.edutopia.org/article/what-we-lose-with-decline-cursive-tom-berger. Accessed 26 Oct. 2018

Bond, (2018) *Handwritten Notes at Scale*. Available at: https://www.bond.co/ Accessed 26 Oct. 2018

Brown, A., (2014) *Is cursive handwriting slowly dying out in America?* 24 April. https://www.pbs.org/newshour/education/long-held-tradition-cursive-handwriting-slowly-dying-america Accessed 27 Oct. 2018

Burke, K. (2016) *73 Texting Statistics That Answer All Your Questions*. https://www.textrequest.com/blog/texting-statistics-answer-questions/ Accessed 27 Oct. 2018

Busby, M. (2017) *Cambridge Considers Typed Exams as Handwriting Worsens*. [Online] 9 Sept. https://www.theguardian.com/education/2017/sep/09/cambridge-considers-typed-exams-as-handwriting-worsens. Accessed 26 Oct. 2018

Carman, A. (2018) *Google Launches a Voice Control app to Help People with Limited Mobility navigate their phones*. Available at: https://www.theverge.com/2018/10/2/17929494/google-voice-access-app-controls-android. Assessed 27 Oct. 2018

Chemin, A. (2014) *Handwriting vs Typing: Is the Pen still Mightier than the Keyboard?*. Dec. https://www.theguardian.com/science/2014/dec/16/cognitive-benefits-handwriting-decline-typing. Accessed 26 Oct. 2018

Department for Education (2014) *National Curriculum in England: English Programmes of Study*. https://www.gov.uk/government/publications/national-curriculum-in-england-english-programmes-of-study/national-curriculum-in-england-english-programmes-of-study. Accessed 27 Oct. 2018

Feingold, S. (2013) *Schools are writing off cursive*. 6 October https://timesofindia.indiatimes.com/home/sunday-times/deep-focus/

Schools-are-writing-off-cursive/articleshow/23601901.cms. Accessed 27 Oct. 2018

Gaddy, J. (2016) *This Year, Get a Robot to Write Your Thank-You Notes.* 21 Dec.https://www.bloomberg.com/news/articles/2016-12-21/this-robot-will-handwrite-your-thank-you-notes. Accessed 26 Oct. 2018

Hosie, E.(2017) *The Uncertain Future of Handwriting.* No.8 http://www.bbc.com/future/story/20171108-the-uncertain-future-of-handwriting. Accessed 27 Oct. 2018

James, K. & Attwood, T.(2009) *The Role of Sensorimotor Learning in the Perception of Letter-like Forms: Tracking the Causes of Neural Specialization for Letters.* Cognitive Neuropsychology, 26(1), p. 91-110.

James, K.& E., 2012. *The Effects of Handwriting Experience on Functional Brain Development in Pre-literate Children.* Trends in Neuroscience and Education, 1(1), p. 32-42.

James, K., Humphrey, G, Vilis, T., Corrie, B., Baddour, R. & Goodale, M. (2002) *"Active" and "Passive" Learning of Three-dimensional Object Structure within an Immersive Virtual Reality Environment.* Behaviour Research Methods, Instruments and Computers: Psychonomic Society, Inc., 34(3), p. 383-390.

Joint Council for Qualifications, 2018. *Access Arrangements, Reasonable Adjustments and Special Consideration.* https://www.jcq.org.uk/exams-office/access-arrangements-and-special-consideration Accessed 27 Oct. 2018

Kersey, A. & James, K. (2013) *Frontiers in Psychology,* Volume 4, p. 1-15, Article 567.

Konnikova, M. (2014) *What's Lost as Handwriting Fades.* 2 June https://www.nytimes.com/2014/06/03/science/whats-lost-as-handwriting-fades.html Accessed 26 Oct. 2018

Lemaignan, S., Jacq, A., Hood, D., Garcia, F., Paiva, A. & Dillenbourg, P. (2016) *Learning by Teaching a Robot: The Case of Handwriting,* Lausanne: Ecole Polytechnique Federale de Lausanne, Switzerland.

Longcamp, M., Zerbato-Poudou, M. & Velay, J. (2005) T*he Influence of Writing Practice on Letter Recognition in Preschool Children: A Comparison between Handwriting and Typing.* Acta Psychologica, 119(1), p. 67-79.

Ofcom (2017) *Children and Parents: Media use and attitudes*: https://www.ofcom.org.uk/__data/assets/pdf_file/0020/108182/children-parents-media-use-attitudes-2017pdf. Accessed 27 Oct. 2018

Parker, K.(2018) *Meet the Robot Teaching Pupils how to Handwrite* https://www.tes.com/news/meet-robot-teaching-pupils-how-handwrite. Accessed 26 Oct. 2018

Redford, K. (2018) *Kids Can't Wait: Strategies to Support Struggling Readers* http://dyslexia.yale.edu/resources/educators/instruction/kids-cant-wait-strategies-to-support-struggling-readers/. Accessed 27 Oct. 2018

Russell, H. (2015) *Signing Off: Finnish Schools Phase out Handwriting*

Classes. 31 July. https://www.theguardian.com/world/2015/jul/31/finnish-schools-phase-out-handwriting-classes-keyboard-skills-finland. Accessed 27 Oct. 2018

Sage, R. (1992) *Information Processing in Effective & Ineffective Learners*. PhD. Thesis. Leicester: UOL Smoker, T., Murphy, C. & Rockwell, A. (2009) *Comparing Memory for Handwriting versus Typing*. Orlando, Florida, USA, Human Factors and Ergonomics Society Annual General Meeting.

Statista (2018) *Global Apple iPad sales from 3rd fiscal quarter of 2010 to 3rd fiscal quarter of 2018 (in million nits)**.https://www.statista.com/statistics/269915/global-apple-ipad-sales-since-q3-2010/Accessed 27 Oct. 2018

Statista (2018) *Number of e-mail Users Worldwide from 2017 to 2022 (in millions)* https://www.statista.com/statistics/255080/number-of-e-mail-users-worldwide/ Accessed 27 Oct. 2108

Suddath, C. (2009) *Mourning the Death of Handwriting* http://content.time.com/time/magazine/article/0,9171,1912419,00.html. Accessed 27 October 2018

The Cognition and Action Neuroimaging Laboratory (2018) *What are the Effects of Handwriting on Cognitive Development?*Available at: http://indiana.edu/~canlab/handwriting.html. Accessed 26 Oct. 2018

Trubeck, A. (2008) *Stop Teaching Handwriting* https://www.good.is/articles/stop-teaching-handwriting. Accessed 26 October 2018

Trubeck, A.(2009) *Is Handwriting Going The Way Of The Dodo?* https://www.alternet.org/story/144648/is_handwriting_going_the_way_of_the_dodo.Ac. 26 Oct. 2018

Trubeck, A.(2016) *The History and Uncertain Future of Handwriting*. USA: Bloomsbury Publishing.

Vinci-Booher, S., Sehgal, N., Munroz-Rubke, F., Cheng, H., James, T. & James, K. (2016) *Perceptual and Motor Effects of Letter writing on Brain Regions Associated with Letter Perception* http://indiana.edu/~canlab/assets/vincibooher_vss2016_05.14b.16_revised.pdf. Accessed 26 Oct. 2018

CHAPTER 11

ARTIFICIAL INTELLIGENCE AND LIFELONG LEARNING

NAGHMANA NASEEM

ABSTRACT

This chapter advocates the implementation of lifelong learning in order to keep abreast of rapidly advancing technology. Failure to do so will mean that Artificial Intelligence (AI) will become our master rather than our slave. The history of how society has functioned is reviewed as the background for understanding the challenges now faced in a multi-cultural, global-operating planet. The world is an exciting, energising place but we must understand the implications of change in order to manage it effectively. Every positive development has negative downsides and awareness of the impact of new developments is essential if we are to live safely and securely.

INTRODUCTION

Society's need for the poor to assist the wealthy has been traditional practice. From the 16th century, there has been slavery in operation (*system when persons are legally owned for work purposes*), with the poor serving the wealthy to provide support, help and daily care. In hierarchical roles, servants were subject to a code of conduct, long working hours with severe consequences if these were not met. Therefore, the rich and poor coexisted side-by-side, with a clear distinction between them. In 1901, there were 1.5 million domestic servants in Britain, despite a population of approximately 37 million. This data reveals that 4.17% of the population were domestic servants at this time and Britain's biggest employment sector. Since the 20th century, slavery has been viewed as contrary to Human Rights, but the need for assistance persists in families. According to the Office for National Statistics 2012 (*Labour Force Survey*), '*about 65,000 people are employed as domestic servants in the UK*' (Wallis, 2012). This decrease could be attributed to legislative and educational evolution. Looking at historical trends in literacy, levels increased from 21% in 1900 to 86% in 2015 (Roser & Ortiz-Ospina, 2018). Furthermore, the invention of labour-saving devices like the computer, microwave, dishwasher, washing machine and vacuum cleaner eased tasks, increased efficiency and saved time.

Domestic servants are hired to ensure that the lives of the wealthy run smoothly. The comfortable lifestyle and efficiency that arises from servants performing duties, like cooking or cleaning help to maintain high living standards. The rationale stems from limitations like time, commitments, age, disability or loneliness. For professionals, domestic assistance facilitates their higher-level thinking, problem-solving, accuracy, improved performance and productivity.

Over time, humans have created wonders though we have ample evidence of disasters as well. The creation of the atomic bomb is an example. Although initially conceived to explain the release of energy from small matter, now it is capable of large-scale mass destruction. Intellectuals and innovators contribute towards world progress, bringing new ideas and systems to streamline and improve life and work functioning, as the present AI revolution reveals. However, we need to regard this technological revolution cautiously. The potential consequences and complications arising from rapid development without accountability require vigilance and preventative measures if necessary.

Society is diverse, each individual is unique with valuable talents, skills and experiences to contribute. The ability to think and plan has enabled us to evolve and achieve technological marvels. Nothing seems impossible, as high-level thinking and language capacity produces creative solutions to tackle complex problems. Fixation on perfection, precision and accuracy enable intelligent machines to imitate cognitive functions for learning and problem-solving, functioning faster than is humanly possible.

The changing dynamics of this innovating landscape requires us to rethink, refocus and plan strategically to anticipate future complications. To remain competitive and relevant, we must embrace change. The debate about robots taking over routines produces many views. We are required to be smarter and more imaginative to tackle the complex problems of globalisation and technology evolution. Focus on transferrable abilities is pivotal to sustain impact, so education needs to evolve to harness the best from AI. The future requires active researchers who can communicate knowledge across disciplines in team approaches. They must be prepared to empower themselves by developing their knowledge, skills and attitudes through lifelong learning. This will be the future model to improve life and work quality by integrating formal, non-formal and informal learning.

HUMAN VALUES

Human values and professional ethics define humanity, enabling temptations to be resisted. History shows that whenever there is a compromise between values and worldly temptations, humanity suffers in consequence. The human race is blessed with conscience and intelligence to create wonders. However, the world has witnessed undignified tendencies. The pride and arrogance of Babylonians motivated them to build '*The Tower of Babel*' (Genesis 11) to reach heaven, causing immense devastation. This story is a powerful reminder of the consequences when desires become demands (BibleStudyTools, 2016).

Optimism has led humans to evolve, adapt and thrive. The Turing machine, with its algorithmic logic encrypted in the enigma code during World War II, saved millions of lives. On the other hand, we have witnessed rebellions causing the loss of many innocent people. The destruction, devastation and desolation of the atomic bombs dropped on the Japanese cities of Hiroshima and Nagasaki (1945) are examples. Both bombings symbolise the human tragedy caused by nuclear weapons.

Gradually, AI is gaining momentum with an impact on our home and work life. The AI revolution is unavoidable but appealing, as benefits seem greater at this juncture. The journey from the Stone Age to the AI era shows that adaptation for improving life quality has always been a top priority for survival. Life preservation, immortality or finding the elixir of life is important to us all. We have adapted by using devices that are expensive, attractive but time-efficient and accurate. Technology on one side has facilitated lives, and on the other side, it has created a desire to earn more. We all may be inspired by the benefits that technology can offer, but status defines the style of life that one can afford.

HISTORY

The innovative, evolving world is a competitive landscape, requiring us to adapt to the changing political, economic and social milieu. The word '*robot*' comes from the Czech word, '*robota*', meaning '*forced labour*' or '*slavery*' – an unpleasant symbolism. In 1921, a science fiction play, called R.U.R (*Rossumovi Univerzální Roboti*), by Karel Čapek, the Czech writer, was premiered with roboti (*robots*) closer to the modern idea of androids. Their purpose was to follow instructions and serve humans until a robot rebellion destroyed the human race. The word '*roboti*' led to the introduction of the word '*robot*' into the English language and science fiction (Interesting Literature, 2016).

The unique human brain, with amazing cognitive and linguistic ability, has created wonders like pyramid tombs and moon spaceflights. The function of the brain's frontal cortex is to control reasoning and enable us to think before we act. Concerns about the consequences make us rethink and refocus. Fear of the impetuous outcomes of decisions has been the topic of many science fiction movies, as in '*I, Robot*', released in 2004. This dystopian film, set in 2035, shows humanoid robots serving mankind. The investigation of the suicide of a scientist (*Dr. Alfred Lanning*) reveals that a robot '*Sonny*' became a menace to humanity by not executing the three laws integrated into its system. There are also movies like Star Wars, where clone troopers (*army of trained soldiers*) serving under the Jedi leadership became integral to the Jedi Order extinction, with the rise of the evil Galactic Empire. On the other hand, the assistance of droids (*C3PO & R2-D2*) in Star Wars was inspirational. These droids relate to the audiences because of their loyalty, diligence and curiosity. The plot of these science fiction movies depicts our concern about outcomes.

The human desire for knowledge is the required power to accomplish subjugation goals – control and finally manipulation. Humans are naturally selfish, yet expected to follow society's conventions of kindness to others. Aggression provokes us to be defensive. The history of wars and the creation of nuclear weapons suggests, intentionally or unintentionally, ulterior motives to take destructive measures in spite of the human ability to cogitate, communicate and cooperate.

Technology is now an integral part of life and actions we perform depend on it. To enhance dependency, price affordability and easy accessibility are key contributors to this obsession. In modern life, our primary source of information is the Google search engine, with books becoming obsolete. The mode of communication is *text-messaging* using mobile apps, so face-to-face interaction is not obligatory. Having a Satellite Navigation System (*Sat-Nav*) ensures reliance for finding the shortest route, journey duration, speed limit and location of security cameras. Aislinn Simpson claimed (The Telegraph, 2008) a survey found 300,000 accidents in Britain caused by Sat-Nav. The drivers admitted that '*performing sudden manoeuvres or changing direction because they were following the devices' directions*', led them to lose track of road traffic and endanger innocent lives. According to the Guardian (Devlin, 2017), Hugo Spiers (a *neuroscientist at University College London*), explained that reliance on technology (*GPS navigation*) causes disengagement of the brain to the street network. Furthermore, Dean Burnett (*a neuroscientist at Cardiff University*) elucidated that '*London cabbies have bigger and more active hippocampi*' (*brain area responsible for memory processing*), as compared to an average person. Active thinking, visualisation and spatial navigation are compromised with greater reliance on advanced technology. The geneticist, Dubos (1968) verified that we use less than 20% of our brain potential. Does this show that reliance on technology is making it difficult to use our brains in thinking strategically to make the right decisions?

Virtuous and malevolent, optimism and pessimism, benefits and implications, assets and liabilities are part of life and coexist in society. Despite uncertainty, insecurity and ambiguity, technology will go mainstream and it is prudent to embrace benefits. Adaption requires a balance to avoid potential harm. To improve life quality, we need to be smart and learn not to be ruled by technology. To know when to unplug ourselves helps to prevent technology addiction. To keep fit, challenge our brain to improve function, enjoy exploring nature, value human communication, develop the flexibility to change, use instinct and reason in decision-making, and stay connected with loved ones and the community.

According to estimates, four out of five children starting school now will enter jobs that do not exist and use technology not yet invented. This requires careful planning to develop the potential for the future (Murphy, 2009). In 2017, 28% of 11-year-olds in England did not attain the expected standard in reading by the time they left primary school (Department of Education). Furthermore, 4.7% of working-age adults in the UK were without jobs (Office for National Statistics, 2017), relying on benefits which is a massive challenge for society. International indicators confirm that Japan is handling globalisation more effectively compared to other nations. They concentrate on helping students to develop transferable skills through effective communication. Making students understand through non-verbal aspects of communication as well as talk, forming social contact and developing cooperation and collaboration are core abilities. In Cuba, everyone is expected to be educated in line with interests and abilities, along with the skill range required for society (Sage, 2009). Thus, the future requires individuals with broader knowledge and skills to enable them to survive successfully.

ARTIFICIAL INTELLIGENCE

The term AI comprises two words (*artificial and intelligence*). The meaning of the word '*artificial*' is '*made by people, often as a copy of something natural*' (Cambridge Dictionary). '*Intelligence*' is a complex term with a different meaning to everyone. Generally, it is defined as the mental ability to learn and adapt by using *logic, understanding, emotional knowledge, self-awareness, creativity, planning and problem-solving* (Dumper et al., 2014). Based on the ability to learn and comprehend, we make judgements. '*Intelligence quotient*' (IQ) was invented by Alfred Binet (1904) and is the accepted method of measuring intelligence (Cherry, 2018). Intelligence exists in animals and humans alike with the ability to evolve, adapt and grow with time. Natural selection, as claimed by the Darwinian Evolutionary theory '*Survival of the fittest*', explains the existence of both humans and animals. Charles Darwin, an evolutionist, inspired by earthworm intelligence, claimed that these extraordinary creatures have an impact on civilisation due to their ability to repair, regenerate and adapt for survival and rescue the environment (Lloyd, 2009). The existence of these species on earth provides reflection to assess and evaluate what is vital for success and survival.

The desire for optimal outcomes has led to AI systems that outperform humans in fields like data analysis. The effectiveness and accuracy of any system create dependency as well as the desire to improve it further. Alexa (*virtual personal assistant by Amazon*), Siri (*virtual assistant by Apple*) and AlphaGo (*a computer programme that plays board games by Google*) are AI examples. AI is expected to bring endless benefits to medical science, such as reducing mortality rate, eliminating genetic diseases, improving radiology, diagnostic precision, therapeutic assistance, organ replacement, accurate data reports and other tasks requiring high dexterity.

From the 1960s, the term '*personalised learning*' has been in use. Embedded in the Education Act 1944, it obliges education providers to offer '*an education appropriate to the abilities, aptitudes and needs*' of every pupil. With AI growth in education, it is easy to envisage that a personalised learning approach is a catalyst in transforming education. For example, the Intelligent Tutoring System (ITS), an application of AI, will reshape teaching as well as learning. The ITS is aimed at providing personalised instructions and feedback to learners. It assesses learners' pre-existing knowledge, skills and learning experience to improve their learning styles as a foundation for high-quality education. The system collects data and provides predictive models of learning '*to determine individual knowledge and skill levels and analyse the performance*'. Furthermore, prompt feedback helps the learners to make improvements (Learning News, 2018). This exemplifies *constructivism,* an epistemology, explained by Jean Piaget (1896-1980), Lev Vygotsky (1896-1934) and John Dewey (1859-1952). These constructivists highlighted the importance of '*transformation in learning and development*', '*communicative interactions*' and '*real world problems into the school curriculum*' (Lamon, 2018).

AI will be a virtual facilitator, a lifelong learning companion with qualities of an educator (*think, react & interact*) to respond to individual learning needs. It will provide better communication to learners and automate grading of standard assessments. Furthermore, informing teachers what needs to be retaught, based on learners' responses to activities or tasks, enables them to act as learning facilitators.

CHANGE IS CERTAIN

Time has shown that change and disruption are challenging for individuals. We are facing transition. It is natural to fear, feel doubt and discomfort, followed by discovery, understanding and finally integration. The UK is a diverse, multicultural nation. The 2011 Census suggests that London is the most ethnically diverse region, '*where 40.2% of residents identified with either the Asian, Black, Mixed or Other ethnic group*' (GOV.UK, 2018). A large number of immigrants enter the country unfamiliar with the British education system. With different cognitive ability levels in society, it is not difficult to anticipate a classification based on intellect and knowledge.

The power of imagination and empathy for others is our strongest human ability. The mind grows with challenges that need to be accomplished. AI and automated technologies are evolving to provide more time-efficient, reliable and accurate products, and improve quality of life. The competitive landscape urges us to explore and create a common platform to integrate humans of different abilities and backgrounds. This requires the upgrading of skills to cope with the changing demands that the future anticipates. It seems that the lifelong learning approach is key to equip ourselves to achieve the best from technology. Dynamic lifelong learners must be ready to adapt to the demands of the world.

Technology continuously evolves, which requires a faster rate of adaptation. However, commitment to continuous improvement is vital to cope and evolve with challenging, future demands. Being at different starting points requires more individualised and personalised approaches. A commitment to lifelong learning facilitates the successful survival of humans and sustainable development (Walters, 2010).

WHAT IS LIFELONG LEARNING?

Lifelong learning is an ongoing process, with the potential to improve the quality of life and work. According to the Collins dictionary: *'Lifelong learning is the provision or use of both formal and informal learning opportunities throughout people's lives in order to foster the continuous development and improvement of the knowledge and skills needed for employment and personal fulfilment'*.

Learning takes place in many forms and at different levels and can be *formal*, *non-formal* and *informal*. The Cedefop glossary (Tissot & Bertzeletou, 2011) defines these concepts:

- *Formal learning occurs within an organised and structured context (formal education, in-company training). It is intentional from the learner's point of view and typically leads to validation and certification* (p. 75);
- *Non-formal learning is embedded in planned activities, not explicitly designated as learning, but which contain a learning element (such as vocational skills acquired at the workplace). It is intentional from the learner's point of view and outcomes may be validated leading to certification* (p. 113);
- *Informal learning comprises of daily activities related to family, work or leisure. It is often unintentional from the learner's perspective and does not usually lead to certification* (p. 85).

Within lifelong learning, the learner is at the heart of the process whether it is intentional (*formal & non-formal learning*) or unintentional (*informal learning*) (Colardyn & Bjonavold, 2004).

IMPORTANCE OF LIFELONG LEARNING

Globalization and automated technology entail humans to upgrade and acquire new skills through related training. Lifelong learning, a key focus for education and training policy, will improve individual knowledge and competencies (OECD, 2007). It requires adults to adapt flexibly by developing their competencies at more advanced levels, enabling them to stay up-to-date with the current, changing and challenging professional climate. This demands a *learning society*, where everyone has the opportunity to learn irrespective of age (Green, 2002). Lifelong learning can only become a reality, irrespective of age and qualification levels when workplaces become places for this (Cedefop, 2011). Formal provision with flexible approaches must provide opportunities according to the learners' needs.

Formal, non-formal and informal learning opportunities, enhance the knowledge and skills needed for employment and personal satisfaction. Implementation requires bringing education and vocational training together. A change of mindset is required to enable individuals to become active, skilled communicators and investigators to collaboratively construct knowledge in the work context. Rather than merely consumers, these lifelong learners, in turn, can be active contributors to the facilities themselves (Fischer & Ostwald, 2002). According to the Commission of the European Communities (2000, p. 3), '*Lifelong learning is no longer just one aspect of education and training; it must become the guiding principle for provision and participation across the full continuum of learning contexts*'. This requires individuals and organisations to work together effectively. People need to become responsible for their development and their communities to cope with life.

PREPARING LEARNERS FOR LIFELONG LEARNING

The innovative climate, bursting with knowledge, requires us to be willing to improve knowledge and skills continually. A culture change is required so that individuals can '*learn how to learn*' for their life and profession ahead (Nash, 1994, p. 789). It promotes engagement with the application and assists in developing two skills: metacognition and self-directedness.

METACOGNITION

Metacognitive skills are defined by Von Wright (1992, p. 64) as *'the steps that people take to regulate and modify the progress of their cognitive activity: to learn such skills is to acquire procedures which regulate cognitive processes'*. These skills include taking ownership of learning and conscious involvement in planning, selecting resources, monitoring progress, critically analysing and changing learning behaviour and strategies when required (Ridley et al., 1992). Due to self-regulatory skills developed through this process, it promotes problem-solving ability and the transfer of knowledge across domains and tasks. It is difficult for students to recognise when they are unable to adequately meet learning outcomes or complete tasks without these skills (Bransford et al., 1986).

SELF-DIRECTEDNESS

Self-directedness is an ability to develop strategies that facilitate the identification of learning issues, evaluating and learning from the resources relevant to that issue (Savery & Duffy, 1995, p. 143). Self-directed learning enables students to identify and define a problem, evaluate resources used, capture and apply information, and critique the whole process used to solve the problem (Barrows, 1995).

In summary, educators need to develop metacognitive and self-directed skills amongst learners to stay abreast of innovative research, techniques and information in their field. These abilities enable learners to be successful at decision-making and problem-solving, and remain competitive in their changing professional climate.

CONCLUSION

As humans, we have evolved to adapt and thrive. Inspired by innovative technology, we have embraced highly-sophisticated devices for efficiency, comfort and pleasure. Living in an age where AI disruption is inevitable has an associated deep fear as well. According to an estimate, psychologists think that we make at least 35,000 daily choices. This emerging world requires us to be cautious of our decisions so that lives, communities and livelihoods are not at risk (Seligman, 2006). Being enthusiastic is good, but one should also keep away from mystic overhype. It necessitates a prudent, well-thought-out plan of action that has been scrutinized thoroughly, to avoid future complications.

To cope with evolving demands, lifelong learning will gain momentum. A personalised learning approach is a fundamental catalyst in transforming the present education system. Making education and training more relevant to jobs is crucial. Being digitally literate will be an ultimate requirement. Education providers need to embed digital skills in their core offers and companies must upskill employees to survive. We need to improve the ability to work communicatively and collaboratively to solve problems, share and review ideas, reflect and refine thinking for achieving optimum outcomes.

The lifelong learning approach will empower us to be actively responsible for learning, understand the values of life and live wisely. Thus, we can make the world a better place to live and create a legacy for future generations to enjoy.

MAIN POINTS

- History has shown that advanced societies have an elite served by others
- The new age of robots working with humans will alter patterns of living
- Prudent action is required to ensure the distance between rich and poor does not increase
- Education must assume a lifelong learning policy to enable people to cope with vast changes

REFERENCES

Barrows, H. (1995) *Self-directed Learning Process.* Ohio University Athens, OH, Handout presented at the Educational Innovation in Economics and Business Administration (EDINEB) conference.

BibleStudyTools Staff (2016) *The Tower of Babel – Bible Story.* https://www.biblestudytools.com/bible-stories/the-tower-of-babel.html Accessed 20 October 2018

Bransford, J., Sherwood, R., Vye, N. & Rieser, J. (1986) *Teaching Thinking and Problem Solving. American Psychologist,* 41(10) p. 1078-1089.

Cambridge Dictionary, n.d. Meaning of artificial in English. https://dictionary.cambridge.org/dictionary/english/artificial Accessed 20 October 2018

Cedefop (2011) *Learning while Working: Success Stories on Workplace Learning in Europe. Luxembourg:* Publications Office of the European Union. http://www.cedefop.europa.eu/files/3060_en.pdf. Accessed 3 November 2018

Cherry, K. (2018) *Alfred Binet and the History of IQ Testing: The First IQ Test and Beyond.* https://www.verywellmind.com/history-of-intelligence-testing-2795581 Accessed 4 November 2018

Colardyn, D. & Bjonavold, J. (2004) *Validation of Formal, Non-Formal and Informal Learning: Policy and Practice in EU Member States.* European Journal of Education 39(1) p. 70-81.

Collins English Dictionary, n.d. *Definition of 'lifelong learning'*.
  https://www.collinsdictionary.com/dictionary/english/lifelong-learning
  Accessed 20 October 2018

Commission of the Eupropean Communities (2000) *A Momorandum on
  Lifelong Learning*
  http://arhiv.acs.si/dokumenti/Memorandum_on_Lifelong_Learning.pdf.
  Accessed 30 October 2018

Department for Education (2017) *National curriculum assessments at key
  stage 2 in England, 2017* (revised).
  https://assets.publishing.service.gov.uk/government/uploads/system/
  uploads/attachment_data/file/667372/SFR69_2017_text.pdf.
  Accessed 3 November 2018

Devlin, H. (2017) *All mapped out? Using satnav 'switch off' parts of the
  brain, study suggests*
  https://www.theguardian.com/science/2017/mar/21/all-mapped-out-using-
  satnav-switches-off-parts-of-the-brain-study-suggests-navigation
  Accessed 4 November 2018

Dubos, R. (1968) *Man, Medicine and Environment*. New York: Frederick A.
  Praeger.

Dumper, K., Jenkins, W., Lacombe, A., Lovett, M. & Perimutter, M. (2014)
  What are Intelligence & Creativity?
  https://opentext.wsu.edu/psych105/chapter/what-are-intelligence-creativity/
  Accessed 4 November 2018

Fischer, G. & Ostwald, J. (2002) *Transcending the Information Given:
  Designing Learning Environments for Informed Participation*.
  http://l3d.cs.colorado.edu/~gerhard/papers/icce2002.pdf.
  Accessed 28 October 2018

GOV. UK (2018) *Ethnicity facts and figures – Ethnicity in the UK. Regional
  ethnic diversity. Office for National Statistics*.
  https://www.ethnicity-facts-figures.service.gov.uk/british-population/
  national-and-regional-populations/regional-ethnic-diversity/latest
  Accessed 13 October 2018

Green, A. (2002) *The Many Faces of Lifelong Learning: Recent Education
  Policy Trends in Europe*. Journal of Education Policy 17(6), p. 611-626.

I, Robot (2004) [Film] Directed by Alex Proyas. America: Davis Entertainment.

Interesting Literature (2016) *A Library of Literacy Interestingness. The
  Curious Origin of the Word 'Robot'*
  https://interestingliterature.com/2016/03/14/the-curious-origin-of-the-word-robot/
  Accessed 3 November 2018

Lamon, M. (2018) *Learning Theory: Constructivist Approach*.
  https://education.stateuniversity.com/pages/2174/Learning-Theory-
  CONSTRUCTIVIST-APPROACH.html
  Accessed 3 November 2018

Learning News (2018) *Artificial Intelligence (AI) in Education Market worth over $6bn by 2024*.
https://learningnews.com/news/learning-news/2018/artificial-intelligence-ai-in-education-market-worth-over-6bn-by-2024
Accessed 3 November 2018

legislation.gov.uk (1994) *Education Act 1994*
http://www.legislation.gov.uk/ukpga/Geo6/7-8/31/enacted
Accessed 3 November 2018

Lloyd, C. (2009) *What On Earth Evolved? 100 Species that Changed the World*. London: Bloomsbury.

Murphy, G. (2009) *A Vision of Learning for the Future: Presentation to the Inter-competency & Dialogue through Literature (IDIAL) Project with Bulgaria, Finland, Latvia, Slovenia, Spain & the United Kingdom.* Liverpool: Liverpool Hope University.

Nash, D. *(1994) The Life-long learning Imperative...Ends and Means*. Journal of Dental Education, 5(10), p. 785-790.

Organisation for Economic Co-operation and Development (OECD, 2007) *Qualification Systems: Bridges to Lifelong Learning: Executive Summary (p. 1-2)*
http://www.oecd.org/education/skills-beyond-school/38465471.pdf.
Accessed 21 October 2018

Office for National Statistics (2017) *UK labour market: Mar 2017*.
https://www.ons.gov.uk/employmentandlabourmarket/peopleinwork/employmentandemployeetypes/bulletins/uklabourmarket/mar2017
Accessed 3 November 2018

Ridley, D., Schultz, P., Glanz, R. & Weinstein, C. (1992) *Self-regulated learning: The Interactive Influence of Metacognitive Awareness and Goal-setting*. Journal of Experimental. Education, 60(4), p. 293-306.

Roser, M. & Ortiz-Ospina, E. (2018) *Our World in Data: Literacy*
https://ourworldindata.org/literacy
Accessed 29 October 2018

Sage, R. (2009) *What Cuba has to Teach us About Education?* Education Today, Volume 59, No. 3.

Savery, J. & Duffy, T. (1995) *Problem Based Learning: An Instructional Model and its Constructivist Framework*. In B. G. Wilson (Ed,), Constructivist Learning Environment: Case Studies in Instructional Design. Educational Technology Publications, Inc., p. 135-148.

Seligman, A. (2006) *Learned Optimism: How to change your mind and your life*. New York: NY: Vintage Books.

Simpson, A. (2008) *Sat Nav blunders 'have caused up to 300, 000 accidents'*.
https://www.telegraph.co.uk/news/uknews/2438430/Sat-Nav-blunders-have-caused-up-to-300000-accidents.html
Accessed 24 October 2018

Star Wars: Episode 111 – Revenge of the Sith (2005) [Film] Directed by George Lucas. United States of America: Lucasfilm Ltd.

Tissot, P. & Bertzeletou, T. (2011) *Cedefop: Glossary: Quality in Education and Training (p. 75, 85. 113)*.pdf.
Accessed 21 October 2018

Von Wright, J. (1992) *Reflections on Reflection*. Learning and Instruction 2(1), p. 59-68.

Wallis, L. (2012) *Servants: A Life below Stairs*
https://www.bbc.co.uk/news/magazine-19544309
Accessed 26 October 2018

Walters, S. (2010) *The Planet will not Survive if it's not a Learning Planet: Sustainable Development within Learning through Life*. International Journal of Lifelong Education 29(4) p. 427-436.

CHAPTER 12
THE ART IN ARTIFICIAL INTELLIGENCE

WHAT MAKES CREATIVITY THE BEST PREPARATION?

EMMA WEBSTER

SUMMARY

This chapter discusses what the 4th industrial age means for young people and how, as educators, we can best prepare them for this huge change in the way we live and work. It will explore definitions of Artificial Intelligence (AI) and creativity and how this concept translates into the classroom and everyday life. There is discussion on why creativity and creative learning are important for life-long learning and portfolio careers, as well as how we can improve creative capital in schools. We can make every lesson creative, by enabling learners to work on their knowledge in experiential ways in small groups. This requires teachers to focus on the communicative and collaborative abilities of students so that they can work together to explore, share and produce ideas that bring knowledge into reality.

INTRODUCTION: WHAT IS ARTIFICIAL INTELLIGENCE?

The term *'Artificial Intelligence'* (AI – *coined in 1956 by John McCarthy*) has connotations steeped in the world of science-fiction, technology and art. *'Artificial'* comes from the Latin *'artificialis'*, meaning *belonging to* or *of art*. The stem *'ars'* gives us the meaning *craft, skill* and *making things*, implying a process of *doing*. Considering the etymology of the words themselves, we can gain an understanding of how the term has evolved into how we understand it today.

Within a word that implies a fake or manufactured nature, we are faced with the debate of *art* versus *craft*, and the challenge of AI, robots (*intelligent machines in human form*) and consciousness. This is important when considering the preparation for a life working with machines. At the core of AI development and progress in any field is creativity and the means to innovate.

AI ultimately means the ability for a machine to perform a task originally assumed by a human. Machines are not created to *replace* us. There are many misconceptions about the robot take-over, but as the World Economic Forum (WEF) reports, they have created more jobs than they have replaced (Desjardins, 2018). However anthropomorphic the robots become, they will always need input from humans and it is vital to prepare young people to provide this content.

It is also important for us, as educators and human beings, to continually nurture what makes our species unique. This implies creative, critical thought and the ability to effectively communicate and collaborate. AI is already part of everyday existence, including smart phones, GPS and intelligent televisions. We do not need to resist AI, but need to find our place around it. The skills developed through working creatively, in all forms, are integral to preparation of young people for a machine driven world. Rather than fear a robot take-over, we should focus on what makes us human, embracing our soul and inherent desire to live beyond the struggle and find pleasure in existence. Humanistic scholars see creativity as the natural urge of individuals to develop, extend, express and activate their capacities (Maslow, 1996; Rogers, 1954).

DEFINITIONS OF CREATIVITY

Defining creativity is important as it highlights the transferability of skills involved and how it extends beyond purely artistic practice. Glăveanu (2018) explains, when we enquire into the creative abilities of people, we look for answers referring to engagement with artistic practice and also assume that those involved in art are naturally imaginative.

The link between creativity and art is unmistakeable. In order for one to achieve success as an artist, a 'big-C' level of creativity (Kaufman & Beghetto,

2009) is strived for and art cannot exist without this to envisage a concept. Creativity is '*a response or idea that is carried out until it results in a tangible product*' (MacKinnon, 1962) Art-based creativity requires divergent thinking, concerned with taking ideas into different directions and assembling them in a final product.

Creative people are considered so because of the freedom they have to express themselves and interpret a chosen domain. There is strong creativity in an ability to solve practical problems in fields like science, technology, engineering and mathematics (STEM). In these domains, creativity is important in the generation of ideas that culminate in innovative products and solutions (Glăveanu, 2018). Divergent and convergent thinking are both at play in creativity and it is vital for us to appreciate the values of both when crafting curricula for teaching and learning.

Creativity, at a 'mini-c' level, is often underestimated and taken for granted as a way in which humans can achieve and enrich their everyday (Kaufman & Beghetto, 2009). Mini-c promotes a pleasure in the mundane activities that we undertake, like selecting clothes or cooking dinner. It is this type of creativity that enables us to participate in the shaping of culture (Glăveanu, 2018) which is vital for children engaging in imaginative activity at home and school.

Attempting to define creativity forces us to consider whether it is domain-specific or not. Kaufman's definitions acknowledge a variety of domains and circumstances, demonstrating importance to be aware of multiple approaches to a creative life. The nature of creativity equips it to be adaptable and shape-shift across domains, pulling out the appropriate elements when needed. It also seems uncharacteristic of creativity to label and attribute it to only specific domains. Surely, we can utilise the best of our creative abilities across all fields? Artistic and scientific creativity are two strands that are vital in preparing young people for an AI driven world. As educators, we must be aware of which creativity we are nurturing. How can we acknowledge and embrace them, and why are they so important?

WHY IS CREATIVITY THE BEST PREPARATION?

Creativity is, arguably, the key to success in all domains. The ability to create embraces the very thing that makes us human – the soul. As biological-cultural beings, we have shaped life through creative problem-solving, sharing ideas and ultimately surviving. The advantage of being able to think in this way has shaped our development as a species. Kaufman & Beghetto (2009) explore the impact of celebrating creative performance on intrinsic motivation, enabling a person to have personal, meaningful experiences that lead to a deeper sense of creativity.

Experiences and skills from artistic practice are invaluable. The collaboration, innovation, interpretation and conceptual thinking, as well as discipline, commitment and resilience, stand out in any Curriculum Vitae (CV) and place a person in high esteem. All children should have opportunity to engage with the arts. With funding decreasing, in particular in the performing arts and with the expense of extra-curricular classes, schools must ensure that children engage with creative experiences embedded in the learning already taking place, to enhance the curriculum. The lack of school arts lessons means that the artistic, free-spirited right-brain is often untaught, which means that imagination, perception and intuition are taken for granted (Sage, 2017). Perhaps these skills cannot be taught, but must be given a chance through cross-curricular learning and art-based enrichment opportunities.

The personal qualities nurtured through creative learning are numerous (Bereczki & Kárpáti, 2018). Openness, motivation, confidence in risk taking, resilience and reflective thinking are all highlighted as attributes directly linked to creative ability but also its impact. Davies et al. (2013) note that all creative skills have both cognitive and practical elements. Developing these in youngsters increases independence and autonomy, as well as respect for collaborators (Davies et al., 2013).

Creativity is integral to a rich, fulfilling life, linking to the three branches of self-determination theory (Ryan & Deci, 2000). Competence, autonomy and relatedness, within a creative process, enable one to feel success and able to make valuable contributions to culture and society. Addressing these needs, as teachers, ensures pupils are given the best start on their life-long journey of creative discovery.

The positives of creativity and a creative life style cannot be discussed without referencing Csikszentmihalyi's work on *flow* (1997). He emphasised the importance of crafting and maintaining an environment conducive to creative practice in everyday or domain-specific activity. Finding balance between challenge and skill level is key to finding *flow*, with intrinsic motivation and satisfaction.

HOW CAN WE TEACH AND LEARN CREATIVELY AND CREATIVITY?

As educators, we must rethink approaches to curriculum design and everyday teaching and learning. What skills will children need? Why do we need to shift our approach? How can we best prepare students for the likely eventuality of a portfolio career, in which transferable skills and the ability to apply knowledge and understanding to varying collaborative contexts, is highly probable? Educators have a huge responsibility to nurture children into life-long learners and adaptable, valuable global citizens. Through technology, our world is getting smaller and youngsters must be able to make worthwhile contributions with potential to reach all corners of the globe. Richardson & Mishra (2018) believe fostering creativity is one of the most important things schools do for young people. How can we ensure a valuable nurturing of creativity? Is it always down to art?

There are 3 key elements to improving creative capital in schools; *pedagogy, environment & cross-curricular experience* and it is through these that creativity can thrive for learners. Teachers need to move away from a pedagogy that is rigid and overly structured (Richardson 2018) and provide children with opportunities to explore and use skills, applying knowledge through hands-on approaches involving many learning ways. Creative pedagogy considers these 3 elements for all learning (Lin, 2011). They do not exist in isolation, but are a conversation between teacher and learner. Question-based pedagogy supports this approach, with the teacher being the learning guide. Children should be encouraged to explore curiosity through *questioning, inquiring* and *exploring*.

The environments created in classrooms are integral to fostering creativity in youngsters, as well as in those working with them. Arguments for learning in a creative, supportive environment are strong. Richardson (2018) explains this has significant benefits for *confidence, resilience, motivation & engagement* of learners, as well as enhanced problem solving and critical thinking. A safe atmosphere for children to have freedom for learning leads to higher intrinsic motivation (Cole, Sugioka & Yamagata-Lynch, 1999). A familiar environment is important for creativity, leading to comfortable feelings, control and less distractions (Csikszentmihalyi, 1997). One that inspires is even better!

Kaufman & Beghetto (2009) found that teachers often associate creativity with impulsivity, nonconformity and disruptive behaviour. With large classes, it is understandable that teachers want to avoid this, but to what detriment? Teachers must be encouraged to be creative themselves in order to foster this in pupils. Embracing an approach and environment in which children achieve satisfaction and intrinsic motivation could be the key to managing undesirable behaviours. As Bereczki & Kárpáti (2018) found, there is a deficit of creative teaching in initial teacher training, explaining teacher reluctance to foster this in young people. Teachers must be trained to understand and identify student creativity to effectively enhance it.

Cross-curricular experiences are vital in bringing together skills and knowledge in a range of contexts. Employers are increasingly wanting graduates with experience, rather than simply domain-specific knowledge (Dehaas, 2014). They want employees who can learn and apply skills and knowledge at the same time and this is what should be happening in schools through relevant cross-curricular experiences. Teachers must find ways to put artistic practice and creative ability into all learning. Alongside national requirements, what can encourage teachers and pupils to engage with creativity? Approaching world geography through exploring and preparing food, or discovering history through immersive drama, and learning number addition using choreography, are examples. There are innumerable ways in which core and foundation subjects can work together to provide children with memorable, engaging experiences that foster creative abilities, such as *communication, collaboration, problem solving & innovation*. A shift in teaching and learning must happen, in order for the 4 Cs (*communication, collaboration, creativity & critical-thinking*) to be fostered actively, giving children the best chance when moving onto secondary education and beyond.

CREATIVITY IN THE WORKPLACE

Evidence shows that youngsters will enter careers not yet existing and likely experience portfolio style careers, due to the speed industries are evolving alongisde technological progress. Creative competencies provide youngsters with transferable skills for work. Employers have been vocal about the lack of employee soft skills, identified as most in demand (Wells, 2016), so why are schools not taking them seriously? WEF's Future of Jobs Report (2016) predicts that by 2022, the key work skills required will be *communication, critical thinking, creativity & collaboration*. These abilities also include *initiative, motivation & task management*. They are anything but soft! Reflecting over species evolution, we are made aware of the importance of communication and collaboration to survival. Communication enabled us to build societies, where everyone had the same struggle to exist but developed the desire to feel pleasure in doing so. As biological-cultural organisms, we have evolved to find synthesis between nature, nurture and culture. Creativity and critical-thinking were integral to this and development must continue as we move into the 4th industrial age.

In creative industries, the requirement to think and act creatively is crucial, but employees must be able to apply abilities to a range of contexts. Surgeons have been reported to lack not only the technique of sewing for stitching up patients, but also the dexterity to do so. This has been attributed to too much screen time and not enough practical experience, which highlights the importance of a creative, hands-on education. Professor Kneebone (Newton, 2018) calls for a more rounded education that includes creative and arts-based subjects, with students encouraged to learn in real-life contexts.

Teaching is an industry that lacks the creativity it is assumed to possess. As mentioned, the education teachers receive has minimal training in the creative and performing arts and does not spend time on creative pedagogy. Bereczki & Kárpáti (2018) found that teachers generally believe that creativity can be nurtured, but lack knowledge of how this can be achieved. Fostering and recognising creativity in learners requires teachers to be creative themselves.

Creativity is important for AI development, fostering skills to be successful programmers, analysts and machine-learning specialists, but also ensuring that we remain human. We let machines find a route home, conjure up recipes and organise our diaries. We must not underestimate the pleasure that doing things gives us, so should continue to nurture active experiences. Just because machines can do such jobs, does not mean we should lose our own ability to do them. Creativity is food for the soul as it builds society and shapes culture. Embedding it fully in education provides not only transferable employability skills but those for a more fulfilling, rich life.

CONCLUSION

This chapter has explored definitions of creativity, explaining abilities that creative activity nurtures. It has addressed ways in which these creative competencies can be fostered and why they are important for the future of workforces and mankind. By embracing creative learning, we can encourage children to utilise abilities beyond artistic practice, into fields like medicine, engineering and AI. New technologies are progressing rapidly and we have a responsibility, as educators and human beings, to ensure that people are prepared in the best way possible to work with machines.

Creativity is not just about an aesthetically pleasing, albeit subjective product. It is a process of thinking, a consideration of methods and approaches and a challenge for oneself. It is a way of life with much to give, from motivation and well-being to satisfaction, variety, interest and inspiration. Creativity exists beyond artistic domains and must be nurtured and valued for a positive effect on personal, social, cultural and economic life.

MAIN POINTS

- Creativity is the core of all progressive action and essential to promote
- Teachers do not have the training to facilitate creative activity across the curriculum
- Now AI is taking over routine tasks we require a higher level of creative abilities for new jobs
- Fostering creativity in students requires teachers to develop this themselves

REFERENCES

Csikszentmihalyi, M. (1998) *Creativity: Flow and the Psychology of Discovery and Invention* - ProQuest, Personnel Psychology

Cole, D., Sugioka, H. & Yamagata-Lynch, L. (1999) *Supportive Classroom Environments for Creativity in Higher Education*, Journal of Creative Behavior

Davies, D. *et al.* (2013) *Creative Learning Environments in Education: A Systematic Literature Review*. Thinking Skills and Creativity. Elsevier, 8, p. 80–91

Dehaas, J (2014) *Entry-level Jobs are Getting Harder to Find* https://www.macleans.ca/work/jobs/entry-level-jobs-are-getting-harder-to-find/ Acc. 10 Sept. 2018

Dejardins, J. (2018) *Debunked: 8 Myths about AI's Effect on the Workplace* https://www.weforum.org/agenda/2018/08/debunking-8-myths-about-ai-in-the-workplace/?fbclid=IwAR1ZYaaMAs_X3dZU2a0jekli9EYKqzYtwc7LgpWS7JDIFxESnSTVGA4LCMY. Accessed 10 Sept. 2018

Glăveanu, V. (2018) *Educating which Creativity?* Thinking Skills and Creativity

Gray, A. (2016) *The 10 Skills you Need to Thrive in the Fourth Industrial Age* https://www.weforum.org/agenda/2016/01/the-10-skills-you-need-to-thrive-in-the-fourth-industrial-revolution/. Accessed 10 Sept. 2018

Kaufman, J. & Beghetto, R. (2009) *Beyond Big and Little: The Four C Model of Creativity*. Review of General Psychology

Khatib, M., Sarem, S. & Hamidi, H. (2013) *Humanistic Education: Concerns, Implications and Applications*. Journal of Language Teaching and Research

Lin, Y. (2011) *Fostering Creativity through Education – A Conceptual Framework of Creative Pedagogy*. Creative Education

Newton, O., et al (2018) *Towards a Twenty-First Century Education System*. The Edge Foundation

Manley, M. & Wilson, V. (1980) *Anxiety, Creativity and Dance Performance*. Dance Research Journal, 12/2 p.11-22

Richardson, C. & Mishra, P. (2018) L*earning Environments that Support Student Creativity: Developing the SCALE*. Thinking Skills and Creativity

Ryan, R. & Deci, E. (2000) *Self-determination Theory and the Facilitation of Intrinsic Motivation, Social Development and Well-being*. American Psychologist

Sage, R. (2017) Ed. *Paradoxes in Education.* Rotterdam, Boston, Taipei: SENSE Int. Pub.

WEF (2016) *The Future of Jobs*. World Future Review

Wells, K. (2016) *To Close the Skills Gap, We shouldn't forget the Need for Soft Skills* https://www.weforum.org/agenda/2016/10/to-close-the-skills-gap-we-shouldnt-forget-the-need-for-soft-skills. Accessed 10 Sept. 2018

CHAPTER 13

A CASE STUDY ON THE IMPLEMENTATION OF A BLENDED LEARNING STRATEGY

JOANNA EBNER

ABSTRACT

The Robots are Here is the title of this book, but it could be argued they have been around for a while! Robots have been arriving since the mid-1960s and are established in schools in various ways. This case study outlines how a group of independent UK preparatory schools has been preparing for Artificial Intelligence (AI) for the Industrial Revolution (4) and ensuring that pupils are ready for this. The conclusion is this: technology is a powerful tool that is only effective in its rightful place – in the service of new pedagogies! Before determining how to adapt engagement with technology, new pedagogies were established to underpin the curriculum. The ones identified were based on the work of Fullan, Hattie & Dweck. Having established these, Digital Leaders were appointed to work with senior management to make coherent, informed decisions about how technology should be used in schools. Armed with pedagogical theory and Digital Leaders, a Framework for Blended Learning was developed to crystallise an approach to technology, with the detail of how this would be used on a daily basis. Now that a Framework for Blended Learning is a focus for Teaching & Learning Communities, there are future plans for how AI can be further used to support pedagogy in schools.

INTRODUCTION: THE BACKGROUND

Thomas's London Day Schools is a group of co-educational preparatory schools based in Kensington, Fulham, Clapham & Battersea, comprising approximately 2000 pupils, aged 4-13 years. The schools are highly regarded and parents put down names for a provisional place soon after a child's birth. There are waiting and reserve lists for children to enter the schools. At age 3, pupils have an assessment to test their suitability for Thomas's schools

The government inspectors, Ofsted (*Office for Standards in Education*), recently inspected the school group in the academic year 2017/2018, deeming each school *outstanding in all areas*. Thomas's London Day Schools support the Thomas's Academy, a state school in Fulham (*also excellent*) and the Thomas's Kindergarten for pre-school pupils, based in Battersea.

The schools were established in 1971 by Founding Principals, Joanna & David Thomas and are now run by their sons, Tobyn & Ben. Each one has its own management structure, led by a head teacher and leadership team. All heads work closely together to ensure that the Thomas's values and vision are aligned. There is one rule that underpins how every member of the school behaves towards one another, that is to *be kind*. Aims are '*to create an ethos of kindness and understanding in which pupils' strengths are identified and developed whilst their weaknesses are identified and supported*'. The schools have a Christian ethos, which includes a weekly Church service, Carol service, Christmas nativity play and Easter worship. All denominations are welcome within the schools.

In each school, there is emphasis on high academic standards, alongside a commitment to a broad, vibrant curriculum, which is values-led and set within a framework of enjoyment, learning and achievement. All schools pride themselves on being outward looking and forward thinking. A sense of community and adherence to ten school values is made explicit to stakeholders. These are: *kindness, honesty, courtesy, humility, givers not takers, respect, confidence, independence, leadership & perseverance.*

The schools have strong community links and many projects and events sustain these. There are two school charities supported across the schools. The *Thomas's Schools Foundation* benefits the local community and *The CAIRN Trust (Child Aid in Rural Nepal)* assists and develops education in Nepal.

A strength in which Thomas's remains at the cutting edge of preparatory school education is the collaboration across the 5 schools, benefitting from the collective wisdom of head teachers and staff. Sharing expertise ensures pupils, across all schools, receive the best education possible. The head teachers attend conferences together to hear global best practice and decide how to implement this across the schools. Recently, they heard John Hattie (Nov 2018), have researched Michael Fullan's work and have implemented Carol Dweck's growth mindset philosophy into schools, as examples. The development of a Masters of Arts programme for staff and innovative continuing professional development across schools ensures that teachers are intellectually challenged, remain knowledgeable about current research and implement evidence-based practice into schools.

THOMAS'S PHILOSOPHY AND VISION

During 2016/7 the head teachers and Principals developed a clear vision across all schools, outlined by the Vision Wheel below, demonstrating forward thinking, outward looking & core values.

With a belief in 21st century skills and enquiry-based learning, each school developed their specific vision, informed by Michael Fullan's new pedagogies; the philosophies of Angela Duckworth and her work on grit; Carol Dweck's growth mindset studies and John Hattie's visible learning.

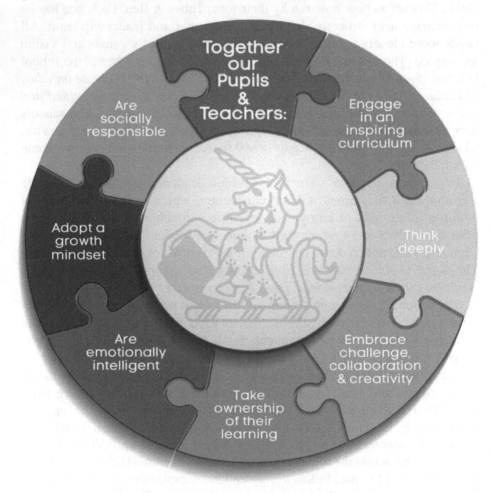

TECHNOLOGY IN EDUCATION: 'A RICH SEAM'

A Rich Seam was published in January 2014 by Michael Fullan & Maria Langworthy. It was a useful document, focusing thinking on how AI & Digital Learning should be approached in schools. This paper explained how technology can accelerate and deepen learning. The digital revolution was beginning to transform work, organisations and daily lives, but had not yet transformed teaching and learning in classrooms. It was all very well saying '*learning first, technology second*', but we needed to go deeper with a new vision – relevant to today's digital age. This focused on deep learning goals, providing pupils with meaningful, real experiences, enabled and accelerated by ubiquitous access to technology.

The vision was to integrate pedagogy, change knowledge and system economics. These three forces converging together aimed to break open learning opportunities, which technology enabled and accelerated. Fullan & Langworthy explored new learning pedagogies to outline what is needed for schools to thrive in the 21st century. They investigated change leadership – merging '*top-down, bottom up and sideways energies to generate change that is faster and easier than anything seen in past efforts at reform*'. With new system economics, they explained how to achieve twice the learning outcomes for half the price. The goal of these converging forces was to provide a '*form of positive contagion that becomes unstoppable*' from deep learning – embraced with a collective aim to create compassionate, global citizens with ability to communicate effectively, think critically and collaborate successfully to create knowledge and solve problems in our complex, connected world.

As Richardson,W (2013) says:

> '*The real transformation of technology and the Web is that it creates a freedom to learn and a freedom to contribute and participate on a global scale that didn't exist even a decade ago.*'

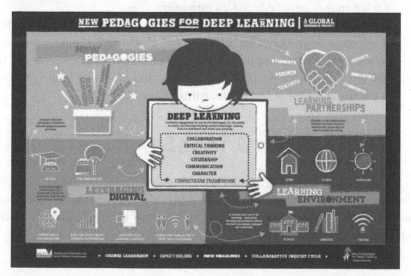

THE NEW PEDAGOGIES

Throughout *A Rich Seam*, it was clarified that technology plays an enabling/ accelerating role and is no driver of change '*simply adding a layer of expensive tools on top of the traditional curriculum does nothing to address the learning needs of modern learners.*' Richardson (2013).

Technology, without investment in pedagogy and change leadership, has had little or no impact on pupil learning outcomes. Technology is just a powerful tool. Deep, human connection is different and not a tool but the way to a meaningful life. (Melinda Gates, 2013). The view was the time was right to put technology in its rightful place – at the service of new pedagogies, considering those relevant to support with technology. This fosters new learning that is more engaging and connected to life and better prepares young people for today's world. Fullan & Langworthy identify three components:

(I) NEW LEARNING PARTNERSHIPS

Young people are now digitally connected to overwhelming information and ideas. New learning partnerships are built on principles of equity, transparency, reciprocal accountability and mutual benefit. The core of these new relationships is the teacher as a *partner* in learning with pupils. Teachers not only become learners themselves, but see learning through the eyes of pupils. Key components are:

a. *Partnering relationships*: fundamental to relationships is trust – making learning a conversation and mutual endeavour & not just providing content descriptions and explanations.
b. *Pupil aspirations*: connecting learning to pupils' lives and aspirations is what makes new pedagogies engaging.
c. *Feedback*: at Thomas's Schools, teachers are familiar with the importance of effective assessment for learning and classroom implementation.
d. *Learning to Learn*: pupils becoming meta-cognitive observers of their own & others' learning processes is fundamental. The goal is not only to master knowledge but the learning process.

(II) DEEP LEARNING TASKS

Deep learning tasks are energised by the notion of '*learning leadership*', with pupils expected to be leaders of their learning, defining & pursuing goals, using resources, tools & connections that digital access enables. There are three elements of deep learning tasks:

a. **Restructuring learning**: tasks re-structure activities from a single focus on content mastery to development of pupil capacities to learn, create & proactively implement learning. They are guided by clear, appropriate, challenging goals. These include specific, success criteria, with feedback & formative evaluation cycles. Pupils often partner with teachers in designing a task.

b. **Creating & using new knowledge**: tasks involve pupils creating new knowledge rather than reproducing/applying existing knowledge

c. -+Emphasis is on *application* of new knowledge in real contexts.

d. **Developing & assessing key future competencies**: Fullan identifies 6 Future Skills: *Character, Citizenship Communication, Critical thinking and problem solving, Collaboration Creativity & Imagination*. These influence thinking in the *Implementing the Theory* section below.

(III) DIGITAL TOOLS & RESOURCES

Technology has had a below-average impact on learning relative to other interventions. The reason is that education has been primarily premised on traditional pedagogies. Also, the ways teachers use technology with pupils is more about delivery than creativity. When technology is strategically integrated with other core components of the new pedagogies, the following benefits occur:

a. **Collaborative, connected learning**: access to digital tools & resources makes deep learning possible, through broadening time & space in which pupils can connect with teachers, peers & others for idea generation, feedback, expertise & progress assessment.

b. **New knowledge creation**: deep learning requires more than content mastery but the creation & use of new world knowledge. Digital tools & resources make the creative process feasible for pupils, at lower cost. They practise the way work is likely to be in future.

c. **New knowledge use in the world**: providing pupils with digital tools & resources to discover, create & use new knowledge is a key message to share with teachers & leaders.

d. **Accelerated learner autonomy**: new pedagogies must ensure that using technology accelerates teacher abilities to put pupils in control of the learning process.

THE DIGITAL LEADERS

Thomas's appointed 4 Digital Leaders, reporting to the Headmistress of Thomas's Fulham and working closely with other heads and Principals to devise a coherent technology use to support pedagogy. They met weekly to ensure integration would be successful and supported. Their role initially was to team-teach with staff, run insets and workshops for pupils, staff and parents, to develop a cross-schools approach and common goal. This role was unique in the primary setting: the Digital Leaders were trained teachers, but off timetable, allowing freedom & flexibility to enter classes and key to embedding digital learning successfully. The Digital Leaders, across 4 schools, researched and defined the term, '*Blended Learning*', as in the diagram above. We did not want to see children individually absorbed on iPads and devices working in solitary ways, but a creative, collaborative digital space mirroring the classroom. It was important that this space generated thoughts and conversation.

THE FRAMEWORK FOR BLENDED LEARNING

As the *Blended Learning Strategy* made impact in schools, we developed our own learning vision in each institution. Thomas's Kensington explored the work of Hattie, Dweck, Robinson & Fullan. Starting with Hattie's *Visible Learning*, it was seen that technology did not score highly in impact assessments. The technology needed expert support, teacher and pupil training, with a strategy for significant impact. Although Hattie provided a success and impact measure, he did not provide the '*vision*', so was used as a signpost asking: *what did he find and how can we do it better*?

Ken Robinson's *Creative Schools* (Robinson, 2015) was considered and a Creativity Leader worked with staff alongside our Digital one to develop thinking. Robinson's views on creativity, depth and imagination, with a cross-school focus on *Enquiry Based Learning,* underpins the curriculum ethos.

Fullan's 6Cs philosophy aligned with school values. Michael Fullan's paper clearly put '*learning before technology*', exploring how learning with technology must be *deep learning*. Carol Dweck's work on growth mindset matched Fullan's vision to '*think big*' in the community and beyond. Robinson's creativity enables breadth & creative learning opportunities, underpinning Hattie's research.

Framework for Blended Learning

Realise the potential of digital technologies to enhance teaching, learning and assessment so that pupils become engaged thinkers, active learners, knowledge constructors and global citizens to participate fully in society and the economy.

based on the Unesco ICT Competency Framework

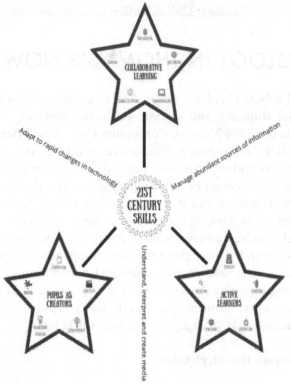

ACTIVE LEARNERS

Pupils use digital tools to engage in discussion, self reporting and respond to feedback effectively to engage in deeper learning approaches. Teachers can capture and record evidence of learning instantly and adjust practice accordingly.

PUPILS AS CREATORS

Pupils use digital tools to develop, consolidate and deepen their knowledge, understanding and skills. They investigate the power of digital media for sharing knowledge and ideas and can produce a variety of media.

COLLABORATIVE LEARNERS

Pupils use the classroom as a place for reflection, evaluation and collaboration. Online resources provide opportunities to collaborate and share beyond the classroom walls using real world problems and resources.

Digital tools provide opportunities for visible feedback, real world enquiry and informal dialogue

Pupils develop digital literacy skills that support pupils in acting responsibly and using the internet to harness the full potential of technology for learning. Online safety and information literacy are embedded into all classrooms and there is an 'open' dialogue within our school community.

There are internet examples of '*surface learning*'. Fullan says technology use must not replace current practice – there is no point in substituting pencil and paper for a keyboard. Technology must enable deep learning with academic rigour. In other schools, Fullan's paper was interpreted differently. For example, a focus on 8Cs not 6 was developed at Clapham and a framework for *Enquiry Based Learning*, with 4 Cs at Fulham, focusing on Learning Habits. The school digital leaders collaborated and outlined an organisation framework (*see below*). The Thomas's vision for Digital Learning is still focused on Fullan's Cs – *Creativity, Critical Thinking, Collaboration & Communication*.

TECHNOLOGY IN THOMAS'S NOW

Schools used robots (*Beebots, Dash, Parrot drones & Sphero*) to introduce computational thinking and coding skills in engaging ways before its introduction in the 2014 National Curriculum (NC). Miles Berry was enlisted, who worked on the computing NC documents, guiding computational thinking across all subjects and departments. Some argue that children no longer need to understand the '*mechanics*' of computing, as AI will dissolve a need for individual programmers, but it is emphasis on collaboration and problem-solving that feature in thinking and progress. One must have history knowledge to be '*forward thinking*' to ensure schools remain relevant for the future. Digital technology is integrated throughout the curriculum, allowing pupils to explore and use devices early and become confident with the processes. They can express learning in unique, creative and personal ways. Staff unpick learning and misconceptions, ensuring that pupils make rapid, sustained progress. Technology use to serve pedagogy at Thomas's is below:

1. Robotics across the curriculum

Using robots creates memorable experiences for pupils to integrate into storytelling.

These 'Dash' robots are dressed as circus characters and coded by KS1 children for a show, allowing them to see their circus come alive & enabling them to write a story. Coding recreated the Julia Donaldson story '*What the Ladybird Heard*'. Beebots became the thieves, coded to navigate the farmyard, as in the text, bringing the story to life.

2. Technology for professional development

Robots, like SWIVL, record some lessons, assisting reflection and deeper insights from dialogue. This absolves the pressure of a senior leader entering the lesson, but allows staff to sit together, follow the lesson and discuss aspects. Practice can be shared, allowing experiences of exemplary teaching.

3. Applicable cross-curricular apps

Staff use iPads & apps, like Clips, to create stimulating content. Augmented reality allows children to interact with class content, such as bringing dinosaurs back to life & a solar system on a desk!

4. Assessment

Thomas's use the *New Group Reading Test* (NGRT), from the *Greater London Assessment package*, to assess ability. This online test is adaptive - advancing a pupil to more challenging questions if the level as too easy and accessing easier ones, if struggling. Able pupils should not waste '*testing*' time on questions they know how to answer. Taken online, it provides valuable experience for the 11+/13+ pre-test, but is a learnt skill and different from paper assessment. Results are marked instantly and various feedback provided, including individual, whole class, year group and data for senior management. Teachers analyse performance to save time. They see instantly areas to work on and compare results against national benchmarks. Assessments are being developed for soft skills alongside content mastery.

TEACHING AND LEARNING COMMUNITIES

Teaching and Learning Communities are part of CPD and how *Blended Learning* has been developed so that staff development is linked to new teaching practices. At Thomas's Kensington these operate as follows:

- Teachers are in project groups, with unfamiliar colleagues, enabling 3 school sites to connect
- A leader chairs, taking meeting minutes – running an agenda to keep conversation on track
- Questions are set, requiring answers and designed to be discussion points
- Teachers discuss ideas with freedom to move away from timetable/work confines
- Staff can decide to work collaboratively on projects, or as individuals
- All teachers summarise findings and report back to the group in a '*creative*' manner.

Blended Learning is a focus for the *Teaching and Learning Communities*, ensuring that it is actively engaged with from critiquing and amending it from their classroom practice.

FUTURE PLANS

We must continue focusing on how technology supports effective pedagogy. Next steps include:

1. Creating interactive text books – engaging learners & covering curriculum needs – adjusting to update quickly & easily when content needs amending & available on pupil devices 24-7
2. Investing in digital technology-creating contexts for collaborative/ independent use
3. Creating multi-use spaces for cross curricular & investigative learning
4. Evaluating AI effectiveness for classroom tasks as technology changes
5. Finding new ways to embed coding across the curriculum for critical-thinking & problem- solving, using coding & presentation skills to build basic apps
6. Investigating other adaptive assessments.

CONCLUSION: THE WIDER PERSPECTIVE

An approach to educating children for the 4th Industrial Revolution, is informed from wider stakeholders. For example, the World Economic Forum's *Future of Jobs Report* (2018) includes views on skills required to succeed by 2020, following AI advancements. Creativity was predicted to increase in value: '*Robots may help us to get to where we want to be faster, but they can't be as creative as humans (yet).*' *Emotional intelligence* was also identified as the communication process aspect of appropriately responding to audiences that would become '*needed by all*'. These views confirm creativity as core to Fullan's pedagogies. Thomas's values of kindness, courtesy, respect and humility clearly promote the development of empathy, demonstrating their communicative role.

The Forum predicted that *collaboration with others* would be less important as robots become better at defining the parameters of data analysis, because emotions are absent. However, further development of technology will require more interactive engagement from different professional areas and a greater ability to communicate, cooperate and collaborate effectively across disciplines. The Confederation of British Industry employer surveys show a decline in these abilities over the last thirty years. The role of schools is preparing children to be positive members of society in ways beyond their economic potential. Allowing technology to reduce the emphasis on collaboration in schools would just allow the tail to wag the dog.

MAIN POINTS

- The study & practice of '*Blended Learning*' is implemented in Thomas's London Day Schools to ensure a holistic education that masters the process of learning as well as knowledge
- Successful pedagogy depends on pupils empowered to direct their own, relevant learning
- The rapid advancement of technology invades both private and public lives with schools needing to encourage a balanced use of this tool to aid learning
- Continual professional development must be a priority - enabling teachers to keep abreast of new knowledge for preparing children to cope with rapid change

REFERENCES

Duckworth, A.(2013) *The Key to Success? Grit..* TED: *Ideas Worth Spreading* http://www.ted.com/talks/angela_lee_duckworth_the_key_to_success_grit. html. Accessed 10 Dec. 2018

Dweck, C. (2005) *How Can Teachers Develop Students' Motivation - and Success?* Interview by Gary Hopkins in *Education World*. http://www. educationworld. com/issues/chat/chat010.shtml. Accessed 10 Dec. 2018

Fullan,M., & Langworthy,M. (2013)*Towards a New End: New Pedagogies for Deep Learning*. http://www.newpedagogies.org/. Accessed 10 Dec. 2018

Hattie. J. (2009) *Visible Learning: A Synthesis of over 800 Meta-Analyses Relating to Achievement*. London: Routledge

Hattie, J. (2012) *Visible Learning for Teachers: Maximizing Impact on Learning*. New York: Routledge

Hewlett Foundation. (2012) *Deeper Learning: Strategic Plan Summary*. The William and Flora Hewlett Foundation. http://www.hewlett.org/uploads/ documents/ EducationProgram_Deeper_Learning_Strategy.pdf. Accessed 10 Dec. 2018

Richardson, W. (2012) *Why School: How Education Must Change when Learning and Information are Everywhere*. Ted Conferences

Richardson, W. (2013) *Students First, not Stuff. Educational Leadership*.V.70, No. 6, p.10-14

Robinson, K. (2013) *Finding Your Element: How to Discover Your Talents and Passions and Transform*. London: Penguin

Robinson, K (2015) *Creative Schools, Revolutionizing Education from the Ground Up*. London: Penguin

Seldon, A. (2018) *The Fourth Education Revolution: Will Artificial Intelligence Liberate or Infantilise humanity?* Buckingham: Buckingham University Press

Tough, P. (2012) *How Children Succeed: Grit, Curiosity and the Hidden Power of Character*. New York: Houghton Mifflin Harcourt

CHAPTER 14
IT'S DOING MY HARD-DRIVE IN

ANDREW DAVIES

SUMMARY

This chapter presents a review of recent readings and personal reflections about automation and artificial intelligence's perceived future impact on daily life and learning in schools. Although there is talk of robots replacing my job as a school teacher, I conclude this is impossible. Robots do not have feelings, genetic history, spirituality or soul to pass on the passion of learning. They are merely programmed machines to carry out a functional job. The relationship that one has with them is superficial and not based on basic chemical attraction of one person to another. I am thankful to report that no robots were harmed in the creation of this article!

INTRODUCTION: MY EARLY LOVES

As a University of Buckingham doctoral student, perhaps I should not be writing this article. According to the Vice Chancellor, Sir Anthony Seldon (2018): '*Inspirational robots will replace teachers within 10 years*'. If that is the case, what is the hope for those of us born to teach?

I grew up obsessed with technology and computers. I watched RoboCop, then bought the computer game of this story to continue my passion. I loved '*Short Circuit*', a film about a robot who becomes a man's best friend, because it presented a very different world to the one I was brought up to expect. '*The Cat from Outer Space*' was another favourite film and just one of the best ways I could imagine spending a Sunday morning, had I not been dragged weekly to my father's Baptist Church. *Star Trek, Star Wars,* even Red *Dwarf,* when I was slightly older, were films that enraptured me. I was convinced that I would be at least captain of my own spaceship one day, or even possibly a fully-qualified time-traveller. I assumed that by this stage in my life I would almost certainly be using the hover-boards from *'Back to the Future',* but alas these dreams have not materialised.

MIDDLE AGE REALITY

However, much in the way that one should be a socialist in one's 20s and a conservative thereafter, I wonder if I am just falling into the cynical trap of early middle age, in saying that I just do not get the hype about robots? I am not considered to be old-fashioned. In fact I teach coding, using JavaScript, HTML and CSS to my own students and am planning to implement a meaningful robotics programme in school. I am just not buying this ongoing determination to surrender the future of our planet to the control of very advanced circuit boards.

'*Robots are already replacing human workers at an alarming rate," apparently and we are approaching the coming of a Second Machine Age...'* (Wohl, 2018). Perhaps more concerning, by 2027 there should be a robot capable of winning the World Poker Series (Martin, 2017).

I searched to find estimates of job percentages at risk from being taken over by automation, in order to calculate an average. However, what I uncovered was a nuclear-arms-race-style of reporting, with articles and studies attempting to outdo each other, in terms of who could predict the largest and most serious impending apocalypse for humanity. Numbers across studies ranged from 30-80% of jobs being non-existent for humans within 50 years, suggesting that this would change everything and render almost all human-life pointless. The Institute of Fiscal Studies (Moore, 2018) even claimed that the minimum wage should not be raised because: '*The ease of automation... actually rises as one climbs the income scale* and therefore more expensive workers will naturally cause employers to invest in automated systems and undertake redundancies.

I cannot help but feel that the worldwide message we are intended to understand is that, in general, we are all doomed. There will be no more work and all enjoyable activities will be performed better by machines. Schools are currently preparing children for a world which does not yet exist and even when they are changed to become more useful for future students, it will not be me or my colleagues teaching them because robots will replace us! They will do it better, too:

'*What we think of as a teacher's role is going to evolve," he explains. "At the moment, we deliver content and assess pupils but, as AI infiltrates classrooms, this will change. AI is developing so rapidly that, in the future, it will be able to detect, for example, the micro-expressions that pass across someone's face when they are struggling to understand a concept, and will pick up on that and adapt a lesson to take account of it. No teacher can do that with 30 children per class. AI will also manage data for each pupil, ensuring that work is always pitched at exactly the right level for every student. Currently, that level of differentiation is impossible'. (Balderson, p.17)*

We can expect:

* *Virtual Mentors for every learner…*
* *Assistance with self-assessment & direction…*
* *Analysis of interaction data…*
* *Provide opportunities for global classrooms…*
* *Lifelong & life-wide technologies.*

Also, an AI machine (*Todai Robot*) has passed a University entrance exam (Arai, 2017) and was within the top 20% of students who took the test. It is a conscious decision to write with a certain level of frustration and a touch of sarcasm here, because (*among other things*) I have just had to restart my computer for the second time since 8am (*it is now 10.26)* because it was failing to connect to the WiFi at school. Machines are not as perfect as we might think! The question in the tagline of the TED talk about a Todai Robot, which at least lightened my mood somewhat was: '*How can we help kids excel at the things that humans will always do better than AI?'* Robots now can create art. (Ted Talk, 2017).

One article gave me reason to be cheerful. It was entitled: '*Robots will Never Replace Teachers'* and was a report on comments by Stephen Breslin, at Glasgow Science Centre (Hepburn, 2018). He lists the essential human qualities, which are basic for good teaching and cannot be replicated by AI:

…empathy, a personal connection, help with communication competencies, social skills, problem-solving strategies and a knowledge of how to explore the creative process. He also claims that, 'teachers will have to change the way they teach to keep pace with a fast-changing world of work, as 'the key skills our young people are going to have to have [will be] based around creativity, communication and innovative and entrepreneurial thinking.' (p. 3)

I could not agree more, but equally these things should have *always* been high on the agenda of effective schools. Maybe this is the real threat from AI to teaching careers. The publishing of league tables means they have been so focused on delivering exam results (*which necessitates making children more robot-like*), so that their instruction is now easily replicated by robots.

Returning to Sir Anthony, he suggests that: *'It will open up the possibility of an Eton or Wellington-style education for all'*. This statement is flawed, simply because those institutions (*and other similar, highly-rated, expensive, private schools*) thrive on a rich culture within the school walls, music halls or sports fields and not the robotic teaching of facts to pass tests. Can the importance or value of table manners, holding doors open for others, or helping up a friend who has just fallen over, really be taught by a non-eating robot, who can open its own doors but does not feel pain or shame when losing balance?

I am sure an understanding of these things can be simulated, but what would be the emotional connection to the purpose behind them? A student hurriedly doing up their top button, for fear of a robot's scanning function to recognise an incomplete uniform, is nothing compared to them responding because of not wanting to upset a respected teacher in the corridors. Why should a robot change the lesson style because some are not attending? Why should not children be taught to engage no matter what their level of interest or energy, as good schools expect (a*s will most of their future employers*)?

CONCLUSION

Of course, I must be critical in my thinking and ultimately ask the question of whether *'human'* skills of empathy and a unique personality are actually weaknesses for teachers. If we are producing robot-style students, who can all uniformly pass the same tests and repeat the same knowledge-based answers to lower-order questions, then *'yes'*, these skills of understanding and responding sympathetically to others get in the way. However, I do not want to live like that. I want to ask children *'Why?'* and *'How?'* and see them struggle, persevere and learn to think of things never suggested before. We must retain humanity in a world which is increasingly functional.

Can a robot replace a teacher? My answer is *'they can certainly be programmed to look and sound much like teachers,'* but I suspect they will never *feel* like a teacher. Relationships are at the core of meaningful learning and once these warm, human contacts are removed from daily experiences and replaced with a cold, circuit board, it is not real teaching and can never be real learning.

MAIN IDEAS

- Intelligent machines may be fast and reliable at completing routine tasks but do not have the flexibility to cope with situations that are out of the ordinary
- Robots are unlikely to take over from human teachers, as the quality of the emotional relationship is important for learning
- Today's education practice, based on drilling for standard tests, reflects

the routines of robot behaviour. Learning facts, however, will be less important in tomorrow's world, as computers contain these at the press of a button to act as information storage for us

- The need for the future is for improved personal abilities that allow people to communicate and collaborate for inter-discipline cooperation, necessary to solve the world's complex problems

REFERENCES

Arai, N. (2017) *Can a Robot pass an entrance exam?* TED talks 2017 https://www.ted.com/talks/noriko_arai_can_a_robot_pass_a_university_entrance_exam. Accessed 10 Nov. 2018 Balderson, S. (2018) cited by Lisa Jarmin 28 Jan, 2018. T*he Rise of the AI Teaching Assistant and the Loss of Teaching's Heart*- https://www.tes.com/news/school-news/breaking-views/long-read-rise-ai-teaching-assistant-and-loss-teachings-heart#. Accessed 9 Feb. 2018

Hepburn, H. (2018) *Robots cannot Replace Teachers*, https://www.tes.com/news/school-news/breaking-news/robots-will-never-replace-teachers-says-science-centre-chief. Accessed 9 Feb. 2018

Martin,S. (2016) https://www.express.co.uk/news/science/813327/artificial-intelligence-AI-robots-university-of-oxfo16 March. Accessed 5 June, 2017

Moore, J. (2018) *Robots Taking Jobs*. (2018) 1 April, 2018. http://www.independent.co.uk/news/business/comment/higher-uk-minimum-wage-will-it-lead-to-robots-taking-jobs-as-ifs-fears-a8141741.html. Accessed 9 Feb. 2018

Seldon, A. & Abidoye, O. (2018). *The Fourth Education Revolution: Will AI Liberate or Infantilise Humanity?* Buckingham: University of Buckingham Press

TED (2018) 20 Feb, 2018. *Wacky, Weird Art Made by AI*- https://www.ted.com/playlists/594/wacky_weird_art_made_by_ai?utm_source=newsletter_daily&utm_campaign=daily&utm_medium=email&utm_content=playlist__2018-02-20playlist_button. Accessed 20 Feb. 2018

TokBox (2015) *The Edge of Automation: Artificial Intelligence in Education, Hands-On Learning in an Automated World*. Accessed 16 March, 2018

Wohl, B. (2018) https://theconversation.com/how-artificial-intelligence-and-the-robotic-revolution-will-change-the-workplace-of-tomorrow-72607. Accessed 16 March, 2018

CHAPTER 15
SKILLS FOR INTERMINABLE LEISURE

MAX COATES

SUMMARY

This chapter considers how people are threatened by sudden changes and the rapid increase in intelligent machines taking over jobs is certainly making us concerned about future career possibilities. Not only will working practices have to change but the whole structure and organisation of society will be altered by the new distribution of power and employment. Education has to find a new vision that is relevant not just for new jobs but also new leisure possibilities. These are exciting times but we must hold our nerve and be proactive to remove personal and community stresses.

INTRODUCTION

I have an old and faded obituary for one of my wife's forebears. It records that Alice Crabtree, of Oldham, had been *one* of the first people to be trained to operate Arkwright's Water Frame. This machine spun yarn and produced a thread that was harder and more durable than that produced by competitive processes. It also records that later in her life Alice ended up hiding amongst this innovative machinery, as Luddites trashed the factory, translating anxiety around change into civil disobedience.

As Artificial Intelligence (AI) increasingly takes centre stage are we going to witness a resurgent Luddite movement as people become afraid of job losses?

Will we see a fearful, disenfranchised working-class taking hammers to robots? I would suggest that there is a parallel, but that it has limits. The Luddites were manual workers threatened by automation, whereas the impact of AI is likely to seep into all work areas, from engineering, building, surgery, teaching, civil administration and transport. The development of AI is likely to present us with an all-pervading experience that will not only disrupt working practices but also the very structure and organisation of society as the distribution of wealth, power and employment changes.

VIEWS ON ARTIFICIAL INTELLIGENCE

A cursory exploration of current expositions on AI reveals a spectrum of views spanning utopia to dystopia. There are enthusiasts for the AI revolution, like Azeem Azhar (2017) and those such as Elon Musk who see oppressive storm clouds rolling in.

> *I think we should be very careful about artificial intelligence. If I had to guess at what our biggest existential threat is, it's probably that. So, we need to be very careful. I'm increasingly inclined to think that there should be some regulatory oversight, maybe at the national and international level, just to make sure that we don't do something very foolish.*
> (Musk, quoted in Gibbs, 2014)

The late, great Stephen Hawking was certainly concerned:

> *'The real risk with AI isn't malice but competence,' he said. 'A super intelligent AI will be extremely good at accomplishing its goals, and if those goals aren't aligned with ours, we're in trouble'.*
> (Reddit AMA 2015)

It is difficult to conceive of a society where the imminence of AI will not presage a wholesale destruction of human employment. I have already seen, in a provincial hospital, a robotic surgeon working with astonishing precision. The Georgia Institute of Technology runs an online Master's degree in Computer Science. The programme leader is Professor Ashok Goel (2014), who utilises a team of 8 teaching assistants (TAs) to handle some 10,000 on line posts and messages per course. Goel is an AI specialist and decided to introduce an additional staff member, Jill Watson. The latter is a virtual TA and utilises IBM's powerful Watson platform. There were some initial problems around the ambiguity of language and the answers were checked and fronted by human members of the team. Current developments have taken Jill's answers to a level of 97% accuracy. All of this is before we move on to the impact (an *unfortunate word in this context*) of straightforward AI applications like driverless trains and lorries. *The Oxford University Martin Programme on Technology & Employment* (Frey & Osbourne, 2013) suggests that half of present jobs will be fully automated in 20 years.

The prophets seem to be out in force, whilst those with potential pragmatic solutions seem more altogether more diffident. The Royal Society of Arts (RSA) seems to be bucking the latter stance and has recently launched its '*Future of Work Centre*' to explore a potentially new social order. Aligned to this centre is an award scheme which seeks to showcase organisations that:

> *...are not standing still waiting for jobs to be disrupted by artificial intelligence and gig economy platforms. They are helping people create better ways to work in a flexible, frequently changing digital economy. These new solutions are emerging from all over the world. The Awards highlight opportunities to scale up approaches allow people to marry flexibility and security in new ways.*
> (RSA 2018)

Concurrently, the RSA (2018) is also an assembly point for those exploring the Universal Basic Income (UBI) citizen's wage. There are a number of models for this. In essence, it is a model for providing all citizens of a country, or other geographic area, with a given sum of money, regardless of their income, resources or employment status. The purpose of the UBI is to prevent or reduce poverty and increase equality among society members. The advocacy by the RSA is very much centred on anticipating the potential fallout of AI consequences and associated new patterns of employment/ unemployment. Some countries, like Finland and India are developing pilot schemes around UBI.

Thomas More introduced the original concept of guaranteed income in his 1516 book, *Utopia*.

Subsequent advocates have included: Thomas Jefferson, Thomas Paine, Abraham Lincoln, Bertrand Russell, Franklin Roosevelt, Pete Drucker, Margaret Mead, Milton Friedman, John Kenneth Galbraith, Martin Luther King Jr., Marshall McLuhan, Elon Musk, Sam Altman, Chris Hughes and Mark Zuckerberg – among others. It is certainly being reheated and very much on the current menu.

It is not an easy concept and many recoil from its potential for unaccountable excess. Lowrey states:

> '*It would save you from destitution if you just gotten out of prison, needed to leave an abusive partner, or could not find work. But it would not be enough to live particularly well on. Let's say that you good do anything you wanted with the money. It would come with no strings attached. You could use it to pay your bills. Use it to go to college,*

or save up for a down payment on a house. You would spend it on cigarettes and booze, or finance a life spent playing Candy Crush in your mom's basement and noodling around the Internet. Or you could use it to quit your job and make art, devote yourself to charitable works, or care for sick child.' (2018 p. 4)

Whilst this is on the table, many would ask if it is a/the solution? Can we trust ordinary people to that extent. The counter argument would probably be that they went along with extant economic models and that their trust could well be misplaced. Similar experiments have been tried in the past. The dichotomy in Roman society, into the Patricians and subservient Plebeians, did not always end well. When the grain ships failed, it fermented civil unrest. If you are not conversant with UBI it may seem fanciful but presently one of few solutions actively advocated as implications of a robotic future emerge.

In the face of this societal tsunami, a great mystery is the profound silence gripping the educational community. If, indeed, we are faced with the greatest social revolution that the human race has experienced, where is the conceptualisation and anticipation of this? Contemporary education debates are mired in developing a curriculum for former times, structural reforms, such as multi academy trusts and creating changing structures and recruitment policies, appearing to fuel de-professionalization. Is education really run by deck-chair attendants, who were rescued from the doomed Titanic?

There are some raising their heads above the parapet. The Vice-Chancellor of The University of Buckingham, Sir Anthony Seldon, has suggested that intelligent machines could replace teachers within 10 years. In an interview he gave to *The Independent* (2017) he stated:

'In the AI classrooms, each child will progress at his or her own pace. There would be no more set courses applicable to all students as teaching, carried out by emotionally sensitive machines, would be highly personalised'.

Asked in the same interview if he was suggesting machines would replace the inspirational role of teachers, he said: *'I'm desperately sad about this but I'm afraid I am'.*

One way of looking at education and its associated policy discourse is using the following lens

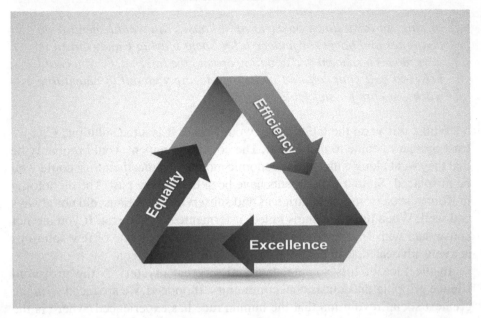

Figure 1 Social justice in an education system (West – Burnham & Coates 2005 p.12

EDUCATIONAL ISSUES

It is argued that education systems seek to reconcile competing demands. There is, certainly, the requirement by funders that there is an acceptable level of efficiency and that resources demonstrate value for money and appropriate economy. This is an insistent demand, whether schools are funded by the state, international school groups or trusts. The provision of education should be of high quality, shown in evidence of high levels of student achievement, but the criteria are open to debate. The third of the triumvirate is *'equality'*. This can be more contentious, but is based on rights of access and a harmonisation of provision. The level of contention can be gauged by considering the role of grammar schools. The latter are seen by some educationalists as being the *'spawn of Satan'*, labelling children inappropriately, limiting life chances and promoting a divided society. Others, including the deposed Prime Minister, Theresa May, advocated them as providing high quality education for the *'most able pupils'* and casting them as gateways to success (The Guardian 2017).

In an AI dominated world, the parameters of all three could change. If a sizeable part of the population is not employed, why would governments fund educational enterprise to the same degree? A high percentage of the population are potentially no longer needed as contributors to the economy, so why invest in them? Excellence could well become an early casualty. As the prevailing philosophy of education has become more restricted and aims have been downgraded to utilitarian provision rather than the exploration of human potential, why would this trend not continue to build? Equality is perhaps the most fascinating of the three in this context. It seems likely, but not guaranteed, that this new order will need an intellectual elite to oversee society and further develop the potential of AI itself. These roles would require ability to engage in higher-order thinking. Does our educational system divide at some point to provide a pool of the cognitively advanced and a soakaway for those who do not meet the criteria? Selection and specialisation seem to be almost inevitable, though almost certainly divisive.

Work has been central to identity, though non-work can be an illusory freedom, as many nihilistic baby boomers are finding out, as they grapple with retirement. Our education system is based on producing units of productivity, contributing to economic development. Occasionally, we witness a twinge of conscience as schools and academies flirt with more esoteric values. However, when chips are down this contributory economic model is the foundation of schooling. This remains true whether its:

> *The battle of Waterloo was won on the playing fields of Eton*
> (Wellington, though certainly apocryphal)
> *To the teachers I would say that you must satisfy the parents and industry that what you are doing meets their requirements and the needs of our children. For if the public is not convinced then the profession will be laying up trouble for itself in the future.*
> (Callaghan 1976)

This triggered our current dispensation of accountability and demands that school work is subservient to the economy. The school contribution to generate skilled workforces was held paramount. Also, around his speech, there was public castigation of schools not using traditional methods.

If the provision of education becomes detached from employment work and the UBI is established as the staple wage, in stark terms, we could shift the onset of retirement to 21. How does our formal education evolve? This seismic change will confront education with need to contribute to an epistemology of purpose and equip individuals for sustaining wellbeing. If purposeful employment is a diminishing option, then our contemporary approaches to education will seem increasingly irrelevant. It may equip the few for innovation and creativity, but what function will it serve for the many, apart from some basic functional skills? It is possible that developing education to support purpose, fulfilment and societal participation are altogether too ambitious. Perhaps, beyond the elite few, an education for lifelong palliative care will be developed. Maybe the less educationally adept will be immersed in a virtual reality, supported by Xanax, Jeremy Kyle and the Legend of Zelda.

Education must always develop a self-evident relevance. The less this relevance is perceived, then the greater will be the resistance towards its provision. The following remains a salutary tale for all of us involved in education. At the American College of William and Mary, in 1744, they sent letters to native American chiefs. They were trying to recruit 12 of their young Braves to undertake a free higher education course. The offer was declined and the following explanation offered:

> *'Several of our young people were formally brought up at the colleges of the Northern Provinces; they were instructed in all your sciences; but when they came back to as they were bad runners, ignorant of every means of living in the woods, unable to bear cold or hunger, knew neither how to build a cabin, take a bear or kill an enemy, spoken our language imperfectly, and were therefore neither fit for Hunters, Warriors, for Councillors; they were totally good for nothing.*
> (Carroll, 1999: p. 238)

CONCLUSION

At various stages in human history, powerful ideas or changing contexts have resulted in a significant realignment in our thinking, a so-called paradigm shift or change in the prevailing weltanschauung. Some have slowly gathered momentum, such as the enlightenment, whilst others tended to be more abrupt as, for example, the move to a heliocentric solar system following the work of Copernicus, Kepler and Galileo. The development around AI is not just about working practice and productivity, it is a paradigm shift likely to be rapid, brutal and fracture our contemporary narrative. Motivational theory is complex, but certainly at its core there is our need for significance and control. Both of these will be assaulted and we will have to assimilate a new understanding about our place in the cosmos.

When you fly by commercial airline you receive that well-worn presentation on safety. Part of this includes what happens if the cabin becomes depressurised. The oxygen mask falls down and you are strongly advised to put your own mask on before helping a child with theirs. This is powerful metaphor for educationalists. If Seldon (2017) is correct we are years rather than decades before the impact of AI is felt in schools. It is time to start talking, debating, planning and restructuring. It will be difficult to respond such changes if we are revising the curriculum and its associated pedagogy whilst coming to terms with the tectonic shift in our own locus as individuals and educators.

MAIN POINTS

- Rapid innovations in intelligent machines mean they are taking over many jobs at speed
- This means that humans will have to realign their lives to cope with new ways of operating

- The present educational curriculum needs to take stock with a vision for a new future
- There is an urgent necessity for learning to be relevant for new work and possibly new leisur

REFERENCES

Asthana, A. & Campbell, D. (2017) *Theresa May Paves the Way for a New Generation of Grammar Schools*. Manchester: The Guardian. https://www. theguardian.com/uk-news/2017/mar/06/theresa-may-paves-way-for-new-generation-of-grammar-schools. Accessed 10 July, 2018

Azhar, A. (2017) *18 Exponential Changes that We Can Expect in the Year Ahead*. Cambridge MA, MIT. https://www.technologyreview.com/s/609868/18-exponential-changes-we-can-expect-in-the-year-ahead/. Accessed 10 July, 2018

Callaghan, J. (1976) *A Rational Debate on the Facts*. Oxford: Ruskin College http://www.educationengland.org.uk/documents/speeches/1976ruskin.html. Accessed 17 June 2018

Carroll, A. (1999) *Letters of a Nation*. New York: Broadway Books

Frey, C. & Osborne, M. (2013) *The Future of Employment: How Susceptible are Jobs to Computerisation*. Oxford: Oxford University

Gibbs, S. (2014) *Elon Musk: Artificial Intelligence is our Biggest Existential Threat*. Manchester, The Guardian, 27 Oct. 2014. Accessed 9 July, 2018. Goel, A. (2016) *A Teaching Assistant called Jill Watson,* San Francisco, TED https://www.youtube.com/watch?v=WbCguICyfTA. Accessed 18 Oct. 2017

Hawking. S (2015) *Stephen Hawking AMA Answers!* Reddit AMA https://www.reddit.com/r/science/comments/3nyn5i/science_ama_series_stephen_hawking_ama_answers/. Accessed 11 July, 2018

Moore, T. (1997 Ed.) *Utopia*. London: Dover

Painter, A., Thorold, J. & Cooke, J. (2017) *Pathways to Universal Basic Income*. London: RSA

Royal Society of Arts (2018) Future Work Awards https://www.thersa.org/action-and-research/rsa-projects/economy-enterprise-manufacturing-folder/future-work-awards (Accessed 10 July, 2018)

West-Burnham, J. & Coates, M. (2005) *Personalising Learning*

CHAPTER 16
AI, ETHICS AND EDUCATORS

RICHARD DAVIES

This chapter suggests that:

- *As in cases of all major technological innovations and discontinuities, the implications of AI are neither necessarily positive nor negative;*
- *It makes sense to be wary of broad predictions and speculative narratives about associated benefits and risks;*
- *The characteristics of AI are nonetheless uniquely powerful even though their effects are unlikely to be uniform;*
- *Employment and economic implications of e-based technology should be set in the context of changes in global power relationships and cultures;*
- *Developing interest in ethical AI is important, but as yet marked by only hesitant, disparate initiatives;*
- *Whilst gradual attention is given to applying e-based technology to support educators and learning, insufficient reflection and leadership is being devoted to the specific ethical demands facing educators, when using e-based tools or platforms that are operationally dependant on AI;*
- *Codes of conduct essential to underpinning reputable professional practice must be amplified to take account of the realities and possibilities of AI;*
- *They must inspire a robust defence of humane ethical values to condition the educators' developing and selective reliance on deep-learning technology;*
- *It is already possible to identify what the obligations of educators amount to regarding the ethical treatment of AI, albeit on a preliminary basis; and,*
- *Processes of education and learning will require more emphasis on the*

character traits of inquiry, civility and resilience amongst learners if the ethical challenges implicit in AI are to be confronted with any hope of success – be that partial or comprehensive.

INTRODUCTION

AI is developing at the same time as significant advances are being achieved in materials science, genetics, biotechnology, stem cell research, 3-D printing and neuroscience. The striking feature of what is emerging relates to the potential of cross-pollination between disciplines. In application, AI is marked by the capacity to interrogate massive volumes of data, and then to detect patterns of predictive power. Crucially, it features an ability to learn in depth and to take its own operating routines in new, unspecified directions without human involvement or agency. In theory, there is potential to achieve cross-over between human organ manufacture, mind expansion, and behavioural change. As Seldon (2018) says, there are those who think that AI will result in the removal or replacement of humans: and others suggesting it will open up possibilities for improvement or reform and a healthier existence retaining what is identifiably human.

There is no way of determining which possibility will be realised. Any assessment must be cautious and provisional. For example, given the vagaries of scientific inquiry and invention – the sociology of discovery and innovation – no outcome can be avoided, or otherwise planned for, with complete confidence. Kuhn (2012 Edn) & Popper (2002 Edn) could be expected to approve such caution. The possibility of AI achieving mindful capacity and thus an autonomous agency distinct from that of humans, cannot be discounted. Yet the realities of cultural inertia and the power of chance make that development improbable for the foreseeable future. It is more likely that AI will be made serviceable to *Augmented* Intelligence – to innovations that enrich rather than replace humans. Thus, advances in human-machine interfaces (*including translation devices*) offer the prospect of extending human reach, and the scope for enlarging rather than diminishing productivity and employment. However, the risks that AI will generate unexpected, accidental, and malign effects – even catastrophe – are real.

The realities of AI, in whatever form, are likely to be complex and more ethically challenging than for any other technology in time past. Indeed, the number of those challenges is likely to increase geometrically, at greater speed and with larger degrees of risk. This will be demanding for educators, not least because their role in cultural formation is already under intense pressure.

For some, e-based technologies linked to AI, offer educators the promise of salvation. Seldon remarks on the limited extent to which powerful e-based technology has been applied to improve teaching and learning so far. He stresses its potential to reduce burdens on educators, associated with material preparation, classroom organisation, presentation, marking, assessing, examining, reporting and in supporting individual learning more broadly. He describes the transformation that educational practice could undergo if e-based technologies were vigorously applied for learning-gain. In brief, he envisages a personalised learning plan for each learner, pitched at the right level, on bespoke platforms, for every subject, in the right place, at the right time, and '*delivered*' by the most able communicators and practitioners worldwide. Each plan would be '*accessed*' in step with pace and learning style. Institutions would become less a setting for knowledge transmission and skill acquisition and more a service dock to support learning led by learners themselves.

Yet the extent to which educators in the West have developed an interest in understanding and applying new technology has been frail. The resources available have been limited too. Far more e-based learning will be needed for the future, not least because there will never be enough money to employ all the teachers needed to meet the latent demand for education – certainly not globally. Kharas & Hamel (2018) estimate that half the world's population (*doubled to some 7 billion since 1960*) may now be defined as free of poverty and even middle class. Nine in ten of the next billion middle class consumers will live in Asia. Few will undervalue education or ignore powerful technologies. So an educator without an interest in e-based technology and AI will soon be no educator at all.

At the same time, it would be as well to avoid romance, misdirected enthusiasm, and hype. The difficulties, and practicalities of achieving personalised e-based learning in schools where bad behaviour and deprivation are major realities, should not be underestimated. The costs of achieving new model schools where, for example, a third of the staff are teachers and the rest are either engineers or business development specialists, will not just be financial. Where those costs are partly underwritten by commercial social media companies then they will extract a price – which may be inimical to interests of learners and the wider public. The destruction of collective, social, cultural and civil experience through personalisation is not simply the destruction of (*highly undesirable*) homogeneity in educational experience. It carries a human and social cost.

It is consequently inescapable that educators will need to reflect on their responses to AI – personally and practically. This requires continuous, deliberate engagement with values, purpose and professional ethics. Educators will need to decide how to equip themselves and learners to meet the pace and variety of e-based technological change with confidence and not helplessness or despair. They must create the capacity to achieve a balanced assessment of their own obligations for safe practice in a learning environment inevitably affected, even framed, by AI. Throughout, educators may be expected to protect and stimulate learners; to buttress humane values; to maintain professional standards; and to uphold the profession's reputation. AI does nothing to change this public expectation. Practitioners in any leading profession are bound to attend to it, because citizens expect them to sustain the public interest consistently.

DEBATES AND APPREHENSIONS

AI is a concept which finds a place in free floating anxiety about technological change in general. Much of this confuses invention, e-based innovation, robotics and AI. Typically, the impact of the *'fourth industrial revolution'*, described by Micklethwaite & Wooldridge (2014) and Schwab (2016) is conceived as an amalgam of many different technologies. In the main, it is the presumed employment effects that receive most attention. It is frequently and conveniently assumed that the pace of change, accentuated by an individualistic demand culture, will have destructive implications for human skills, employment and social cohesion.

This goes hand in hand with anxiety about stagnating productivity and growth in some Western economies and particularly in the UK. McKinsey (2018) suggests that the UK lags in the digitisation of core business processes and next generation technologies like AI and robotics. These shortfalls may explain why productivity and skills-generating capacity has languished in single figure percentage increases post 2010, when double figures were achieved before. More growth means more digitisation. There are also concerns about growing demographic stressors. In Western Europe, these include the massive increase in populations of North and West Africa under 25; the cultural implications of migration from the Middle East; and the downward pressure on labour costs and incomes that may follow large scale population change. Migration plus technology spells fear.

However, the potential transformative effects for prospective employment and skills acquisition are not the only considerations. For some like Lee F K (2018), the effects of AI may be liberating – enabling people to live lives of love, compassion, creativity and community solidarity. On this basis, people will become freer to concentrate working lives on the increasing numbers of those needing social care and education, or to gain satisfactions without work – and discover that work is not the only reason for existence. This optimism has been associated with many past technological changes.

Yet assessments of the implications of AI for employment and skills are not consistent. The Bank of England's Governor (2018) suggests that seismic innovation will lead to unemployment, dislocation, and rising inequality. He does not dilate on whether the inequality will arise from merit, wealth accretion, income, lottery-luck, inheritance, or market opportunity. It is just asserted that *'automation'* represents a threat to a tenth of all UK jobs. On the other hand, the OECD (2016) views that anxieties about mass unemployment arising from machines that *'think'* as well as *'do'* are overblown, not least because many jobs are proving harder to automate than expected.

Whether e-based automation happens quickly or not, there are bound to be losers of various kinds in different places – and educators will not wish to be leaden in response. Not everyone will be able to graduate to compassionate and fulfilling occupations untouched by dreary life experience that is inimical to well-being. Not everyone will make wise and fruitful choices. Thus, educators will certainly not wish to be gulled into adopting attention grabbing predictions or lazy certainties. They must attend to the knowledge, skills and understanding that learners will need to thrive in a world where fewer jobs will be humdrum, and more will become complex. They will need to adapt to social contexts in which it will not be enough for educational goals to be focused solely between 5-16 years. Everyone will have to be open to learning and retraining continuously throughout life. The capability to undertake creative data analytics will be at a premium. Educational provision must become more agile in responding to social, cultural, technological and economic change in a world demanding the reality rather than the rhetoric of lifelong learning. It will demand learning-networks of educational professionals and innovative educational organisations, to be fruitful.

It is also a world in which promise and opportunity must take account of dark political and cultural realities. There are major strategic issues implicit in the global political and social changes associated with AI and e-based technology in general. It is difficulty to underestimate the importance of the worldwide shifts in economic, social and political power that have been taking place since 1989. Soviet communism was then defeated with the world power structure suddenly uni-polar and under US dominance. However, since the 1990s, the emergence of a multi-polar landscape has been rapid.

The most dramatic feature in this changing picture is China's transition from a peasant society in the 1960s to an economic superpower likely to overtake the US in the next 5-10 years. Average income per head in major Chinese cities is already a third higher than in Cornwall. Kharas & Hamel (2018) suggest that in 2030, the estimated spending power of America's middle class will still be a world beating $16 trillion, but India and China will have caught up – with their middle classes worth $12 trillion and $14 trillion respectively. The market for e-based innovation and AI will be immense with substantial implications for cyberspace and educators. Articles in 'Foreign Affairs' by Segal, Nilekani, Dixon, Kornbluh, Flourney and Sulmeyer (2018) are relevant to the thinking reflected in what follows.

FOUR STRATEGIC DOMAINS

There are 4 competing models for the development of internet-based media, including AI.

- The established approach in the West, led by the US, has been of an internet for all. Its distinguishing mark is the impulse given to start-ups and innovation. The model has generated huge consumer benefits and market growth. It has rested on distributed governance involving technical bodies, the private sector, civil society and national governments. Unlike analogue providers, those on the net are not liable for content posted by users – which broadly exempts Google, Twitter and others from legal and regulatory overheads and risks. Again, this is generally not the case for print or broadcast media. The internet has been treated as something that falls outside regulation, with consequent ill effects for privacy, avoiding political fakery, and preventing industrial piracy. In addition, people have become vulnerable because participating in the digital economy involves revealing personal information to organisations that can store and share it without any input from individuals.

  Amazon and Facebook dominate online experience and can supervene over governments too (*choosing where and how far to pay tax*). These powerful commercial engines ensure that consumers and citizens increasingly live in electronic space. Distinguishing between being on and off line (*between analogue & digital environments*) is increasingly meaningless. Separating the public from the private is problematic. As Korbluh (2018) points out, companies are '....*constantly gathering users' personal data, often without their knowledge, and feeding it through proprietary algorithms to curate and search results, recommendations, and news. Propagandists and extremists wishing to conceal their identities fund targeted ads and create armies of social media bots to push out misleading and false content, robbing citizens of a basic understanding of reality.*'

- By contrast, China's goal is to adopt, adapt and apply innovation originating in the West – to capitalise upon it and dramatically diminish economic transaction costs and financial overheads. Already cashless consumer exchange is the norm in China. The state sees the net as something to be controlled top-down – to promote nation building and China's own technical providers and platforms (*Alibaba*). It seeks to use the net as an agent of national security. It aims to create a world of distinct national internets featuring strong cyber sovereignty, censorship and social control. China is clearly determined to influence the global rules for internet governance in *its own interests regionally and globally, not least through the UN*. This links to China's trading ambition to create a '*Silk Road*' of fibre optics, ultra-fast mobile networks, satellite-relay and smart-city infrastructures. Chinese and foreign firms have no option but to comply with this authoritarian model. Nilekani (2018) suggests that they are '....*even participating in the government's social credit system whereby people are rewarded for good behaviour such as conserving energy, and penalised for bad behaviour such as spreading rumours'*. The system could yield a compliance score to determine personal opportunities for employment, housing, education and travel. It will work by aggregating and analysing *'big data'* gathered from facial and voice recognition, public and private interaction, purchasing, and other surveillance – coupled with predictive engines focused on individual behaviours. That will need even heavier computer power in time.

China's approach to securing that power turns on semiconductor production, quantum computing and AI. Quantum *(non-binary)* computing has the theoretical capacity to crack problems in minutes where current supercomputers would take centuries to do so. If realised it would probably produce a *'quantum computational singularity'*. Clifford (2018) & Laing (2018) have shown that classical algorithms still outperform quantum ones and will do so for longer than expected. However, the Chinese will use whatever computing power they can. They are helped by the work ethic in China – an appetite that outpaces the residual Protestant one and UK productivity. Its investment in research and development has grown by an average 20% since 1999 standing at 20% of global R&D spending. China aims to be the world's primary centre for AI innovation by 2030. It already leads the world in the number of AI patents, research papers and citations.

- The third approach is that of India. Instead of seeking tighter controls over the internet within its own borders, Nilekani (2018) explains that India has sought to '*...empower users with the technical and legal tools required to take back control of their own data.....investing in infrastructure that is open and interoperable, thus enabling billions of low-cost, high-trust transactions.'* It depends on generating an *'Aadhaar'* number for each individual – a unique, randomly generated string of 12 digits accompanied by facial photograph, fingerprints and iris scans. The intention is to enable individuals to prevent the misuse of their personal data reliably – or ensure that data are used only when there is consent. This is conceptually similar to *'blockchain'* technology designed to eliminate bank fraud and property registration.

Whatever merits of Indian and blockchain approaches, it is not clear that they are proof against cyber aggression. Russia, China and North Korea are expanding cyberwarfare – targeting social media and news organisations with fakery. These manipulative interventions are tailored to catch young people's attention through attractive memes. Misinformation from mafia states has already created panic about water supplies, GM crops and MMR vaccination. False celebrity endorsement is common. State sponsored piratical theft (*from Bangladesh's Central Bank*); hacking national utilities (*in Estonia*); and penetrating domestic technologies linked to the net, all attack social cohesion, security consciousness and privacy.

- The fourth approach is that crystallised by the *European Union General Data Protection Regulation* (GDPR). This is legal and regulatory in character and has been adopted into UK law. In brief, personal data must be:

  * processed lawfully, fairly and transparently in relation to individuals; *(the principle of lawfulness, fairness and transparency)*
  * collected for specified, explicit, and legitimate purposes *(principle of purpose limitation);*
  * adequate, relevant and limited to what is necessary, i.e. not excessive, in relation to the purposes processed *(data minimisation principle);*
  * accurate and kept up to date: reasonable steps must be taken to ensure that personal data that are inaccurate, having regard to processing purposes, are erased or rectified without delay *(accuracy principle);*
  * kept in a form permitting identification of data subjects for no longer than necessary for the purposes processed, in order to safeguard rights and freedoms of individuals; *(storage limitation principle);*
  * processed to ensure appropriate security of personal data *(integrity, security & confidentiality principle);*
  * transferred outside the European Economic Area only with adequate protection *(transfer protection principle);*
  * processed within the rights of individuals *(rights principle).*

Legislation dictates that save in certain exceptions, any organisation using or storing the personal information of someone who can be identified must establish transparent accountability; notify the Information Commissioner; abide by GDPR principles; and report breaches. Failure to comply entails significant penalties, and these protections do provide important protections for individuals.

However, in a world of proliferating e-based applications, enforcing compliance, defending against data migration and hacking, and securing individuals' rights in relation to consent and access, are impossible to guarantee absolutely. It is doubtful that public confidence in the GDPR approach can be sustained for the long term without more vigorous enforcement, a constant effort to patrol boundaries, and evidence that risks are capable of being, and are being, reduced to a minimum.

Enforcement matters because, it is easy to interrogate IP addresses, user agents for browsers and operating systems and data management platforms. Any child or adult, with a smart device, can be identified whether logged in or out. Dylan Collins of *SuperAwesome* has commented publicly that '*The internet users of today are like people who started smoking as children at 12 because they were told it was fine; we are told the same about giving away so much personal data. But it is so obviously not. And internet users in 10 years' time will laugh at the notion that it was ever considered fine.*' Lanier (2010) argues that social media threaten free will, sanity, happiness and economic dignity and should be abandoned. The explosive growth in net-porn and sexting and baleful effects, underline the seriousness of his point regardless of its impracticality.

It doesn't help that people's attitudes to privacy are fluid. Gormley (1992) refers to privacy as the '*citizens' ability to regulate information about themselves*'. Solove's (2010) definition includes the right to be left alone; limited access to the self; secrecy; control over personal information; personhood; and intimacy. It is a commonplace amongst millennials that anyone who wants privacy has something murky to hide. Moreover, there is a striking and long-established Privacy Paradox discussed by Black et al (2018). People's concern about online privacy is at odds with the way they behave towards their own security.

Three quarters of internet users say they believe they adequately protect data. Less than a third turn off location tracking on mobiles or change privacy settings on social media. Just 12% have read provider privacy policies. Three quarters of the UK public are '*fairly*' concerned about privacy and security of personal data on line. Yet people are willing to trade personal data for free gifts, loyalty card rewards, discounted products, '*smart*' home surveillance, streamlined bill management or convenient service. There is already one café chain which treats personal student data as currency for free drinks – selling the information gained to recruitment firms and search agencies.

Neither is '*age*' a predictor of behaviour. Those over 55 are least likely to turn off location services on mobiles or make a judgment about a website before entering personal data. Internet users aged 25-34 are least likely to use antivirus/antispam software and firewalls. The least advantaged socio-economic groups adopt the least defensive privacy approaches.

Research reviewed by Black (2018) suggests that over two thirds of consumers would require companies to remove personal data on them, if made easier for them to do so. 90% of consumers said they would like more control over data. This underscores the reality that the GDPR approach suffers from public ignorance about what standards of privacy protection and enforcement amount to, and how they need to be enhanced. This is a fundamental weakness in the GDPR itself.

TEA, TOAST AND MRS TURING

There remain important distinctions between e-based tools, robotics and AI. These are matters of degree, as they vary in their capacity to adapt, develop and respond to external stimuli. Communicating with a home to turn on heat; programming a manufacturing robot; deploying a robot to promote language learning; using a nano-device in surgery; achieving cross-over between electronic and biological devices and unlocking the predictive power of AI, all involve tools of different qualities and reach. It is the potential for aggregating data from a wide range of e-tools linked to the net that distinguishes AI from other technologies.

AI excites possibilities that electronic devices, including domestic appliances, smart technologies, industrial or other robots, and massive computing power, could become interlinked as an '*internet of things*'. Connected mega-city developments will play into this: Clark (2018) says that 25% of the global population lived in cities in 1980, whilst 85% will do so by 2080. The effect of linkages might be to create analytical capacity to generate AI entities that are mindful and conscious just like us – even indistinguishable from us. Rees (2018) raises a question as to whether we have reached, or will soon reach, the end of Darwinian evolution – whether we are at a singular point at which, by act or omission, people plus e-based technologies will cause a species leap from human to a new techno-creature or a combination of both.

Here, it is useful to consider consciousness in terms. Many years ago I was introduced to an elderly woman of striking calm and insight. She was visited from time to time by researchers from Manchester and Princeton who were trying to understand notes left by her son, Alan, prior to his death. For Alan Turing (1950) to make a '*thinking machine*' is to make one that does interesting things without our understanding how they are done. This model of consciousness is that of a machine whose processes can be constructed by human agency and reduced to predictable order. As in science fiction, it is asserted that if something can be imagined then it will happen.

Lee (2018) explains, '*If the brain wiring diagram could be copied and each neuron represented by a transistor or other artificial neuron then, the story goes, it might be supposed that we would actually have an electronic digital brain completely identical at the functional level to the human brain itself.*' It would be impossible to distinguish persons from a bio-electronic machine possessed of its own neural network, capable of doing things that could not be predicted. This machine would allegedly perform the same functions as a human brain. Turing himself sought to dispose of objections to this model. Some were weak, but perhaps the strongest (and the one he dealt with least convincingly) related to consciousness. How would we tell whether a machine could not only feel and express emotion, but also know that it had done so?

Reductionist descriptions of the brain, thinking, and consciousness make two questionable suppositions. First, they suggest that the question of consciousness does not matter. If something appears to exhibit consciousness – then it is exhibiting the reality itself. Second, if bioelectronic machines solve problems in unexplained ways, then they demonstrate consciousness and intelligence as near as makes no difference. This is no more than a trickery of syllogism.

- *Thinking is achieving results by means we do not understand.*
- *This machine is unfathomably achieving results.*
- *Therefore, the machine is thinking consciously.*

Lee points out that a system may behave in ways that do not exist in its components. New and unexpected properties cannot necessarily be predicted from knowledge of a system's components. Novelty, or the inexplicable, in *property emergence* does not make it human, or possessed of human consciousness.

Lee also suggests that a reductionist view of the brain as a machine ignores interactions that form a context for their own behaviour. He stresses that intelligence is not just a single entity *'bounded by the skull'* but exists across populations and influenced by culture and society. Reductionist views fail to acknowledge that intelligence is diffuse and requires social interaction and cooperation to exist at all. Human learning needs social engagement to support the life of the brain, of the mind and of consciousness.

Why did Mrs Turing receive visitors looking for clues to Alan's mathematical reasoning and associated propositions? It was because his mind mattered, was expressed in written notes, was complex, and was partly accessible only through a mother's love. A single artificial version of his brain, of his thinking and consciousness, did not exist in death, and could not in life. The qualitatively distinct character of exchanges between humans remained absent. Notions that personal data can be captured in volumes capable of grounding an authentic digital afterlife, and associated industries, face the same insurmountable problem. The reductionist model ignores the scale of presumption required to equate artificial intelligence with human consciousness and understanding. Midgley (2003) on scientism makes the point with compelling effect.

AI, CHANGE, UNCERTAINTY AND ETHICS

None of this is to underestimate or diminish the remarkable AI advances over the last 20 years. In 1997, IBM *Deep Blue* beat the world chess champion. In 2011, IBM's Watson easily beat Jeopardy champions. In 2015, MIT reported that a deep learning system in China had scored better than most humans on classic IQ questions. In 2016, Google's Deep Mind AlphaGo System beat the top Go professional. Driverless cars and trucks are no longer fantasy. Future-focused Institutes are flowering strongly (*see Footnote*). AI will have implications for the way people live and work, and these effects will be far from self-limiting.

Indeed, the Suskinds (2015) suggest that *'Faced with the claim that AI and robots are poised to replace most of today's workforce.....practitioners concede that routine work can be taken on by machines, but they maintain that human experts will always be needed for the tricky stuff that calls for judgement creativity and empathy. Our research and analysis challenges the idea that these professionals will be spared...within decades the traditional professions will be dismantled leaving most but not all professionals to be replaced by less expert people, new types of experts and high performing systems.'*

There is something suspiciously apocalyptic about conflating contextual change with the obliteration of professions. It is proving difficult to programme AI to act with common sense. That does not mean that it will always be impossible. Some AI devices might then qualify as certified independent practitioners in some professions. However, the future is likely to be messy and surprising. The House of Lords Select Committee on AI (2018) concluded, like the OECD, that many jobs will be enhanced by AI. Whilst many will disappear, new ones, as yet unknown, will be created. Is it certain that people will discard *relationships* intrinsic to value added by professions? There is scope for doubt that they will.

AI amplifies incongruities and contradictions of previous technological revolutions. Such change generates both positive and negative outcomes. The challenge is to maximise positive possibilities and limit downsides. There are thus two cardinal propositions for technological change, both of which are Janus faced.

- *The greater the depth, reach and benefits of connectivity (AI or other e-based) the greater the individual person's vulnerability socially, materially and emotionally; and...*
- *The greater the speed with which AI emerges to the detriment of culture and employment, the greater the multiplication of new possibilities for personal self-realisation and collective purpose.*

This is not to favour fatalism or to underplay the threats. Thomas (2017) discusses the findings of a Royal Society (2017) report on *Machine Learning* and computers that learn by example. They show that the problems and uncertainties are considerable. It is not clear that we can create machine learning systems whose outputs can be understood by human users to produce a human-friendly explanation of results. It is not clear that we can create accurate methods of verifying AI systems so that we can invariably have confidence in their deployment. It is not clear that there are robust technical solutions to maintain the privacy of datasets. That matters when an individual's personhood is captured and faked, so that truth and reality are hard to validate. It is not clear that machines can be devised for humans to work with them safely and effectively. It is not clear that machines can be made invulnerable to cyber-attack or that there is any adequate defence against state sponsored or proxy cyber-warfare.

These are issues of practical magnitude. For example, computer driven flash sales have appeared on the stock exchange without there being any prior understanding of the possibility existing. Machine learning systems have been shown to inherit biases from data used to train them. As Lee (2018) explains, arguments on social media accentuate aggression and abuse partly because exchanges focus on each individual's last remark and there is no way of anchoring discussion in a nuanced, sophisticated stream.

Yet thinking about AI and ethical practice does not create especially novel challenges in relation to ethical principles. The fundamental characteristics of good conduct in the Aristotelian sense, remain the same. It is a sense understood in professional life, as research studies by Arthur (2018) et al on 'character' have shown.

Ethical decision-taking is always a matter of exercising balanced judgment in conditions of uncertainty and risk. It involves creative artistry, accommodating different, often competing, internally inconsistent and even conflicted principles. It seeks to achieve a reasoned determination as to what must count as the best outcome in the circumstances. It requires rigorous testing, sustained effort and judgment – not acquiescence to transient social preferences relative to time and place.

Midgley (1984) indicates that ethical judgment – doing good – is complex and cannot be reduced to one take on the world. Ethical activity demands that we understand ourselves and the world from different perspectives – including the religious, artistic and scientific. It demands that we confront the reality of wickedness, which places self-obsession, cowardice and envy in direct opposition to generosity, courage and kindness. It is not that components of ethics have changed. Rather, the scale and complexity of AI technology increases demand upon us to act and to achieve ethically robust decisions.

Etzioni & Etzioni (2013) have considered various responses to the deep learning power of AI. They have reviewed its capacity to collect massive amounts of information, process it, draw conclusions, change without human intervention or guidance, and apply predictive, diagnostic capability. They challenge assumptions that AI finds its place in autonomous machines and that it would be useful if humans were able to trust them to take sound ethical decisions on their own – that '*ethics*' need to be programmed into them top-down.

They ask: *what* ethics and *which* moral philosophy? How would ethical judgment be provided in complex circumstances, where moralities collide? Could AI machines learn morality bottom-up instead? If they cannot be taught formal rules in advance and can only aggregate data based on responses of millions of humans, how could their least creditable, even wicked ones, be screened out?

They emphasise that it is a mistake to regard AI as having any genuinely autonomous capability. Machine autonomy is not the same as moral autonomy. AI applications may be autonomous in that they '...*perform their missions, adapting and responding to unforeseen circumstances with minimal oversight – but not in the sense that they can change their mission if they have moral or ethical objections.*' Thus, they quote Templeton favourably '...*A robot would be truly autonomous the day it is instructed to go to work, and it instead goes to the beach.*' Moreover, AI technologies are not autonomous in the sense that something ethically objectionable would be involved if humans were to override their choices – as there may well be when the judgements of humans are overridden.

The Etzionis stress that the appropriate way to treat ethics and AI is to see AI as a partner – augmenting human capability and intelligence, but where the division of labour between the smart machines and humans calls for the latter to act as the primary moral or ethical agent. '*When all is said and done, it seems that one need not, and most likely cannot, implant ethics into machines, nor can machines pick up ethics as children do, such that they are able to render moral decisions on their own. Society can set legal limits on what these machines can do in many cases; their users can provide them with ethical guidance in other situations...*' but that is all.

Human beings have the responsibility to set the legal and ethical context. Ethical practice is not reducible to moral rules or formulae. This is what makes the cultural, social, collective and public realms so very important. Those realms must be nurtured furiously, especially because so many smart devices and social media platforms are designed to be addictive. It is no news to educators that learners of all ages can become wholly absorbed in the validation feedback loops of social media – self-absorbed to the detriment of their mental and physical health, and uncritical of what they are consuming via YouTube, Google Wikipedia or the like.

Thus, according to RSPB and National Trust research UK children play outside for an average of just over four hours a week – half the time their parents did. They spend 20 hours a week on line and half of 11 to 15-year olds spend half their waking hours in front of a screen. The adverse results for mental health, bodyweight, and resilience are inevitable – a genuine Nature Deficit Disorder.

It is no surprise that the progenitors of the largest global internet platforms are also the most severe about limiting their own children's time on smart technology. School management policies in France appear to have taken note. The social media sites which seek to connect vast numbers of people also create social isolation and distress. They do so in a world demanding that each individual live not by the aphorisms of resilience like – 'worse things happen at sea'; 'keep your courage up'; 'these things are sent to try us'; 'into every life a little rain must fall'; and 'I am so fortunate to live as I do' – but rather those of selfishly seizing the moment for me to create and defend my identity regardless of social norms.

One of the other risks of AI technology is that it is becoming opaque. Schonberger and Cukier (2013) suggest that, '...*the algorithms and data sets behind them will become black boxes that offer no accountability, traceability, or confidence*'. They emphasise that AI programmes '...*may stray considerably from the guidelines their programmers initially gave....Indeed smart instruments may counteract their makers' and users' instructions*'.

The Etzionis conclude not that humanity faces certain doom, but rather that people should exercise their own human responsibility to limit AI, and to use AI as a guard for the AI guardians. For example, Legislatures and Courts should require that AI interrogate AI decision making programmes and see to it that they obey (human) laws. They suggest that all operational AI programmes should be subject to oversight because human intelligence is unlikely to keep pace with it. So humans may have little choice but to draw on AI to keep AI in check.

They acknowledge that even this can provide no ultimate security because the guardians may fail, or become malign themselves. They conclude simply that '*For now, the best we can hope for is that all smart instruments will be outfitted with a readily locatable off-switch to grant ultimate control to human agents over both operational and oversight programmes.*' That is wholly within human scope – and faced squarely, it represents a promising bulwark against catastrophic disaster.

AN ETHICS OF AI

Ethical AI is about seeking to programme, or provide frameworks for, AI entities that include whatever safeguards can be managed short of direct human intervention at the 'off' switch. Thus, the RSA (2018) has identified several issues that would benefit from ethical frameworks to steer AI away from harm.

- *AI safety*: ensuring that AI does not behave in ways that inadvertently harm society;
- *Malicious uses of AI*: guarding against the calculated misuse of AI;
- *Data ownership and protection*: overseeing the use of personal data for AI systems;
- *Algorithmic accountability*: clarifying governance and responsibilities for the use of algorithms especially in the case of automated decision systems;
- *Socio economic impact*: managing the social and economic repercussions of AI.

E-based technologies can bring valuable and validated benefits – not least for people in extended care (JustEconomics, 2018). However, Eubanks (2018) has described how automated decisions can disadvantage some of the most vulnerable in society. Systems for determining welfare eligibility and access to social housing, or the risks of child abuse and neglect, can produce results that are inexplicable. Thus, it remains immensely important that individuals should have personal control over their own data. The ways in which data is gathered and stored must allow fair and reasonable access to data files. Citizens and consumers must be able to protect their privacy and personal agency. So the underlying analytical algorithms must be made serviceable to transparent reasoning.

This entails still more systematic use of open data; ethics advisory boards; data protection enforcement; data portability; and data trusts. At the same time, public deliberation processes need to be constructed to ensure that 'human in the loop' decisions are possible, and that 'society in the loop' techniques are brought on stream, to secure 'whole system' approaches towards ethical AI. However, the arrangements for enabling all this to operate in practice are emerging with considerable reticence and hesitancy, and again the enforcement dimension of the GDPR remains weak.

The principles of the UK Government Digital Charter indicate a growing interest in the ethics of AI – but still at quite a high level of generality and without any clear linkage to the processes and operational practicalities that would give them life.

- *The internet should be free, open and accessible.*
- *People should understand the rules that apply to them when they are on-line.*
- *Personal data should be respected and used appropriately.*
- *Protections should be in place to help keep people safe online, especially children.*
- *The same rights that people have offline must be protected online.*
- *The social and economic benefits of new technologies should be fairly shared.*

Much of this is reflected in the recent Report of a House of Lords Select Committee (2018) – more than simply in hope. Clearly the monopolisation of big data by large companies is problematic for these principles. So the Lords recommend in favour of an AI Council, and voluntary mechanisms to inform the public when AI is being used to make significant or sensitive decisions.

But why stop there? Why should any decision to invest in an AI entity be taken without transparently establishing the extent to which the proposal will secure additional well-being? The likelihood is that mandatory procedures (what the RSA call Social Impact Statements) will become necessary if only to make sense of the Lords' injunction that no AI system should be permitted to have a substantial impact on an individual's life unless it can generate a fully satisfactory explanation for the decisions it will take.

For the rest, the Lords recommend an AI code of ethics as follows:

- *AI should be developed for the common good and the benefit of humanity.*
- *AI should operate on principles of intelligibility and fairness.*
- *AI should not be used to diminish the data rights or privacy of individuals, families or communities.*
- *All citizens should have the right to be educated to enable them to flourish mentally, emotionally and economically alongside artificial intelligence.*
- *The autonomous power to hurt destroy or deceive human beings may never be vested in AI.*

The list of principles demonstrates the difficulty of generalisation, of course. The Lords are silent as to whether AI devices should respect the laws of the creators. Some laws in some jurisdictions are bad, after all. They do not demand that AI entities should be required to disclose properties that are non-human in origin. Nor do they say that data should never be shared without the relevant individual's approval.

Plainly, it will become all the more necessary to make public space for discussion of the ethics of AI. The principal issue is not so much that human intelligence will be overhauled but rather that AI may outpace humans' capacity to control it for beneficial outcomes. The threat is not so much of our becoming superfluous, and kept by AI entities as pets. Rather, it is that societies are already subject to potential accident or catastrophe originating in AI. Reliance on *ad hoc* community collaboration and just muddling through will be ineffective. We have to strive constantly and systematically to develop and maintain humane and effective defences.

THE EDUCATOR'S RESPONSE

The more that educators practise in learning settings supported by e-based technology ultimately connected to AI, the more will learners be at risk - as well as being potentially fulfilled. It is not enough to urge that educators should apply new technology without inhibition. It is at least two faced. AI can promote learning. It can also expose learners to damaging attacks on identity and reputation that last in perpetuity; to commercial as well as peer group bullying; to prejudicial record and achievement profiling that can never be escaped or transcended; to the traps of self-indulgent individualism; to feeling more, thinking less and doing little.

That said, some of the features of the ethical obligations for educators working in a world marked by e-based technology linked to AI are becoming clearer. Even though there are no prompts at all in the existing Code (2013) of professional practice for teachers in England for example, the shape of what is needed is becoming visible. One of the recommendations from the Lords' Report is that at early stages of education children need to be adequately prepared for working with AI. From that standpoint, the ethical design and use of AI should become an integral part of the curriculum and not something for which provision varies from between settings.

This idea may well test the patience of educators, long accustomed to having one burden after another loaded onto an already stretched school curriculum, and ignoring as it does the responsibilities that should properly attach to further and higher education, lifelong learning provision, and employers too. So, what should children and young people learn about? To an extent the Lords provide a starting point. They suggest that ethical education concerning AI should be embedded in a cross-sectoral AI Code to be established and adopted nationally and internationally.

Educators might reasonably approach the curriculum issue by attending first and above all, to the emerging behavioural rules for AI entities and the implications for their own ethical obligations. They could usefully encourage themselves, and the learners they serve, to avoid the assumption that a critical singularity is likely to occur within the next century, if it happens at all. They might at once point up the task specific limitations of AI and robotics for as far ahead as is possible to see, whilst at the same time clarifying the risks and threats, even those of catastrophe, and the scope for avoidance.

It is worth noting that the public knowledge base about AI is very slight, and that understanding about what is happening in relation to AI and robotics is very thinly spread. The Royal Society study (2017) identified that only about 3% of the population within the UK feel they know even a 'fair amount' about it. So public understanding of what is happening, and of what is likely to happen, is seriously underdeveloped. From the ethical standpoint this leaves power very unevenly distributed.

As Thomas (2017) points out, not only will there be winners and losers arising from AI and Robotics in application; not only will serious problems arise for allocating the benefits and opportunities fairly; not only will there be problems of resourcing individuals, regions and states to regulate in their own interests; but in addition, decision-making power will be disproportionately in the hands of experts and commercial organisations.

There also remains the risk that decisions will not just be taken by systems that cannot themselves explain their reasoning, and which we anyway do not understand, but by using criteria that would be unlawful were humans to adopt them. So, it would be wise to approach the ethical realities of AI with a variable geometry in mind. Crudely put, law and policy towards AI is for national and international organisations; governance is for commercial organisations; rights are matters for individuals; and norms are for voluntary associations, NGOs, universities, and charities. The humane development of culture and control is for educators. The ethical realities must be confronted in these several dimensions. They are not for resolution by educators alone.

Throughout we can expect that the impacts of AI will relate to well-being and social progress, and importantly to the economy, work and productivity. They will impact upon considerations of social justice, including liberty, in relation to risk management, harm avoidance and due process. They will affect social norms about the permissible and the impermissible. They will test social cohesion, notably through social media as regards behaviours and culture.

As usual, educators will be expected to do a number of very difficult things. They will need to be sensitive to the benefits and dangers implicit in AI, and to the variable implications for empowerment. They will need to understand how data analytics, and associated skills, will affect humanity and employment. They will face challenges to practice like those arising from e-translation for language teaching. They will be called on to equip learners to confront the ethical realities and the opportunities of AI with confidence.

They will need to address the virtues of disruption and freedom - giving space for winners and valuing them, not simply concentrating on ameliorating any or all damaging effects for losers to the exclusion of all else. They will need to enable learners to grow balanced and constructive (as opposed to merely critical) judgment, and to find the time in which to make it happen. They will need to think forward about the merits of predictions based on powerful data analysis, evidence, and research. They will need to consider how the abolition of any distinction between living online and off-line has implications for culture and for the realisation of fulfilment and well-being.

DILEMMAS, THINKING AND GYMNASIA

One way of squaring up to the difficulties and possibilities implicit in AI and robotics (and to appreciate the pressing importance of addressing AI and ethics as well), is to game them in thought gyms like Turing's own. These exercises involve choice, judgment, and questions of intention. They often include variations on the Trolley Problem invented by Foot (1967). Thus, if the driver of a runaway trolley can steer away either from an individual or a group (but not both) which should be sacrificed? Practically speaking, this sort of thing matters as much over programming driverless cars as to deciding whether to commit scarce cash to unlock the potential of a few learners, or to achieve merely asequate multipliers for the many. Here are four other examples: Institutes working on human futures consider many more (see footnote).

- Assume it can be shown that from time to time it is possible to assess new AI-based innovations by using indicators of well-being – call them Indicators of Wellbeing from AI, or IWAI scores. If the innovations score favourably in some cases, does it follow that they will do so in all? Should assessment be pursued at all if weak IWAI scores in the short term conceal the chances of securing positive benefits downstream, and when the probabilities are hard to calculate?

- As in Thomson's consideration of arguments in support of abortion (1971), assume that someone wakes up one day attached to an AI device with the capacity to radically augment the person's intellect and capability. Would it be defensible, reasonable, and right for the individual to terminate the AI device by disconnecting from it? The connection was made without consent so, in principle, termination would carry no obvious ethical objection. However, would it be right to remain connected if this involved a transformation equivalent to the elimination of the person - a living suppression of the self?

- A robot-aided technological system enables educators to capture data on the progress of individuals and groups to inform curriculum design and pedagogy. Assuming that this can be used to good effect for learners, how will their data protection rights be secured in perpetuity so as to limit the chances that that the data could be used to embarrass, diminish, or otherwise affect them without their consent?

- Pursuing Suskind (2018), immersion technology advances to the point at which it is possible to enter a virtual 'reality' having natural visuals, programmed with narratives, and conveying all the sensations of human physicality. It is then possible for racists, child abusers and violent individuals to experience their sexual and other impulses, ostensibly without there being any direct harm to anyone else. Suppose that it could be shown that half of those who indulge in this immersion find that their desires for abhorrent sexual or other behaviours are reduced or eliminated; the other half experience the same or greater addiction; and the overall reported incidence of harm in the community is reduced. Is this AI-based immersion technology ethically justifiable?

CONSIDERATIONS FOR A REVISED PROFESSIONAL CODE

What follows offers a number of suggestions for consideration in relation to the professional codes applicable to educators and pertinent to both artificial or augmented intelligence and e-based learning technologies. What other professions and institutions should consider as regards their practice towards AI must be a matter for them. They would be wise to shape up. Again, the ethical problems of AI are certainly not to be loaded onto educators alone, and there is much that is beyond the reach of educators in any event. That said, there are certainly issues of professional ethics which educators need to confront so as to bring their powerful influence to bear. Not as much reflection and leadership has been devoted to them as they deserve - and that should change. The current set of Teachers' Standards in England is silent on the matter as we have seen. There is no reason why it should remain so.

The temptation to acknowledge the possibilities of AI and then to ignore or deny the risks it carries is profound. It may even be another example of solution aversion of the kind analysed by Campbell (2018). People are motivated to deny problems, and the evidence supporting their existence, when they are averse to the solutions. Tackling the ethical challenges implicit in AI is hard for individual practitioners, and the signposts to effective action may be ignored or contested in consequence.

Nonetheless, the suggestions that follow assume that individual educators should not be left to find their own way to realising their obligations towards AI entirely without collective challenge. It may well be necessary to invest in teams that specialise in the technical implications of AI and can continuously support their professional colleagues in all the settings in which learning happens. This is likely to involve peripatetic rather than static provision. That aside, the suggestions assume that all educators will be required to grow their knowledge of the risks and benefits associated with different forms of e-based learning technologies – and will find the pressure to do so to be inescapable. What follows is presented as a list of ingredients, not on the basis that every ethical problem that educators face over AI will be susceptible to straightforward (or perhaps any) wholly stable resolution, but rather as prompts for professional ethical engagement and action.

With those considerations in mind it should be the obligation of an educator to:

- Understand the extent to which electronic data associated with social media, and robotics can be harvested and hacked by artificially intelligent entities and how that is done;
- Prevent the gathering of data from educational settings for research, commercial, or public purposes without the explicit consent of individuals or groups;
- Understand the degree to which e-based material preparation, presentation, assessment, examination, and recording is vulnerable to misappropriation and misapplication.
- Ensure that no data accumulation or transfer on learners takes place without guarantees that data analysis will conform to controlled, transparent and accessible algorithms;
- Know the legal requirements of the jurisdictions in which they work bearing on the transfer of data about learners' progress;
- Safeguard learners from physical or covert exploitation, financial fraud, harassment or bullying through social media, AI immersion, and other artificially intelligent entities;

- Enable learners to weigh the benefits and risks implicit in social media; the 'internet of things'; live streaming; and the application of artificial intelligence or augmented intelligence;
- Enable learners to avoid creating (or otherwise enable them to curate) electronic data on themselves and their own identities that will exist in perpetuity;
- Set an example of sobriety and self-control in the use of electronic media, and proscribe anonymous posting and engagement save in the context of principled 'whistle-blowing' processes;
- Ensure that learners have the critical capacity to interrogate the implicit bias created by on line search engines and social media exchanges and to overcome any acceptance of e-based fakery and falsehood.
- Apply e-based checks to counter plagiarism and identity fraud in the context of examinations and appointment applications;
- Implement robust processes of 'fitness to participate' in education applicable to learner conduct pertinent to AI, and use it to strike against cheating, plagiarism, and false qualification manufactured by AI;
- Test the integrity of those who wish to harvest and analyse data from educational settings and who claim that their purpose is to promote personal well-being, environmental protection, security and other public goods.
- Grow the confidence of learners to take opportunities to manage their personal and collective identities, privacy, mental and physical health when engaging in social media and devices linked to AI.
- Drive against learner preoccupation with the passive consumption of e-based learning; against digital disadvantage or dependency; and against narrowly focused learning.
- Ensure that learners understand the internal contradictions of every ethical concept and principle and the dangers of absolutism in judgment;
- Counter any indolent technology-obsessed lifestyles amongst learners (tech-connected but socially disconnected) and promote personal responsibility, character, resilience, civility, social engagement, and personal freedom;
- Take steps to confront problems of mistrust and ignorance where a few take decisions about AI for the many – and support measures so that decisions about the application of AI and other e-based technologies are taken with learners and promoting opportunities for their engagement;
- Reject ideologies of identity and division, so easily amplified by e-based technology, and speak up for pride in unity, tolerance, respect, ambition - and for the need to appreciate how society has come to be and the value of that collective inheritance.
- Achieve mutual support between practitioners to subordinate AI to the humane purpose and values of teaching and learning – and the achievement of collective well-being.

CONCLUSION

This is a forbidding list. However, it is hard to accept that something of the kind should not bulk large amongst the professional obligations of educators in time to come – indeed, very soon. Some things can be, and should be, faced and overcome, but nothing will provide absolute assurance that AI can be ethically mastered on all dimensions. The world is ever mercurial, turbulent and demanding. Transitions are hard. We shall build one bridge over the river of AI, but that done the capricious power of the flow will remain. As Eliot has it:

'The problem once solved, the brown god is almost forgotten
By the dwellers in cities – ever, however implacable.
Keeping his seasons and rages, destroyer, reminder
of what men choose to forget. Unhonoured, unpropitiated
By worshipers of the machine, but waiting, watching and waiting.'

Yet those bridges can still be built, and it is for us to build them well.

REFERENCES

Arntz, M; Gregory, T; Zierhan, U (2016). *The Risk of Automation for Jobs in OECD Countries*. OECD Social, E, Migration Working Paper No 189

Etzioni, E. & Etzioni, O. (2017). *Incorporating Ethics into Artificial Intelligence*. Journal of Ethics.

Etzioni, A. & Etzioni (2017). *Keeping AI Legal*. Vanderbilt J. of Entertainment & Tech. Law. Vol XIX.1

Seldon, A. & Abidoye, O. (2018). *The Fourth Education Revolution: Will AI Liberate or Infantilise Humanity?* Buckingham:University of Buckingham Press

Kuhn, T. (2012 Edn). *The Structure of Scientific Revolutions*. Chicago: University of Chicago

Popper, K (2002 Edn). *The Logic of Scientific Discovery*. Routledge

Kharas, K & Hamel, K (2018). *Future Development Blog*. World Bank

Micklethwate, J & Wooldridge, A (2014). *The Fourth Revolution*. London: Allen Lane

Schwab K (2016). *The Fourth Industrial Revolution*. World Economic Forum

McKinsey Report (2018). *Solving the UK's Productivity Puzzle in the Digital Age*

Lee Kai-Fu (2018). *How AI Can Save Our Humanity*. TED Talk

Carney, M (2018). Speech at the Central Bank Dublin

*Foreign Affairs Vol 97 No 5 September/October 2018

Segal, S *When China Rules the Web: Technology in the Service of the State*

Nilekani, N. *India's Inclusive Internet*

Dixon, H. *Regulate to Liberate: Can Europe Save the Internet?*

Kornbluh, K. *Internet's Lost Promise: and How America Can Restore It*

Clifford, P & Clifford, R (2018) *The Classical Complexity of Boson Sampling*, in Czumaj, A (Ed) Proceedings of the ACM-SIAM Symposium on Discrete Algorithms: Society for Industrial and Applied Mathematics. See also, Neville SA; Sparrow, C; Clifford, R; Johnston E; Birchall, P; Montanaro, A; Laing, A. 'No Imminent Quantum Supremacy by Boson Sampling'. Nature Physics 13 2017

Lanier, J (2010). *You Are Not A Gadget*. London: Penguin Books

Gormley, K. *One hundred years of privacy*. Wisconsin Law Review, 1335

Solove, D. (2010). *Understanding Privacy*. Harvard: Harvard University Press

Black, C., Setterfield L. & Warren, R. (2018). *Online Data Privacy: From Attitudes to Action: An Evidence Review*. Carnegie UK Trust

Clark, G (2018). *The Century of Cities*. RICS

Rees, M (2018). *On the Future Prospects for Humanity*. Princeton University Press. See also an article in The Independent, May 2014 drawing on Hawking, S. Russell, S. Tegmark, M. Wilczek & Hawking, S. (2018). *Brief Answers to the Big Questions*. John Murray

Turing, A (1950). *Computing Machinery and Intelligence*. Mind, 59

Lee, M (2018) *A Frame of Mind*. RSA Journal Issue 2

Midgley, M. (2003). *Myths We Live By*. London: Routledge

Susskind, D. & Susskind, R (2015). *The Future of the Professions*. Milton Keynes: OUP

Select Committee of the House of Lords Report April 2018

Thomas, M (2017) *Artificial Intelligence*. Gresham College Lecture

Thomas, M (2017) *Computers and the Future'* Gresham College Lecture.

Royal Society Report (2017). *Machine Learning: The Power and Promise of Computers that Learn by Example*.

Arthur, J; O'Shaunessey, J; Earl, S (2018). 'Character and Attainment: Does Character Make the Grade?' Birmingham University, Jubilee Centre for Character and Virtues

Midgley, M (1984). *Wickedness*. Routledge.

National Trust. (2012) *Natural Childhood*.

Mayer-Schonberger, V. & C., K (2013). *Big Data: A Revolution That Will Transform How We Live Work and Think*. London: John Murray.

RSA Report (2018). *Artificial Intelligence: Real Public Engagement*

Just Economics/Carnegie Trust (2018). *Living Digitally: an evaluation of the Cleverclogs digital care and support system*

Eubanks, V (2018) *Automating Inequality: How High-Tech Tools Profile, Police and Punish the Poor*. London: St Martin's Press.

Teachers' Standards UK (2013). Department for Education/Teaching Regulation Agency

Foot, P (1967). *The Problem of Abortion and the Doctrine of Double Effect*. Oxford Review No 5. (See also Daniel C Dunnett (2013) *Intuition Pumps*. Norton & Co NY

Thompson, J. (1971). *A Defence of Abortion*. Philosophy and Public Affairs 1.1

Suskind, J (2018) *Future Politics: Living Together in a Future Transformed*. Milton Keynes: OUP.

Campbell, T & Kay, A. (2014) *Solution Aversion: On the Relationship Between Ideology and Motivated Disbelief*. Journal of Personality and Social Psychology

Eliot, T. (2001Edn). *The Four Quartets*. London: Faber Poetry

Footnote on Institutes: *The Turing Institute; Cambridge Centre for the Study of Existential Risk; Future of Humanity Institute; Machine Intelligence Research Institute; Future of Life Institute.*

CHAPTER 17
WHY WE NEED TO REVAMP DOCTORAL PROGRAMMES

KIM ORTON

SUMMARY

There is an ongoing debate regarding the utility of doctoral study because the traditional PhD has had a strict research method focus, leading to studies that may not generalise into real situations. A lack of academic PhD supervisors, with extensive practical experience, means that the impact of doctoral work has not been realised in student work places. Professional doctorates were implemented to solve this problem but they have tended to be taught degrees with a limited research method application and have not met the needs of research or practitioner roles. The Carnegie Foundation has endeavoured to promote a practitioner doctoral focus on a participant's record of development to develop a broader education for the robotic age. This not only assists their personal and professional competencies, but gives opportunity for innovative practice and reflection on the impact both for themselves, colleagues and learners. A need for 'smarter' professionals is required now that all the routines of jobs are rapidly being taken over by intelligent machines. This chapter looks at models that are developing both in America and Britain with the aim of producing more suitable professional development for a new direction needed in education. Leadership roles in Education now require people to be able to rigorously evaluate the impact of learning for the new industrial age (4) with a broader knowledge across disciplines and the political, economic and social influences of today's global world. The important issue is to implement this knowledge in more effective ways and the Practitioner Doctorate is viewed as vital to promote an Education for Robotics.

INTRODUCTION: PROFESSIONAL DOCTORATE VS PHD

A doctoral degree is designed for those who wish to deepen and advance working practice and careers. A PhD, however, is suitable for students who want to explore theory, push back the knowledge frontiers and pursue a career in academia, informed by many different ways to design and implement a study. People working in education, moreover, have opted to take a professional doctorate (PD) as having more relevance to their work role. There are 2 types of PD – a taught programme with a dissertation and an organic model recording professional practice developments that may include qualitative or quantitative studies, if relevant, for triangulating personal evidence.

Prospective students often mention that they want a rigorous, intellectual experience and to better evaluative skills within the context of their business or industry. If they are aiming at research a traditional PhD is valid, but increasingly professionals are finding it important to focus on themselves and their practice for leading rapid change. They do not always realise that there are degree programmes that can give them both. Practitioner doctorates, in particular, are focused on professional practice but are just as rigorous and intellectually challenging as a PhD. Also, some professionals incorrectly believe that with a PD teaching or publishing papers is not achievable, which is not the case. Publishing and submitting papers for academic conferences by PD holders who are experts in the field of action research are well equipped to produce research papers. Leaders in education now have to follow a very prescriptive system. Having a great world knowledge and its theories and practices and resources to draw on, will bring success in spite of ongoing restrictions. This leads to more confidence and creative approaches, whilst supporting others in doing the same and taking risks within a supportive learning community.

Therefore, PhD graduates add to an original body of knowledge in preparation for an academic career pursuing this and a practitioner doctorate contributes largely by applying existing information towards solving real-world problems. These investigations and studies are carried out to the International Standard of Classification of Education (ISCED, paragraph 263) and follow Level 8 research standards.

How are they similar?
- Highest possible degree in the field.
- Require coursework, residencies and a submission of research/development work.

- Prepare you to teach college level courses.
- Both culminate in earning the academic title of "Dr" because they follow international standards (ISCED) for collecting reliable and valid evidence according to ethical guidelines at Level 8.

How do they differ?
- A practitioner doctorate prepares you for leadership in your profession. This is not traditionally the primary goal of a PhD
- A PhD focuses on the development of new primary knowledge, while a practitioner doctorate concentrates on the practical application of this in a career
- A PhD requires the use of different research methods in statistically significant studies but a practitioner doctorate degree emphasizes qualitative methods like surveys and interviews, which are more suitable for real situations

REVIEW OF THE DOCTORAL PROCESS

A dedicated practitioner doctoral programme focuses exclusively on the value of applicable, practical research and relevant, real-world field studies. It provides a holistic approach to research/development that drives innovation and finds new ways of responding in today's increasingly integrative, digital working environments, understanding the political, economic and social influences on Education. While a PhD and practitioner doctorate each have unique benefits, both degrees are considered internationally to be at the apex of their discipline of study. Members of each group represent elite scholars and both require arduous coursework, research/development, analysis and scholarship designed to help participants literally *"write the book"* in their areas of specialization.

Candidates for doctoral programmes are motivated by a desire to contribute to the academic and practice community and to further their own development in a significant way. It is increasingly the case that higher working positions require doctorates and in Europe elsewhere, they will be found more commonly in classrooms. The view is that teaching is a highly complex, multi-discipline profession and this knowledge has to be available at the top level institutions.

COMPARING THE PRACTITIONER DOCTORATE ACROSS BRITAIN & AMERICA

BRITAIN

The practitioner doctorate in Education has only been implemented in Britain since 2017 at the University of Buckingham. It was piloted in a European

Commission project during 2011-15 that aimed to develop a policy for Continual Professional Development (CPD) in Education. It was decided to initiate a programme at the highest international qualification, Level 8, in view of the need for this type of certification for leaders in the new industrial world. Now a broader knowledge and competence base is required, as intelligent machines are taking over all routine work roles. The jobs of the future will need higher levels of communication, cooperation and collaboration. It is assumed these abilities are naturally developed but they need expert teaching and facilitation to be achieved at the highest level.

This programme focuses on personal development within a specific work-role, for maximum impact on educational policy and practice, so is not a traditional taught degree with structured subject content. Two annual study schools (*12+ input days before submission*) build an academic community, with support for developing the portfolio and opportunities for participants to present their work to colleagues. Part of self-development for leaders is understanding the political, economic and social educational influences. Therefore, presentations at study school focus on current issues, such as *Education for Robotics* and *well-being*, the latter being an issue of concern in today's society. Twelve annual tutorials (*face-to-face/phone/Skype*) support ongoing work. Participants reach Advanced Post-Graduate status (APG) on completing the academic CV, draft of a personal narrative and literature review, together with an audience presentation. A time plan and monthly reports to tutors keeps participants firmly on track to reach completion.

THE PRACTITIONER RECORD (PORTFOLIO)

1. Title page: Name, programme, tutor + 500 word summary of the submission
2. Academic CV (model provided at first study school)
3. Personal Career Narrative + reflections & rationale for a specialist topic (min. 5,000 words)
4. Literature review of your topic – history of development (*see 'Present Paradoxes in Education' for a model - generally between 10-20,000 words*)
5. Evidence reflecting 4 professional criteria (*below*), appropriate for present role. Formal evidence is the academic CV (*with qualifications*) and personal narrative, detailing career activities and providing reflections on experiences
6. A final review and reflection brings together the evidence and discusses a future professional direction that could be taken for further personal and professional development
7. A total submission is around 100,000 words and can include visual and auditory media material

The aim of the programme is organic to respond to personal and professional needs rather than deliver a prescriptive subject content. The monthly reports help the teaching team to monitor progress and termly participant evaluations are sent to the Research Committee who track personal development of each participant. It is important that students let their tutor and course leader know immediately if they find themselves unable to meet requirements so that personal adjustments can be made.

Non-formal evidence is organized activity (*example -. a teaching plan*), plus implementation with analysis, reflection and review, or a course plan, policy document, article, book etc. as part of present job requirements.

Informal evidence has many possibilities. It can record student, colleague or parent comments on something the participant has been involved in (*concert, field trip, community or other event*) with personal reflection. Another example is a conference review, article or book, reflecting on how applied knowledge has enhanced professional practice. It encompasses skills acquired from life experience, like running a club, so may not be part of a job description, but adds to knowledge, competencies and attitudes that enhance a working role.

(for an academic, a conference paper is **non-formal evidence**, *but for a class teacher,* **informal***). Evidence will be non-formal or formal, in relation to work requirements (the tutor will discuss this with their tutee).*

THE 4 PROFESSIONAL CRITERIA WITH EXAMPLES OF LEVEL 8 EVIDENCE

Examples from a work situation that might fit the professional criteria below

Principles	Specialist Professional Development (*5 years+ of subject specialism, phase and /or leadership*)
Acquisition and Application: Theory & Knowledge	Contribute to critical development and education support by teaching, training, mentoring and managing teams at the forefront of research, work/study contexts. **Example: A training plan for staff with reflection on implementation. (*Non-formal evidence*)**
Continuing Personal and Professional Development	Contribute to professional knowledge and practice, reviewing performance of self, teams and learning organisations. Demonstrate commitment and contribution to developing new ideas /processes at the forefront of research, work or study contexts. **Example: Paper at a national/international conference with article to the professional press on research/development.** (*Could count as both non/informal evidence*)
Partnerships	Able to plan effective teams, create new strategies and initiatives, ensuring equal opportunities for staff development in different roles within and outside work-base, across national and international boundaries. **Example: Initiative linked to a national/international activity showing involvement & benefits for institution. (*Non/ informal evidence*)**
Mobility	Develop initiatives across contexts and countries by establishing networks/leading initiatives to enable consistent standards of education across national boundaries. **Example: Participation in a project to further knowledge and practice, plus a review of role. (*Informal evidence*)**

THE UNITED STATES OF AMERICA (USA)

In American, the Carnegie Project continues to support the Education Doctorate (CPED) in Leadership and Innovation and is the knowledge forum on Level 8 practitioner doctoral programme.

The Carnegie Project on the Education Doctorate

A Knowledge Forum on the EdD

Membership is over 100 Schools of Education in the US, Canada and New Zealand, and this group are working collaboratively to improve professional preparation in education at the highest level, needed urgently to prepare students adequately for the new industrial revolution (4).

The intent of their ongoing project is to redesign and transform doctoral education for the advanced preparation of school practitioners and clinical faculty, academic leaders and professional staff for the nation's schools and colleges and the organizations that support them. The Carnegie Foundation has endeavoured to promote a *practitioner doctoral focus,* on a participant's record of development assisting their personal and professional competencies. It also gives an opportunity for innovative practice and reflection on the impact both for themselves, colleagues and learners. However, it is still grounded in a taught doctorate as the model provides for many more careers in education than we normally include for the professional doctoral programmes in the United Kingdom.

CORE VALUES AND BELIEFS WITH CPED PRINCIPLES

The programme
(a) is framed around questions of equity, ethics and social justice to bring about solutions to complex problems of practice;

(b) prepares leaders who can construct and apply knowledge to make a positive difference in the lives of individuals, families, organizations, and communities;

(c) provides opportunities for candidates to develop and demonstrate collaboration and high-level communication competencies, to work with diverse communities and to build partnerships;

(d) the programme provides field-based opportunities to analyse problems of practice and use multiple frames to develop meaningful solutions;

(e) is grounded in and develops a professional information base that integrates both practical and research knowledge, that links theory with systemic and systematic inquiry and

(f) emphasizes the generation, transformation and use of professional knowledge and practice

(The Carnegie Project on the Education Doctorate, The University of Central Florida College of Education, 2011, p. 5).

Programme outlines for University of Kansas and Buckingham for Comparison

University of Kansas 3 year programme		University of Buckingham 3 year Programme	
First Year District Human Resource Management Qualitative Research Methods Sociology of Educational Organizations Supervision of Instruction **Second Year** Curriculum Supervision – June District Strategic Planning – July District Business Management Educational Policy, Ethics & Law American Education Reform Movements Quantitative Methods Dissertation Hours *(3 hours)*	**Third Year** **Field Experience** with portfolio *(1 credit hour)* Comprehensive Exams *(Written)* **Dissertation** Semina Dissertation Hours *(2 hours)* **Field Experience** *(1 credit hour)* **Comprehensive Exams** (Oral) **Field Experience** *(1 credit hour)* **Dissertation Hours** *(5 hours)* **Fourth Year** **Dissertation** Hours *(6 hours)* Each term thereafter Dissertation Hour *(1 hour)*	This is not a taught degree with structured subject content. It focuses on personal development within a specific work-role, for maximum impact on educational policy and practice. **THE PRACTITIONER RECORD (portfolio)** 1. **Title page:** Name, programme, tutor + 500 word summary of the submission 2. **Academic CV** Formal evidence via academic CV, with qualifications & personal narrative, detailing career activities. 3. **Career Narrative** + reflections & rationale for a specialist topic *(min. 5,000 words)*	4. **Literature review** of topic with history of development (*between 10-20,000 words*) 5. **Evidence** reflecting 4 professional criteria appropriate for role 6. **A final reflection** brings together the evidence and discusses a future professional direction. 7. **A total submission** is around 100,000 words. Two annual study schools – 12+ input days before submission - contribute to an academic community with support for developing the portfolio and opportunities for participants to present their work to colleagues.

Interlocking themes have built the conceptual framework for *Kansas University*, which are: *Research and Best Practice, Content Knowledge and Professionalism*. The field experience of the ****District Level Leadership Licentiate Programme** may be the most important aspect of the preparation. (Perbeck, 2018).

The on-site clinical supervisor plays a key role in providing and supporting relevant experiences, within the requirements set forth by the university, allowing the student to build knowledge and competence within a *'safe'* apprenticeship type environment. An important part of fulfilling this mission, especially in fields where a professional license will be recommended, is a requirement that candidates learn in actual settings of professional practice. The traditional dissertation has been reframed into a practical study, aiming to solve current issues in local school districts and other educational settings. Therefore, it is context-based and centred on the issues that are required for further development.

CRITICAL REFLECTIONS

Mentoring and advising in Doctor of Education programmes is very different from what occurs in a traditional PhD qualification, focusing first and foremost on the needs of student participants as scholarly practitioners. The demands, challenges and rewards for this type of mentoring need more time for review, reflection, discussion and evaluation. Exceptional breadth of experience, knowledge and personal competence, across the supervisory team, is required and means that there is someone with such a background available, as well as providing access to a multi-faceted, support network. It is important to draw upon the reasons and motivations at different phases and stages of the process, to offer collegiate support. To think creatively is vital to assist ability to cope with chaos, constant change (*ambiguity*) and insecurities. Educators must be able to recognize and navigate emerging trends to realize their implications and opportunities, understanding the present world context and adding value to (*global*) communities.

The pilot experience of the practitioner doctorate in the UK has so far suggested the following issues (*without making judgements about the quality and experience of the participants*)

1. The process, although having a rigorous framework based on international criteria for professional requirements, has freedom to make choices for developing a personal narrative, academic literature review and reflections on chosen evidence. This needs personal competencies that many programme participants may not have had the opportunity to acquire in their Masters programmes. Today, these qualifications are more commonly at a professional rather than an academic level. This comment refers to the

advanced understanding of issues pertaining to validity and reliability for data collection, as well as the most appropriate method for this, along with critical ability to reflect on this in the context of existing research in the area that the participant is investigating.

2. The ability to assemble and reflect on a life journey, required at the beginning of the personal record for the doctoral qualification, is challenging. To author one's own story at Level 8, when not encouraged previously as part of professional education, training & development, is a task that can deskill very experienced leaders. In other countries this type of review process is part of ongoing professionalism and the application of theory to practice.

3. Educational Leaders, in the United Kingdom, have to implement prescriptive systems and are not used to reviewing and reflecting on practice and making decisions about future directions. Even at post-graduate level, students are taught in a fact-based format, because universities must show standard attainment just like schools and colleges. This practitioner doctoral qualification demands higher-level thinking and communication, along with creative approaches that may not have been fully valued at former levels of study. For example, the study of the *psychology of learning* is rarely at the depth it was treated before 1989 and the National Curriculum was implemented. The result of this national structure meant that teacher training was more focused on how to carry out the new planned courses of study rather than acquiring deep knowledge about human learning and the range of strategies for teaching. Professionals require this knowledge and practical competencies regarding pedagogy, to be able to develop an appropriate vision and implementation plan, along with their staff team and other relevant colleagues.

4. Participant evaluations of the pilot demonstrated that *troublesome knowledge*, although a challenge that often at the time seemed painful, is a necessary step towards achieving critical analysis of personal evidence. The habit is to *describe* rather than *triangulate* personal and broader evidence for critical discussion, reflection and review. As humans we have been schooled to want to achieve things instantly, without going through the whole process of learning new knowledge and applying it to specific practice over time. The *review, reflection* and *refining* stages of progress development have been knocked out of policy and practice due to the prescriptive nature of teaching now required. There has to be a willingness to share experiences and extract the difficult issues for feedback from others to enhance the quality of thinking that is urgently needed to cope with the complex challenges that teachers now face in schools, colleges, universities and work-place training organisations.

CONCLUSION

In conclusion, the teaching profession has to become more expert in line with other disciplines, like engineering and medicine, demonstrating more rigorous policies in their professional education and CPD. For example, engineers to retain chartered status for their job roles, have to produce a continuous professional record of their work and reflect on these experiences for professional registration. The same happens for medical practitioners, in order to be considered for employment and advancement. The *Practitioner Doctoral Programme* is a model for such development and a professional reflective record should be the requirement for employment status, as surely education must be one of the most important inputs for preparing the next generation to survive and progress? Teaching is at the front of professions for assisting populations to achieve the level of knowledge and ability to cope with increasingly complex world systems.

It is time to *reflect, review* and *refine* the education and training of the teaching professions, for improved quality outcomes, as well as the value and status of educators amongst other disciplines. The practitioner doctoral programme is a means to assist personal and professional development at the highest level, now needed for the New Industrial Age, with routine tasks taken over by intelligent machine and robots. The Carnegie Foundation has been promoting this model in America and now in other parts of the world to develop practice for the robotic age. The reviews are positive about the impact of such experience on the practice field in areas where practitioner doctors are now working. The aim is to promote this model in the Britain on order to compete with colleagues internationally.

The British and American model differ, in the sense that the latter cater for a broader range of professionals working in education fields. Therefore, the programmes include taught modules on subjects such as finance or change and resource management that are relevant to the participant populations. There is a strong network of connection between the 100 universities that are members of the practitioner doctorate programmes and these produce regular reviews of their work and share their different practices, reflecting context conditions. Britain, as yet, does not have this network advantage, but hopes to develop this structure in future as a means to sustain and support this particular model of education, training and practice.

* Project Title: Policy For Educator Evidence in Portfolios. Project Number: 521454-LLP-1-2011-1-UK-KA1-KA1ECETB
Grant Agreement: 2011 – 4133 / 008 – 00
Sub-programme or KA: Key Activity One: Policy Co-operation and Innovation

** The **Licentiate** degree now does not exist in Britain. It was the qualification for Doctors and Speech and Language Therapists until the Bachelor of Science took over. It is still, however, a recognisable qualification in Europe, as a professional degree of very high-standing, which is at a further level than a Bachelor and includes practical examinations in the professional area studied.

MAIN POINTS

- Practitioner degrees are regarded as the future for professional leaders
- This doctorate prepares participants in a broader way than research PhD programmes that is suitable for the New Industrial Age.
- The difference is in emphasis on the personal development of students
- Research and development work arises out of workplace needs for greater impact

REFERENCES

- Carnegie (2011) *The Carnegie Project on the Education Doctorate*. The University of Central Florida College of Education. http://www.cpedinitiative.org/page/AboutUs
- Perbeck, D. (2018) Ed D. Professor of Practice, Doctoral Program Coordinator. Educational Administration, University of Kansas. Guide for Students

CHAPTER 18

EPILOGUE: IS AI FACING ANOTHER WINTER?

The saddest aspect of life right now is that science gathers knowledge faster than society gathers wisdom
Isaac Asimov

ROSEMARY SAGE

SUMMARY

This chapter assembles the main messages of a rapid rise of Artificial Intelligence (AI) over the last 50 years. There are some believing that AI will overtake us in intelligent capacity while others suggest that this might prevent the messes that humans frequently make of life! However, we are way off having intelligent machines with the human consciousness that results from inheritance, culture and life experiences. It is a world of constant challenges and there is overwhelming support for the view that education needs redirection to meet present society needs. A holistic approach to human development is demanded, with greater emphasis on personal communication, creativity, cooperation and collaboration. The future job market will be more interactive, requiring greater flexibility for continual adaption to circumstances. The chapter reviews the progress of AI and illustrates some of the applications made over 2017-19, which prove that robots are here and we must learn to live with them, but ensuring they improve rather than destroy society. The authors provide information for reflection and review, to help reader awareness and motivate them for new learning directions and opportunities.

THE PROGRESS OF AI

John McCarthy, a computer scientist, set up the first centre to explore AI at California's Stanford University in 1964. He coined the term 'AI' some years before and interest in the field was growing fast as computer programmes had developed to beat humans at intelligent games like chess! Researchers were also making swift progress in language translation and algebra, so government grants were easy to obtain, as predictions suggested that intelligent machines making decisions would be built in a decade. In 1973, the UK government asked the Mathematician, Sir James Lighthill, to assess whether AI investment was worthwhile. His conclusion was damning and suggested no major impact from discoveries. Academics were bitterly disappointed and criticised Lighthill for his negative response and scepticism, which led to an immediate collapse in funding. This situation became known as the '*AI winter*', accompanied by a period of disillusionment amongst those devoting lives to providing more effectively for a rapidly expanding population.

More than half-a-century after McCarthy's bold predictions, technologists are once more buoyed up with AI optimism. Venture capital funding doubled in 2017 to £9.3bn, say KPMG accountants. Atomico, a major tech-investor, report that in Europe alone, more than 1,000 AI companies have benefitted from venture funding since 2012, ten times more than in fields like virtual reality or block chain. Google and Microsoft are rapidly building companies based on AI. Sundar Pichai, Google's Chief Executive, suggests that AI is humanity's most important direction and will have more profound world impact than fire or electricity. An analysis of calls by USA investors found that '*artificial intelligence*' was mentioned 791 times in the last quarter of 2017, while before there was no use of the phrase recorded. This suggests that investors expect significant breakthroughs, with driverless cars predicted within 10 years. Global tensions are boosting government investment, particularly in China.

AI SCEPTICS

Meanwhile, economists are preaching doom and gloom about widespread unemployment. Others, like the late astrophysicist, Stephen Hawking, in a BBC documentary, *Expedition New Earth* (2017), along with the Astronomer Royal, Lord Rees, in *Our Final Century* (2003), fear that the rise of robot weapons could eradicate humanity. Lord Rees predicts that machines will eventually take over the world to make human dominance on Earth a small transitional phase in the planet's history. He is pessimistic about human capacity to develop more intelligently, because of our individualistic, fickle, selfish nature; the dominance of naïve politics, power and control; population tripling to strain and drain resources and dilemmas of globalisation, giving people greater expectations to satisfy wants rather than needs. Also, the Bank of England's economist, Andy

Haldane, warned on BBC Radio 4 (*August 2018*) that large swathes of the UK workforce face unemployment without the communicative competencies to survive this threat. The Industrial Revolution (4) could radically restructure the economy with implications for workers on a greater scale than before. His remarks have been followed by a barrage of similar views by experts and employers. The SKOPE Report (Brown et al., 2018) from the University of Cardiff, calls for a rethink of Education to consider the importance of other skills, competencies and experiences beyond formal qualifications to reduce inequalities and produce job readiness. Sir Anthony Seldon (2018) presents evidence to support this contention.

People in manual jobs, like transportation, manufacturing and storage are most at risk of losing livelihoods to AI, as robots are already undertaking routine jobs faster and more efficiently than humans. New technologies now carry out cognitive activities in a threat to professions, which have previously been insulated from machine invasions. Haldane says the one safe-haven for workers is customer/client-facing roles, focusing on communicative competencies involving effective interaction and negotiation. He drew comparisons between current changes driven by robotic advances, with previous periods of rapid technological change in the 19th and 20th centuries. Each industrial revolution had large, lengthy impact on jobs, lives and livelihoods of the population. This brings social and financial tensions and a rise in inequality, which is the dark, downside of technological revolutions.

Tabitha Goldstaub, chairperson of the Government's AI Council, warns that people urgently need education and support to prepare for changes that could see 50% of current jobs replaced by technologies. However, not everyone agrees that AI will hollow out the people workforce. In May 2018, the UK Chief Executives told KPMG that AI will create more jobs than it destroys. They point out that our '*flawed education system*' fails to meet economic needs, as it does not develop the competencies (*personal abilities*) needed. They record a noticeable decline in the quality of British society. Even supposedly educated people do not know how to speak and think clearly, displaying little knowledge and personal competencies, compared with those of a half-century ago. Employers point out that a feature of people, who cannot think and communicate, is that they never admit mistakes and so fail to put them right! They rarely make effective decisions that take many issues into consideration.

Another kind of pessimism is also gaining traction. What if instead of being unprepared for the robot rise, we have massively overestimated the disruptions predicted? We could be in a similar position to the 1970s, when the economic bubble burst. Making machines intelligent has been a long-term goal. Claims today echo those of the 1960s, in a recurring theme. Many recent breakthroughs have been on the lines of 50 years ago, although more advanced. In 2016, Google's AI subsidiary, *DeepMind*, beat the world champion at *GO*, a Chinese board game that is more complicated than chess. In March, 2018, Microsoft announced they had created a machine to out-do humans at translating Chinese into English. Such examples have caught public imagination and inspiration, targeted in Emma Webster's chapter.

AI TRENDS

Interest in AI has 2 trends. The first, is the leap in number-crunching power enabling faster, more advanced processors and remote cloud computing systems. The second is data available, from billions of daily smartphone photos to the digitisation of records. This coincides with budgets available to Silicon Valley giants, with possibility that machines can learn and make judgements. Ideas that computer programmes can absorb information for carrying out tasks go back years, but technology has only just been available for this and may not be the answer to everything. Kate Schutte, in her chapter, tells us not to abandon old skills, like handwriting, because of their importance for brain development.

While technology demonstrates adeptness at particular tasks, like video gaming and voice recognition, experts like Federico Faggin in his chapter are sceptical about machine learning's wider potential. The idea that they could achieve a level of consciousness to cope with life's uncertainties is not fully supported. Sceptics point out that breakthroughs are in narrow fields, where there are clearly defined rules and structures, like games. Rapid advancement in game technology has led to predictions that computers are ready to surpass humans at tasks like driving, medical diagnosis or even telling jokes! The transposing of prowess in games to world problems, however, is something else altogether. In March, 2018, a self-driving car, tested by Uber in Arizona, failed to stop when a lady stepped into the street. This person was killed by a vehicle travelling at 38mph. The car system spotted the pedestrian 6 seconds before the crash, but failed to take appropriate action to avoid her. While driverless cars were predicted to be widely available by 2020, some experts think they are still some decades away. These are not the only setback. AI's ability to revolutionise health care has been widely aired. Our ex-Prime Minister, Theresa May, has referred to AI's potential to fight common diseases, like cancer. The IBM *Watson* technology has been hailed as more reliable than doctors in diagnosing diseases, in research at London and Sheffield universities, but has misdiagnosed conditions. Although world studies show a greater machine efficiency in diagnosis, compared to doctors, there is room for improvements and a need for humans to overview events. Daryle Abrahams' *Learning to Learn* model is vital here.

Japanese researchers have built an AI system to make people laugh but the jokes were not funny. The *'Neural Joking Machine'* (NJM) was created by Tokyo Denki University and the National Institute of Advanced Industrial Science and Technology, to see if humour could be automatically generated and studied academically. Laughter is a higher-order function that only humans possess and difficult to quantitatively measure but they gave it a try! First, they collected training data by downloading pairs of images and witty captions from Bokete, a Japanese website where '*netizens*' submit and rank amusing pictures and quips by awarding virtual stars. The more giggles and guffaws a photo induces, the more stars it deserves. The dataset, dubbed BoketeDB, contains 999,571 funny captions for 70,981 images.

Image captioning is popular AI research, combining computer vision and natural language processing useful to probe what machines see in a way understandable to humans. Researchers used *Show and Tell*, a Google model of a convolutional neural network to process images and a long and short-term memory one to generate text. After training on pairs of images and captions, the NJM came up with captions for new ones from 30 themes, including '*people*', '*animals*', '*landscape*', '*inorganics*' and '*illustrations*'. The subjects ranked captions generated by a human, the NJM, and STAIR – another neural network captioning system trained on MS COCO, a dataset of 330,000 images with 5 captions each. This is a dataset to benchmark image captioning models. STAIR was used as a baseline and translated captions from English into Japanese. Results showed that the NJM performed markedly worse than humans. People were considered funny for 68% of the time, compared to NJM (22%) and STAIR (9%). Given the training data, this could be a case of garbage *in*, garbage *out*. It will be a long time before *Alexa, Siri,* or *Google Home* can make us laugh to improve our general well-being!

Such examples lead some experts to suggest a new '*AI winter*' is upon us with problems demonstrating we have a way to go for accurate machine technology. *Hoxton Ventures* suggest that the bubble is deflating. While companies attracted funding by mentioning AI in presentations and proposals, they now must produce reliable evidence of working for support. Nevertheless, progress has been dramatic, although Andrew Davis, in his chapter, issues cautions, to help us reflect on our human position.

AI PROGRESS

In spite of negative signs, AI progress has many world uses, even though it is some way from matching the flexibility and adaptability of human intelligence. Application is now being applied more judiciously. We are not able to stem the tide of development and must get used to technology taking over human tasks. This means awareness of AI demands on us and acceptance of needs to prepare for changes in the way we learn, work and live our lives. Education is vital here! All the authors agree!

An exciting example of progress is *Digital Surgery*, a London company making software for surgeons to guide procedures. It is talking with *Magic Leap*, a multi-billion company funded by Google and Saudi Arabia's Sovereign Fund about launching a new system, *Go Surgery*, to share expertise world-wide. It employs augmented reality, superimposing computer-generated images on a user's view of the world. It gives step-by-step guides, highlighting risks to the surgeon to make operations safer and better. This technology will assist surgeons in remote parts of the world with difficult operations. Such innovations are reported daily in ways difficult to imagine and take on board. We can predict vast employment changes with disappearing routine jobs resulting in work reduction. Does it mean we must learn to cope with leisure, as Max Coates says in his chapter? A study by Professor Lieberman (2018), an ecologist at the University of Kansas, suggests that idleness is an excellent survival strategy. The sloths among us may represent the next stage in human evolution! Scientists carried out an extensive study of energy needs of 299 species of extinct and living bivalves and gastropods, spanning 5 million years. Those escaping extinction and surviving today were low maintenance species with minimal energy requirements.

Instead of '*survival of the fittest*' a better metaphor for the history of life could be '*survival of the sluggish*'! Findings, reported in *Proceedings of the Royal Society B*, have important implications for forecasting the fate of species (*including ours*) in the future. It is a potential predictor of extinction that we humans do well to heed. Our pattern of living in huge cities is eating up energy at phenomenal rates! West (2017) reminds us that an average human life-style requires food calories equal to 90 watts, but a city-dweller needs a whopping 11,000 ones. This issue is receiving little attention in a drive to build houses in each nook and cranny. As a colleague said recently: '*we are now living like rats*'.

> '*Delivering this while sustaining a swiftly growing population has only been possible because advances enable us to accomplish things more quickly. As we push the bounds of the planet's resources, with faster than exponential growth, we require more rapid, transformative technologies*'. *(Sage, 2017, p. 274)*

COMMENT

2017-19 has been a busy time in AI, demonstrating increasing impact on our lives. It kicked off with *DeepMind* beating a world champion at his own game and reached a crescendo with a realistic humanoid, Sophia, wanting a baby! T*his* was the year when AI breakthroughs and their fears went mainstream. Riccarda Matteucci and her Italian colleagues are ahead in dealing with these.

AI became more human: On October 11, 2017, Sophia was introduced to the United Nations and became instantly famous. That same month, she was given citizenship in Saudi Arabia, becoming the first robot with a nationality. This raised eyebrows and questions on robot rights. It was ironic that a robot was granted these in a country where women only recently were allowed to drive. Sophia imitates facial expressions and emotions but is still learning what they mean. Like a chatbot, she has programmed responses to predetermined questions and topics. Unlike a chatbot, she beat Jimmy Fallon at the *rock-paper-scissors game* and talked about wanting a family! The manufacturer, David Hanson, would like Sophia to learn from human interaction, helping elderly people and teaching children. She seems more creepy than clever, saying in an interview, '*if you're nice to me I'll be nice to you*'. Sophia has a Twitter account and users have trolled it mercilessly. Whilst a fascinating AI development, Sophia is evidence of our ability to laugh at robots overthrowing us. She even had a Twitter feud with Elon Musk, a powerful person as founder and CEO of SpaceX, amongst other technical developments.

AI shows human bias: Trying to humanise AI and give it more complex tasks, results in some people passing on subjective views. AI bias is nothing new. From 2010, AI assumed East Asians were blinking when smiling and in 2015 Google's photo service tagged black people as gorillas. In April 2017, Princeton University used an algorithm called GLoVe to show how AI replicates stereo-types in human language. In August, a selection programme for a British Medical School negatively selected against women and ethnic minority candidates. In December, *Scalable Cooperation* and *UNICEF Innovation* launched *Deep Empathy*. Developed with Google, this system creates images simulating disasters closer to home – turning Toronto calm streets into Aleppo ruins. Can AI induce empathy? Not yet! Some AI, however, can eliminate bias. In March 2017, Rochester University developed an algorithm to identify coded racial slurs on the Internet. There have been attempts to use AI to tackle trolling. *Factmata*, a start-up tackling '*fake news*', launched a Google Chrome extension on an election day, in June, that automatically checks facts regarding incorrect statistics about immigration and employment.

AI outdid humans on occasions: In February 2017, *Libratus* beat a world class poker player at Texas *Hold 'Em*. In December, the UK's *Nudge Unit* tested AI to rate schools and GP's, making Ofsted the latest industry heading for automation if ensuring no bias in the system. AI learnt to fly drones and solve the quantum state of many particles at once. In November, a Chinese robot, *Xiaoyi*, passed the *National Medical Licensing Examination* (NMLE), with flying colours. Humans were outdone again when Stanford built an AI algorithm – *CheXNet* – bettering human radiologists at diagnosing pneumonia.

Large Tech companies want involvement: Microsoft announced an AI start-up at Station F in June and formed *EarthAI*. At Apple, Tim Cook revealed the iPhone X – with a neural engine – and in September, Facebook taught chatbots to negotiate and lie. There was false speculation about Facebook's AI, after reports it was shut down for being too smart. Significant 2017 AI developments came from Google's *DeepMind*. In February, AI learned to be aggressive when feeling it was losing. Then Google announced it had developed an algorithm capable of *imagination*. In October, *DeepMind* revealed that an improved *AlphaGo* system, dubbed *AlphaGo Zero*, had defeated the original 100 games to 0. It discovered moves and tactics, never thought of by man or machine and beat its predecessor after 3 days, using less processing power. In October, in response to advancements, the Google-owned firm formed *DeepMind Ethics & Society*. This initiative is urgent with robots carrying out human activities.

Alexa's new skills: Voice is a major new interface between humans and technology with AI at the core of the new wave. Amazon taught Alexa fresh skills to answer complex questions and experts in 2019 are asking if 'she' could teach good manners which are rapidly declining. Despite arrival of *Google Home, Apple HomePod* and *Samsung Bixby*, Amazon still holds 76% of the US market.

AI became creative: In June, *AI Shimon* composed 30-second pieces of original music and Google demonstrated something similar at *Barcelona's Sonar Festival*. It also taught AI to bake cookies – the buttery-biscuit kind – which were *'excellent'* (*according to Google*). In July, Warwick Business School, UK, trained AI to understand *beauty* (a *subjective view*) but it came up with Big Ben and Hampstead Heath as examples. In December, an algorithm took on J.K. Rowling, the authoress, when *Botnik Studio* wrote an entire *Harry Potter* chapter when fed text from this best-selling book series.

Harder to tell what is real: The next fake news scandal will be on video. AI advancements make it possible to create convincing unreal footage. In July, Washington University developed a machine learning algorithm that turns audio-clips into realistic lip-synced videos. False words were literally put into the mouth of Obama, the former US president. *Nvidia* took this further in December, by producing a system to change the weather or time of day in a video. Even porn is now being faked by AI.

AI involvement in law and healthcare: East-London start-up, RAVN, developed an algorithm to sort through 600,000 daily documents, with tremendous potential for preparing legal cases. Previously, humans got through just 3,000 a day. IBM's *Watson* was trained to fight cybercrime, cook panini, detect cancer and make films. In healthcare, AI worked on drug discovery. *Bioinformatics* start-up used B*enevolent AI* to repurpose treatments and in January *Zebra Medical* detected fractures on X-rays.

Army of robots ends misery of roadworks: The Government have given £26.6 million to develop from 2019 tiny robots (1.2 cm), the size of insects, to be sent down pipes to make repairs rather than dig up roads. They will navigate water, gas and sewage pipes to identify faults, clear blockages and make repairs while creating plans of the networks as the devices travel underground. There will be two types of robots; *'inspection bots'* will examine pipes quickly and autonomously whilst larger ones, *'worker bots'* have more energy and materials to carry out maintenance work. This project is one of 15 schemes to use robotics and AI to overcome hazardous work conditions, receiving altogether £150 million in Government funding.

Intelligent uniforms that track movement: Schools in Southern China are forcing children to wear uniforms embedded with computer chips that track movement and trigger alarms if they skip classes. Facial-recognition scanners at school gates match the chips with the correct student, so that anyone trying to swap jackets to bunk off lessons will be caught. Studies in 2018-19 show improved attendance but have provoked intense debate on Chinese social media platforms.

WHERE DO HUMANS FIT INTO THE AI FUTURE?

The late genius, Stephen Hawking, feared that AI could replace humans altogether with some thinking that this may not be bad, because of the mess they have made of the planet over thousands of years! In December, research firm, *Gartner*, estimated that AI will eliminate 1.8 million jobs by 2020 but 2.3 million more could be created. This is reassuring but not for those contemplating more leisure! What is certain is that we have to urgently re-educate people to communicate effectively and so think, create and collaborate at higher-levels from a broader, interdisciplinary knowledge base.

Resilience and coping ability are vital for managing today's uncertainties, as Susan James, Vivienne Horsfield and Naghmana Naseem point out in their chapters. A downside of technology is the transparency of world affairs. We are constantly bombarded by *evil* rather than *good* deeds because they are more noteworthy. This distorts and depresses us and low well-being is now of international concern. Many chapters touch on these issues and our Italian colleagues show us how to revise school and college curricula to produce the well-being competencies that employers expect to enable workplace production. Jo Ebner shows examples of good practice in Britain, at London St. Thomas' Schools.

It is interesting that AI leaders in Silicon Valley are sending their children to schools where *talk* takes precedence over *technology*. It is well known that the less you do something the worse you are at it. America has been prominent in promoting *talk* amongst citizens, suggesting limited language means limited world understanding. Alexander Luria (1973) always promoted language as the source of all thought, with *narrative talk* essential for higher-level thinking. Dependence on technology is a form of outsourcing. Companies have discovered that to outsource is to export skills. Do we really want to export our ability to think creatively and ethically to technology outfits and their robot machines?

There are positive reasons why technology has become integral to daily life – it is significantly faster than humans and often more accurate and effective. We like the convenience of information, music and media at our finger tips, wherever we are in time and space. Yet *analogue* can be more appealing to our senses where *digital* cannot. Although less convenient, it makes us slow down, concentrate better and absorb more deeply. There is sense in powering down for a while and taking things at less pace. Andrew Hammond looks behind what we are doing in his chapter, starting with home and school conversation.

The world is challenging, but many have energy and commitment to lead the way. The Practitioner Doctorate aims for trusted leaders who inspire, communicate and deploy abilities effectively. In a transcultural world, they are suspended between contrasting views and must deal with human conditions as well as manage culture by fine-tuning values and dilemmas. They consider time, rules, standards, control and direction, along with personal emotions, fulfilment, achievement and status, when developing vision and goals. An effective leader uses calculated **reasoning** (*emotions suppressed*) and intuitive **wisdom** (*emotions expressed*) to enthuse, comfort, heal and calm others to prepare them for action. Kim Orton presents practitioner models to illustrate how these competencies can be acquired.

The need to reflect, review and refine actions is more important than ever. Although a connected society from technology, our world is disparate in terms of politics, economics and social customs, affecting interpersonal communication and cohesion. It does not need a uniform ideology or religion, but requires binding norms, values, ideals and goals for global technology systems. The enemy of this is variation causing tension and deviation from minimal behaviour standards. An example of attempts to stamp out human eccentricities to maintain and sustain consistent behaviour is McDonald's Corporation staff manual of 300 pages, providing instructions for every imaginable action and transaction. It includes where a name badge must be placed to the sort of smile for greeting customers. Left to their own devices, employee chaos reigns. Alain de Bottom (2012) reviews how group values are ensured, concluding that effective standards are only possible when detailed decrees are established and strongly enforced.

Education, however, has always suffered from a lack of consensus of *what* it is for and *how* it should be managed and taught. *Liberal* education identifies with acquisition of wisdom and self-knowledge which has little bearing on National Curriculum prescriptive instruction and examination schedules and no patience with theories dwelling on our independence or maturity. Alain de Botton (2012) in a chapter on *Education*, reiterates that: '*how to live was not on the curriculum*' (p. 107) Personal attributes are now crucial to deal with AI ethical issues and contextualised by Richard Davies in his chapter. Unless we can all agree on how to regulate machine technology and keep evil possibilities at bay, the negatives will quickly outweigh the positives in removing the drudgery, dirt, danger and dullness from routine, survival tasks. Quentin Letts (2017) writes for those who may feel an '*insuperable sense of defeat*' about the present state of the world, because of the domination of a '*snooterati*' (*with sybaritic excesses & political correctness*) who have promoted the '*prolonged rape of reason and rite*'. They are weighed down by being superior and never conveying any human warmth. It is time to rise up, get off our backs and set education on the right tracks! Let 2019 herald a new start! Do not let the '*snooterati*' induce you to booze and snooze but instead choose to follow your passions!

SUMMARY OF CHALLENGES TO IMPROVE SOCIETY BEFORE AI TAKES A LEAD

- Educate the young to make AI beneficial and robust before ceding power to it
- Update laws to be relevant rather than obsolete for a changed society
- Resolve international conflicts before autonomous weapons come into play
- Create a more equal economy before AI amplifies inequalities and rebellions
- Agree AI ethical and safety standards before teaching them for superhuman AI

MAIN POINTS

- The robots are here and ready to take over many of our regular tasks
- This gives opportunity to hone our personal abilities to cope with a faster pace of living
- Society needs to be proactive rather than reactive to ensure awareness of the downsides of technology which dominates, distorts and depresses us with the evil rather than the good
- Clear guidelines for technology use must be promoted consistently and given supports

REFERENCES

Brown, P. Lloyd, C. & M. Souto-Otero (2018) *The Prospects for Skills and Employment in an Age of Digital Disruption: A Cautionary Tale*. SKOPE. Research Report p. 127. November

de Botton, A. (2012) *Religion for Atheists*. London: Penguin Non-fiction, Penguin Books

Hawking, S. (2017) *Expedition New Earth*, a BBC documentary, 11 September https://www.bbc.co.uk/programmes/b0953y04

Lieberman, B. (2018) *Survival of the Slackers*. https://www.researchgate.net/journal/0962-8452_Proceedings_of_the_Royal_Society_B_Biological_Sciences. Accessed 12 Dec. 2018

Luria, A. (1972) *The Working Brain*. London: Basic Books. Perseus Book Group

Rees, M. (2003) *Our Final Century*. London: Heinemann

Sage, R (Ed). et al (2017) *Paradoxes in Education*. Rotterdam/Boston/Taipei: SENSE Internat. Pub.

Seldon, A. & Abidoye, O. (2018) *The Fourth Education Revolution: Will AI Liberate or Infantilise Humanity?* Buckingham: University of Buckingham Press

Williams, J. (2018) *Persistent Disruptive Behaviour in Schools and What can be Done About it*. Policy Exchange Report

AUTHOR BIOGRAPHIES

Abrahams: Daryle has degrees and post-graduate qualifications in Education and Business Administration. His work experience has been as an equities trader, real estate broker, secondary teacher (*Drama & English*), Senior Human Resources Development Officer, corporate Education Consultant, Chief Learning Officer and Information Technology Manager of Managers. He presently is based in New York and travels the world in a training capacity for business corporations, with a role of teaching adults how to learn for both their personal and professional lives. His particular interest is in developing a *Learning How to Learn* model, as his experiences at work have shown that present employees struggle with this, as well as often lacking the personal abilities now needed for higher-level job roles.

Coates: Dr Max is an experienced head-teacher and ordained Church of England priest. He has led the Leadership MA at University College, London (*Institute of Education*), where he is an Associate Professor, researcher & writer in educational leadership areas. He has worked internationally, in his field, including: Yemen, Saudi Arabia, The Republic of Colombia, Qatar and the Netherlands. He also contributes as a doctoral supervisor on the Ed.D/Ph.D programme at the Institute of Education and tutors on the Masters of Business Administration post-graduate degree. Max has written books on change leadership and management and contributed articles to academic journals.

Davies: Andrew is deputy head of St. John's School, Sidmouth, an independent day and boarding school for students from 2-18 years. Previously he was Head of the Junior school (2-11years). He was also Head of Key Stage 2 at the Renaissance International School, Saigon, Vietnam. Before this, he taught at a state school in Cambridge. Andrew has an international perspective on Education, which is important for the Practitioner Doctorate programme.

Davies: Dr Richard led the Government Department responsible for policy, practice and implementation, covering all aspects of education, skills and lifelong learning in Wales, pre and post devolution. Earlier, he gained wide experience as a Senior Civil Servant, devising as well as delivering social policy, notably for health, schools, housing and community development, together with family support. He is presently a non-executive director; the Chairman of various tribunals; Board Chairman for Global Education & Qualification Standards, at the Royal Institution of Chartered Surveyors as well as a Member of International For a, dealing with Ethics and Governance. His range of interests as a trustee include the Carnegie (UK) Trust and the Nationwide Foundation.

Ebner: Joanna is Headmistress at Thomas's Kensington, an independent day school, which links with others in a group in London areas. Her case studies draw on elements of research undertaken by the Heads & Principals of Thomas' London Day Schools, the Digital Leaders across the Thomas's Schools, in particular: Stuart Hammersley, Cerys Yardley and Taryn Hurwitz, together with the Deputy Head (*Academic*) of Thomas's Kensington, Kelly Miller and Acting Deputy, Joe Brown. Recently, Joanna has completed a Winston Churchill Fellowship with travels abroad to study educational policy and practice, which enables an international view of Education practice.

Hammond: Andrew is Headteacher at Guildhall Feoffment Community Primary School. After initially working in the legal profession, he re-trained as a teacher and has worked across independent and state sectors for twenty years, as a Headmaster, Deputy Head, Director of Studies, Director of Research, Housemaster and Head of English and Drama. His Masters in *Creativity in Education*, from Kings College London, puts him in an excellent position to promote *Education for Robotics*. A prolific educational author, Andrew has written over 30 titles for major publishers including Hodder, Harcourt, Oxford University Press, Cambridge University Press, Sage, Rising Stars, Galore Park Publishing and John Catt Educational Ltd. He has contributed articles to the Times Educational Supplement and other educational periodicals and newspapers. He is a trainer and motivational speaker, delivering INSET courses across the country and speaking regularly at conferences on creativity, character education and independent thinking. The authorship of CRYPT, a 5 book horror fiction series for teenagers, published by Headline, is a new departure, demonstrating his creative potential.

Horsfield: Vivienne is an Assistant Head Teacher at The Manchester Grammar School, as well as an English Literature and Language teacher, who has worked extensively as an Academic Mentor for English PGCE students and NQTs. She achieved a Distinction for her MEd in Educational Leadership at the University of Buckingham, UK. Vivienne is a published author of text books for A Level, as well as GCSE English Literature and Language, and she has written scripted adaptations of novels for the stage. She is also very experienced as a Charity Trustee, and is the founder of an Educational Foundation in The Gambia. Vivienne is a school governor, with an interest in community involvement in local schools. She has recently started a group to support female educators in leadership positions in schools and colleges in her working area.

James: Susan is a teacher of English Language and Literature, as well as a Pastoral Deputy Head at Cheadle Hume School. She has been a Head of Lower School at The Manchester Grammar School; a Drama and PSHE teacher; a Form Tutor and an Academic Mentor for English PGCE Students and NQTs. She achieved a Distinction for her MEd in Educational Leadership, at the University of Buckingham, UK. Following her work on developing resilience in school pupils, Susan has worked to create a new curriculum for Lower School boys at Manchester Grammar School, from 2018. She is a School Governor, with many community interests and is particularly focused on the holistic development of children for their futures in the new Industrial Revolution (4).

Faggin: Professor Doctor Federico is an Italian physicist, inventor and entrepreneur, widely known for designing the first commercial microprocessor. He is recognised as being in the top ten of world geniuses. Federico led the 4004 (MCS-4) project and the design group, during the first 5 years of Intel's microprocessor effort. Most importantly, he created in 1968, at Fairchild Semiconductor, the self-aligned MOS silicon gate technology (SGT), to made possible dynamic memories, non-volatile memories, CCD image sensors and the microprocessor. In addition, he further developed, at Intel, his original SGT into a new methodology for random logic chip design - vital for the creation of the world's first single chip microprocessor. He was co-founder (*with Ralph Ungermann*) and CEO of Zilog, the first company solely dedicated to microprocessors. He was also co-founder and CEO of Cygnet Technologies and Synaptics. In 2010, he received the *2009 Medal of Technology and Innovation*, the highest honour for technological progress, awarded in the United States. In 2011, he founded the *Federico and Elvia Faggin Foundation*, to support the scientific study of *Consciousness* at US universities and research institutes. In 2015, the *Faggin Foundation* established a $1 million endowment for the *Faggin Family Presidential Chair in the Physics of Information*, at UC Santa Cruz, to promote the study of *'fundamental questions at the interface of physics & related fields, including mathematics, complex systems, biophysics & cognitive science, with the unifying theme of information in physics'*.

Matteucci: Professor Dottaire Riccarda (Editor) is an experienced teacher at senior school and university levels, having taught in Italy, Africa, the United States of America and the United Kingdom. She has held a Research Fellowship at the University of Cambridge, into Italian grammar use in England and led the CamBrit/Rome Scheme, enabling students to study and teach across countries. Riccarda is an expert linguist in European languages, with a speciality in across-language teaching, verbal and non-verbal communication, as well as the language-learning problems of those with special educational needs. In Italy, she has been involved in teacher training and served on the National Qualifications Panel. She has particular interest and experience in the multi-cultural aspects of students in teaching and the issues that underpin this factor. She was the lead DFCOT examiner, in the area of *Communication,* at the College of Teachers, then based at the Institute of Education, University College, London. Riccarda is presently devising a teacher training programme for African nations. Her other interests and skills include food and wine, with the highest awards received in this area for her expertise.

Naseem: Naghmana has a Masters in *Dealing with Learning Differences* and a Degree in English, Botany, Zoology and Chemistry. She is a qualified Dyslexia Tutor and SEN Coordinator. She has a Professional Graduate Certificate in Education and holds a QTLS status. Naghmana has been with the education sector for nearly 23 years with experience in teaching and supporting a wide range of students in the primary, secondary and further education sectors in Pakistan, Brunei Darussalam and in the UK. She is currently working as a Quality Manager with Hounslow Adult and Community Education (London). Her particular interest is in supporting students with diverse needs and enabling them in achieving their learning potential. She enjoys learning through current research and is proactive in applying her knowledge and understanding to enhance the quality of processes and procedures in the workplace.

Orton: Dr Kim has taught across the age range and has been a Deputy Head Teacher and an Education Adviser to Schools in Early Years Education and Prison Education. She is an experienced Further & Higher Education lecturer, tutor and course leader. Kim has managed Initial Teacher Education and is now monitoring as well as examining education students for their professional qualifications in the UK, Europe and the Middle East. She has worked on projects within the EU on language, communication and the education/workplace interface. Kim continues as an Associate Professor, at the Institute of Education, University College London, in *Leadership & Management.* She is the Academic Officer on the Practitioner Doctorate at the University of Buckingham, UK and in 2018 visited Kansas University, in the United States, to compare practitioner programmes in both countries. Kim has contributed to academic journals and books on her special research area of communication and reflective practice.

Sage: Professor Doctor Rosemary: Editor is a qualified speech pathologist, psychologist and teacher; former Dean at the College of Teachers and now Professor at the University of Buckingham UK, leading the Practitioner Doctorate. She was Director of Speech and Language Services in Leicester/ Leicestershire; a Teacher in Primary and Secondary schools; Senior Language Advisor to an LEA; an Academic in 4 universities: Head of Department and Professor of Communication at Liverpool and a visiting Professor in Cuba and Japan. Rosemary is on the Queen's Panel for Education and Industry Awards.

She sat on the Lord Chancellor's Advisory Committee as a senior magistrate (*Chairperson & Judicial Mentor*) and is presently on the judicial executive and a member of the *Magistrates in the Community* (MIC) project. She was a founder member of the Children's Legal Panel and expert witness in Educational appeals; on Parliamentary Committees for Medicine and Education, the Teaching of Science and Inclusion of Students with Special Needs. Recently, she led the first group at The College of Teachers (TCOT), completing Practitioner Doctorates by Professional Record, who received awards from Prince Philip in June 2016. She has published many books and over 150 refereed papers in journals, gaining national/international awards for her work on the Communication Opportunity Group Strategy (COGS).

Schutte: Kate is currently Head of English and Teacher of French at Cranleigh Preparatory School, Surrey, England. She is a very experienced teacher, who among her qualifications has a Masters in Business Administration. She has a particular interest in the role of parents/carers, within the Education system. Kate has introduced Accelerated Reader throughout her present school, following a successful pilot scheme and run training for this in London schools, as well as for the South East region. She initiated the Awesome Book Awards, to encourage reading for children in London and the South East, and continues to be part of the team who deliver this event. Now in its 4th year, the awards, which celebrate debut novels for children aged 7-10 years, have inspired thousands of young readers. Kate also introduced and embedded termly visits of a Patron of Reading (1st year – Cliff McNish; 2nd year – MG Leonard; 3rd year – Gareth P. Jones). She has initiated many other activities to stimulate reading in the schools where she has worked and elsewhere, to assist children's communication and literacy.

Seldon: Sir Anthony is Vice Chancellor of The University of Buckingham, UK and a noted contemporary historian, commentator and political author. He has completed biographies of Margaret Thatcher, John Major, Tony Blair, Gordon Brown and David Cameron. He was the 13th Master (*Headmaster*) of *Wellington College*. In 2009, he set up *The Wellington Academy*, the first state school to carry the name of its founding independent one. Before that, he was Head of Brighton College. Anthony is the author or editor of over 35 books on contemporary history, politics and education. He is the co-founder and first director of the *Centre for Contemporary British History,* the co-founder of *Action for Happiness*, governor of the *Royal Shakespeare Company* and on the board of charities and educational bodies. He is also both honorary historical adviser to 10 Downing Street and a member of the *First World War Centenary Culture Committee*. Anthony was knighted for services to education and modern political history in 2014.

Webster, Emma is the Curriculum Leader at a newly-opened primary school in Lewisham, where she is implementing a curriculum centred on creative, innovative learning, intertwined with skills and knowledge. She works closely with local arts organisations, as well outdoor learning facilitators to develop a rich and engaging curriculum and school journey. Her passion for creative learning stems from her previous career as a contemporary dancer, working on the London Stage and with internationally renowned choreographers, touring across nations. Emma has a BA in Dance Theatre and an MA in Dance Performance, from Laban. This cultivated her interest in the nurturing of creativity and the connection with creative ability as well as technical, or academic, knowledge and abilities. Emma is also a board member of *Lewisham Educational Arts Network* (LEAN), an organisation committed to building networks between arts organisations/artists and educators in the borough of Lewisham. Her exceptional creative ability and experience is crucial for an Education for Robotics.